Southern Living®

HEALTHY Hearty COOKBOOK

Southern Living®

HEALTHY Hearty COOKBOOK

Oxmoor House®

Library of Congress Catalog Number: 99-85813
ISBN: 0-8487-1946-8

Printed in the United States of America
Second Printing 2000

Editor-in-Chief: Nancy Fitzpatrick Wyatt
Senior Foods Editor: Susan Payne Stabler
Senior Editor, Copy and Homes: Olivia Kindig Wells
Art Director: James Boone

Southern Living® Healthy Hearty Cookbook
Editor: Kelly Hooper Troiano
Assistant Foods Editor: Suzanne Henson, M.S., R.D.
Copy Editor: L. Amanda Owens
Associate Art Director: Cynthia R. Cooper
Senior Designer: Melissa Jones Clark
Director, Test Kitchens: Elizabeth Luckett
Assistant Director, Test Kitchens: Julie Christopher
Recipe Editor: Gayle Hays Sadler
Test Kitchens Staff: Gretchen Feldtman, Natalie E. King,
       Rebecca Mohr, Jan A. Smith, Kate M. Wheeler, R.D.
Senior Photographers: Jim Bathie, Charles Walton IV
Photographers: Ralph Anderson, Tina Cornett,
       Cheryl Sales Dalton, William Dickey, Colleen Duffley,
       J. Savage Gibson, Brit Huckabay, Sylvia Martin,
       Howard L. Puckett, Bruce Roberts, Becky Luigart-
       Stayner, Jan Wyatt
Senior Photo Stylists: Cindy Manning Barr, Kay E. Clarke
Photo Stylists: Virginia R. Cravens, Mary Lynn Jenkins,
       Leslie Byars Simpson
Director, Production and Distribution: Phillip Lee
Associate Production Manager: Vanessa Cobbs Richardson
Production Assistant: Faye Porter Bonner

CONTRIBUTORS:
Indexer: Mary Ann Laurens
Editorial Assistant: Sally E. Inzer

Cover: Hearty Lasagna (page 129)

Page 2: Pork Chops 'n' Gravy (page 115), Roasted Garlic
Mashed Potatoes (page 182), and Marinated Two-Bean Salad
(page 159)

We're Here for You!

We at Oxmoor House are dedicated to serving you
with reliable information that expands your imagi-
nation and enriches your life. We welcome your
comments and suggestions. Please write to us at:

Oxmoor House, Inc.
Editor, *Southern Living® Healthy Hearty Cookbook*
2100 Lakeshore Drive
Birmingham, AL 35209

To order additional publications, call
    1-205-877-6560

We Want Your Favorite Recipes!

Southern Living cooks are simply the best cooks,
and we want your secrets! Please send your
favorite original recipes and a sentence about
why you like each one. We can't guarantee we'll
print them in a cookbook, but if we do, we'll
send you $20 and a free copy of the cookbook.
Send each recipe on a separate page, with your
name, address, and daytime phone number to:

Cookbook Recipes
Oxmoor House
2100 Lakeshore Drive
Birmingham, AL 35209

page 18

page 40

page 143

page 230

Contents

Countdown to a Healthy, Hearty You!

Join us on a journey to better health. We've identified ten things you can do to boost your overall health and well-being. Here's the countdown:

10 **Pamper Yourself:** Get permission to treat yourself well (page 8).

9 **Simplify Your Life:** Learn tips to get you started (page 10).

8 **Make Time to Play:** Kick back and enjoy yourself (page 13).

7 **Know Your Numbers:** Zero in on your body's specific needs (page 14).

6 **Appreciate Simple Pleasures:** Remember that it's the little things that count (page 17).

5 **Make Healthier Shopping Choices:** Experiment with gradual changes (page 18).

4 **Sneak in Some Exercise:** Seize any opportunity (page 20).

3 **Descend the Food Pyramid:** Use this guide to good food choices (page 22).

2 **Set Realistic Goals:** Make a plan for ensuring success (page 24).

1 **Use the Recipes in This Book:** Get started with our nutritional information (opposite page) and seven savory menus (page 26).

Put Our Recipes to Work for You

You'll find over 250 healthy hearty recipes in this book that offer great taste, while being considerably lower in fat and calories than traditional recipes. Each recipe has a nutritional analysis that includes calories, fat, protein, carbohydrate, cholesterol, and sodium. We've also included food exchange values for people who use exchanges for diabetes or weight control. These exchanges correspond to the food groups in the USDA Food Guide Pyramid (page 23). Use the chart below for the number of exchanges you should consume from each food group daily, based on a diet of 30% or fewer calories from fat.

DAILY FOOD GROUP EXCHANGE GUIDE

Approximate Daily Calories	Fat (maximum servings)	Lean Meat (recommended servings)	Milk (nonfat) (recommended servings)	Starch (recommended servings)	Fruit (minimum servings)	Vegetable (minimum servings)
1200	3	4	2	6	2	3
1400	4	4½	2	7	3	4
1600	5	5	2	7½	3	4½
1800	6	6	2½	8	4	5
2000	7	6	3	9	4	5
2200	8	6	3	11	4	5
2600	10	7	3	13	5	6
3000	12	8	3	15	6	6

The chart above shows the number of servings recommended from each food group at 8 calorie levels. To determine the total number of calories you need each day, multiply your current weight by one of the following factors:

To Determine Calories Needed to Maintain Weight:

Age 20 to 29: weight x 13 = calories needed
Age 30 to 39: weight x 12 = calories needed
Age 40 to 49: weight x 11 = calories needed
Age 50+   : weight x 10 = calories needed

To Determine Calories Needed to Lose Weight:

To lose a pound a week, subtract 500 calories a day from calories needed to maintain weight.

Whether you're simply trying to eat healthfully or to shed a few pounds, these numbers will help get you where you want to be.

10 *Pamper* Yourself

Your state of mind is as critical to your overall health as diet and exercise. Make time for simple pleasures that relax and rejuvenate your spirit when the going gets tough. Read on for ideas to help make your life more relaxing.

what to do in those solitary moments?

• *Get started on that best-seller you've been wanting to read.*

• *Light a scented candle—try one formulated especially for relaxation and stress reduction.*

• *Soak in a tub filled with bubbles or your favorite bath oil.*

• *Tune in to your favorite music.*

• *Enjoy a glass of wine—or try a new wine.*

• **Get at least 8 hours of sleep each night.** Challenging days are easier to face when you're well rested.

• **Spend time alone.** Whether it's 10 minutes or an hour, time alone allows opportunity for reflection among the hustle and bustle of daily routines.

• **Bask in fresh air** and sunshine by taking a leisurely walk.

• **Take a spa vacation.** Revel in others cooking healthful meals for you, planning your exercise regime, and spoiling you with spa specialties such as massages, facials, and wraps.

• **Splurge on a manicure and pedicure.** Or do your nails yourself.

• **See a new exhibit** at your local museum.

• **Catch up with a friend** at your favorite lunch spot.

• **Reward yourself** for sticking to your new stress-free, healthful lifestyle with a great sweater, a new shade of lipstick, deluxe linens, or a bottle of new perfume.

9 Simplify Your Life

Balance is the key to making things run more efficiently at home, at the office, and in the kitchen. These tips will help you prioritize things, reduce clutter, minimize time in the kitchen, and maximize your pursuit of healthful pleasures.

at the office

· · · · · · · · ·

• *Set aside time each day to go through your mail. Sort in batches, according to what's hot, what needs to be filed, and what's junk. Then act upon each stack.*

• *Eliminate desk clutter. It's amazing how in control you feel when you can actually see the top of your desk.*

• *Stop and smell the roses—pluck one for your desk along the way.*

• *Identify superfluous activities that rob you of valuable work time, and eliminate them so you can work more efficiently.*

• *Keep a photo of loved ones on your desk. Seeing those faces helps you focus on what's important in the grand scheme of things.*

At Home

• **Organize yourself with to-do lists** rather than trying to commit your schedule to memory. You won't forget things, and you'll gain a great sense of accomplishment by checking off items as they are completed.

• **Learn to say no**—you don't have to join everything. Participate in projects in which you feel you would make the most impact. Putting your best effort toward one project will make more of a difference than having a finger in several things.

• **Limit social engagements,** and spend more quality time with your family.

• **Clean out the closets.** Donate items that haven't been worn in over a year. You'll gain more room and provide for others who are less fortunate.

• **Chunk the junk mail** as soon as you sort it so that it won't pile up. Make sure you and family members aren't receiving duplicate publications. You'll save on clutter, and you'll save a few trees.

In the Kitchen

• **Use aluminum foil** to line broiler pans for easy cleanup.

• **Buy precut veggies** at the salad bar or in the produce department to save time on chopping and slicing.

• **Keep chopped, cooked chicken** as well as ½-cup portions of chopped onions and bell peppers on hand in the freezer.

• **Make weeknight meals easy** by serving an entrée that cooks quickly on the stovetop or in the oven. While it cooks, prepare a simple salad or vegetable.

• **Become a weekend cook.** Freeze a few meals on weekends, and during the week, all you have to do is thaw and reheat.

• **Use your slow cooker!**

kitchen time-shavers

. . . .

• *Get rid of kitchenware you never use. Pare down to basic items that will save you time and energy, such as kitchen shears, a food processor, an electric slow cooker, a good knife set, a microwave oven, zip-top plastic bags, and nonstick skillets.*

• *Use kitchen shears to make tasks easier and faster. They'll snip fresh herbs, chop tomatoes in a can, and trim the skin and fat from chicken or meat.*

• *Marinate meat and poultry in a heavy-duty zip-top plastic bag to eliminate dirtying an extra bowl.*

Make Time to *Play* 8

Recreation allows you to kick back and have a good time. Best of all, there are no deadlines or chores—just plain and simple fun. And you might even get a little exercise without realizing it.

• **Learn a new sport.** The possibilities are endless. Whether it's tennis or golf, fishing or sailing, horseback riding or canoeing, running or hiking, the important thing is that you're having fun. You may even make some new friends.

• **Explore your hometown.** Play tourist for the day, and visit places that you've never seen before. Take in the latest museum exhibit, catch a game at your local sporting arena, or tour historical homes in your area. You'll learn a lot and gain a greater appreciation of your hometown.

• **Plan a picnic.** Pack healthful fare, and get outside to enjoy the fresh air. The change of pace allows you to take in all that nature has to offer.

• **Bring back Sunday afternoon drives.** Who knows where the road will lead? Along the way you may discover quaint shops, the perfect diner, or an exceptional view. Just don't forget your map—or camera!

• **Organize a block party.** It's a perfect way to get to know your neighbors while enjoying great food and fun. Get everyone involved with the planning and cooking. Keep notes on what you did as

everyone will probably want to turn this into an annual event.

• **Gather family and neighbors for a softball game.** You'll enjoy the camaraderie, while getting a good dose of exercise.

• **Plan family vacations to emphasize sports and fun.** Take along bicycles to explore the area, and don't forget your tennis rackets. No matter what season you take your trip, there's always an activity to include—hiking in spring or fall, snow skiing in winter, and lots of water sports in the summer.

• **Visit area farms.** Some have petting zoos and horseback riding. Others allow you to pick fruits and vegetables, select the perfect pumpkin, or chop your own Christmas tree.

• **Have fun in your own backyard.** Who says you have to go to a foreign land for adventure when you can venture out back for an exciting camp-out. Set up tents or sleep under the stars, grill hot dogs and burgers, and don't forget the marshmallows! Afterwards, share ghost stories around the "campfire" for a memorable evening.

7 Know Your Numbers

To take good care of yourself, you first need to know what you're working with. Make an appointment with your physician to find out how you stack up health-wise. He can identify potential problem areas you may need to focus on to help you stay healthy.

Keep Cholesterol in Check

Too much cholesterol in your blood increases your risk for heart disease. Have your cholesterol checked regularly, and work with your doctor to keep your heart healthy.

CHOLESTEROL COUNTS

Total Cholesterol
Less than 200 mg/dl = Desirable
200–239 mg/dl = Borderline high risk
240 mg/dl or greater = High risk

HDL *("Good" Cholesterol)*
40–50 mg/dl = Ideal for the average man
50–60 mg/dl = Ideal for the average woman

LDL *("Bad" Cholesterol)*
Less than 130 mg/dl = Desirable

Triglycerides
Less than 200 mg/dl = Normal triglycerides
200 to 400 mg/dl = Borderline-high triglycerides
400 to 1000 mg/dl = High triglycerides
Over 1000 mg/dl = Very high triglycerides

Bone Up on Calcium

Calcium is important for building and maintaining strong bones. Teenage and young adult women particularly need to eat a diet rich in calcium to reduce the risk of osteoporosis later in life. Women are also encouraged to get a bone density test during premenopausal years as a guideline to determine risk for osteoporosis. Then you can talk about whether medication or lifestyle changes will be necessary to take care of the problem. Make sure you're getting enough calcium by following the chart at left.

RECOMMENDED DAILY CALCIUM

Children *(4–8 years)*	**800 mg**
Adolescents and young adults *(9–18 years)*	**1,300 mg**
Adults *(19–50 years)*	**1,000 mg**
Adults *(51 years and over)*	**1,200 mg**
Pregnant or nursing women	**1,000-1,300 mg**

Size Up Your Ideal Body Weight

Body Mass Index (BMI) is a height-weight calculation that you can use to determine if your weight is in a healthy range. BMI is a more accurate measurement of your body fat than the former "ideal" weight charts.

To use the BMI table below:
1. Find your height in inches on the left side of the table.
2. On the row corresponding to your height, find your current weight.
3. Then look at the numbers at the very top of the column to find your BMI.
4. Use the BMI and Health Risk table below (blue box) to determine your health risk.

BODY MASS INDEX

BMI	19	21	23	25	27	30	32	34	36	38
Height					**Weight (pounds)**					
58"	91	100	110	119	129	143	152	162	172	181
59"	94	104	114	124	134	149	159	169	179	188
60"	97	107	117	127	138	153	163	173	183	194
61"	101	111	122	132	143	159	169	180	191	201
62"	103	114	125	136	147	163	174	185	196	206
63"	107	119	130	141	152	169	181	192	203	214
64"	111	123	135	146	158	176	187	199	211	223
65"	114	126	138	150	162	180	192	204	216	228
66"	118	131	143	156	168	187	199	212	224	236
67"	121	134	147	159	172	191	204	217	229	242
68"	125	139	152	165	178	198	211	224	238	251
69"	128	142	155	169	182	203	216	230	243	257
70"	133	147	161	175	189	210	224	237	251	265
71"	136	150	164	179	193	214	229	243	257	271
72"	140	155	170	185	199	221	236	251	266	281
73"	143	158	174	189	204	226	241	257	272	287
74"	148	164	179	195	210	234	249	265	281	296

BMI AND HEALTH RISK

Below 18.5 = Underweight
18.5 to 24.9 = Healthy Weight
25.0 to 29.9 = Overweight
30+ = Obesity

For example, if you are 5 feet 7 inches (67") and weigh 147 pounds, your BMI is 23. This means you have a low risk of developing a weight-related disease, such as heart disease or Type 2 diabetes.

managing your weight

. . . .

Maintaining a healthy weight through diet and exercise helps to prevent the development of such diseases as Type 2 diabetes, heart disease, stroke, high blood pressure, and certain cancers.

• To maintain your weight, refer to the equation on page 7 to find out the average number of calories you need each day.

• To lose one pound, you need to burn 3500 calories more than you take in (you need a calorie deficit). For example, reduce your calorie intake by 500 calories a day (that's as simple as passing up two glazed donuts). If you do that for seven days (500 x 7 = 3500), you'll lose one pound.

time-out

. . . .

Treat yourself to a daily time-out. Reenergize your mind as well as your body by doing things that change the tempo of your day, such as reading poetry, walking, meditating, or playing the piano.

Appreciate *Simple Pleasures*

6

Reassess your life, and affirm the value of what you have. These hints help you refocus your mind, body, and diet on the simple pleasures that life offers.

Lifestyle

• **Slow down and savor everyday moments of life.** This applies to any situation, whether you're eating or going from point A to B. Appreciate simplicity, and admire the world around you.

• **Make peace with your life.** Instead of facing each day with frustration and anxiety, deal with daily challenges and unexpected pressures head-on with a more calm, realistic approach. You'll be less likely to overindulge in self-destructive behavior and instead maintain intellectual readiness and wellness as you begin each day.

• **Honor your relationship with your partner.** Don't just share your problems—have something joyful to share, too.

• **Gather the family every night for dinner.** This requires commitment, but the extra effort reinforces a stronger relationship and self-worth for the whole family.

• **Listen to your favorite music** on your commute home. It will help you relax.

• **Unwind by changing into comfortable clothes once you're home from work, and snack on fresh fruit or fruit juice.** Experts say that a little natural sugar can help brain metabolism and let you wind down naturally.

• **Challenge yourself mentally at least once a day** by doing things that are new to you, such as working crossword puzzles, playing cards or chess, or reading. Studies show that regular mental stimulation can stave off short-term and long-term memory loss in old age. The key is to keep your mind active.

• **Laugh.** Plain and simple, laughter is integral to good health. Scientists say that laughter may go a long way toward battling stress and fighting illnesses. It can boost immunity, oxygenate the lungs, and condition the heart. According to one Stanford University professor, a hundred laughs produce about the same aerobic benefit as 10 minutes on a rowing machine or 15 minutes on a stationary bike.

Diet

• **Don't starve yourself if you're dieting—it doesn't work.** Just try to cut back on calories and fat and control those portion sizes.

• **Indulge *occasionally*** on favorite foods often written off as taboo.

• **Eat breakfast.** It will help you maintain a healthy weight by preventing overeating later in the day, and it gives you the boost of energy you need in the morning.

• **Drink at least 8 cups of water daily.** Water is calorie-free, and any nonalcoholic and noncaffeinated beverage counts toward daily intake.

• **Serve simple side dishes,** such as rice, steamed vegetables, potatoes, or a tossed salad, with an entrée that may take extra time to cook.

Exercise

• **Learn to enjoy exercise.** Your body needs it. Just 20 minutes a day of exercise can lower your heart-disease risk.

• **Don't go overboard with regimentation.** Vary your exercise routine and the foods you eat so that you won't get tired of them.

• **Tune in to the world around you.** Yoga and meditation can relax and energize you. In turn, you'll be less likely to do anything that brings you down, such as eating an unhealthful diet or leading an unhealthy lifestyle.

• **Focus on your healthful accomplishments.** Instead of feeling guilty about missing a workout, congratulate yourself for exercising the other days during the week.

5 Make Healthier Shopping Choices

It's easy to make healthful shopping choices if you make the changes gradually. Experiment with one or two products at a time, and keep the changes quiet—your family doesn't need to know! Read on for other ideas.

• **Shop the perimeter of your supermarket.** You'll be more likely to select fresh vegetables and fruits, healthful dairy products, and lean meats and poultry over processed foods that tend to be in the middle of the store—plus you'll save money and maximize nutrition.

• **Be sure to read labels and make low-fat substitutions in the kitchen,** but don't be sold on every food that's labeled fat free. Remember that even though a food is fat free, it still contains calories—and those can add up quickly.

• **Introduce your family to low-fat snack alternatives,** such as popcorn, raisins, and yogurt.

• **Remodel your favorite recipes.** By gradually using less fat and sugar, you probably won't notice a difference. And try mixing nonfat products with their regular counterparts if the flavor of nonfat foods doesn't appeal to you. Refer to the chart at right for substitution ideas.

HEALTHFUL INGREDIENT SUBSTITUTION CHART

Instead of . . .	Try . . .
Baking chocolate (*1 ounce*)	**3 tablespoons dry cocoa plus 2 teaspoons sugar and 1 tablespoon water**
Butter, margarine, shortening, vegetable oil (*1 tablespoon*)	**½ the amount called for in recipe or 1 tablespoon reduced-calorie margarine**
Cheese (*1 ounce*)	**½ the amount called for in recipe or 1 ounce reduced-fat or part-skim** (*with 5 or fewer grams of fat per ounce*)
Chicken broth, canned, regular (*1 cup*)	**1 cup reduced-sodium, fat-free, canned chicken broth**
Cream or half-and-half (*1 tablespoon*)	**1 tablespoon fat-free evaporated milk**
Cream of mushroom soup (*1 can*)	**1 can reduced-fat cream of mushroom soup**
Egg (*1 large*)	**¼ cup egg substitute or 2 large egg whites**
Ground beef (*1 ounce*)	**1 ounce ground round or 1 ounce lean ground turkey**
Mayonnaise (*1 tablespoon*)	**1 tablespoon reduced-calorie or fat-free mayonnaise or 1½ teaspoons reduced-calorie mayonnaise mixed with 1½ teaspoons plain nonfat yogurt**
Pecans, chopped (*½ cup*)	**¼ cup toasted** (*this works with any type nut*)
Sour cream (*½ cup*)	**½ cup plain nonfat yogurt or ½ cup nonfat sour cream** (*for baked goods add 1½ teaspoons flour to each cup of yogurt or nonfat sour cream*)
Whole milk (*1 cup*)	**1 cup fat-free milk**

Sneak in Some *Exercise*

Squeezing fitness into your already busy schedule isn't as hard as you may think—even if you have a low-level commitment to exercise machines and gyms. Just 20 minutes of an activity a day can make a difference, so seize any opportunity to move around. Here's how:

24 reasons to exercise

. . . .

- *burns up calories*
- *increases your heart rate*
- *increases your good cholesterol (HDL)*
- *improves your cardiovascular fitness*
- *improves muscle strength*
- *gives you a rosy glow*
- *strengthens bones*
- *improves muscle flexibility*
- *increases your range of motion*
- *increases oxygen supply to your brain*
- *gives you more energy*
- *strengthens your lungs*
- *helps you sleep better*
- *lowers blood pressure*
- *improves circulation*
- *allows you to consume more calories without gaining weight*
- *improves your posture*
- *strengthens heart muscles*
- *relieves stress*
- *keeps you away from the refrigerator*
- *boosts your self-esteem*
- *gives you a chance to enjoy the outdoors*
- *improves endurance*
- *clears your mind*

- **Do stretching exercises,** sit-ups, push-ups, or use an exercise machine while watching television.

- **Hide that remote control.**

- **Vacuum, dust, and clean those windows!** Turn housework into a workout while listening to your favorite tunes.

- **Take your children** to the park *and play* with them.

- **Walk your dog**—it's beneficial for both of you.

- **Make reservations at a hotel that has a pool or an exercise room** when you travel. Or pack a jump rope, and do some jumping. On vacation trips sign up for walking tours of local attractions and scenic highlights.

- **Make the most of your lunch hour.** Take a 15-minute walk around the office building before eating lunch. If the heat or the cold gets to be too much, try mall walking or stair climbing in your office building.

Keep Motivated
The key to sticking with an activity is to do so because you enjoy it and not because it burns the most calories. Try new activities that will peak your interest to get out and have fun! Try . . .

- **Yard work.** Alternate arms when raking leaves for a better workout. Both you and your yard will benefit.

- **In-line skating.** It improves muscle tone and burns calories without pounding your joints, and it's easy to learn.

- **Bicycling.** This is a great workout that the whole family can enjoy.

- **Fun-runs.** You'll be helping a charity as well as keeping fit. If running is not your speed, sign up for one of the many charitable walk-a-thons.

- **Softball.** Many communities and businesses sponsor local teams. Share in the camaraderie of good competition while getting to know others.

DID YOU KNOW?

By sticking to your half-hour run three times a week for a year, you'll lose 12 pounds of fat. Here are other incentives that require the same time commitment:

Swimming	**12 pounds**
Aerobics	**9 pounds**
Walking	**9 pounds**
Weight lifting	**5 pounds**

THE ACCIDENTAL EXERCISER

There are plenty of ways to exercise around the house to burn off that piece of pie you had for dessert.

Activity (per 10 minutes)	Calories Burned for Women (132 lbs)	Calories Burned for Men (176 lbs)
Washing windows	31	42
Weeding	45	60
Moving furniture	60	80
Scrubbing floors	55	73
Shoveling snow	60	80
Cleaning gutters	50	67
Running up stairs	150	200

Descend the *Food Pyramid*

The Food Guide Pyramid was developed by the U.S. Department of Agriculture (USDA) to be a visual guide to healthful eating. It outlines the number of servings needed each day from each food group. Healthier foods form the base of the pyramid, so center your focus there.

The placement of food groups in the pyramid corresponds with the recommended number of daily servings. For example, you should strive to eat the most servings from the group at the base of the pyramid—breads, cereal, rice, and pasta. These foods supply vitamins, minerals, complex carbohydrates, and dietary fiber—all important nutrition components that contribute to overall health. Eat the fewest from the group at the top: fats, oils, and sweets.

FOOD GUIDE PYRAMID
A Guide to Daily Food Choices

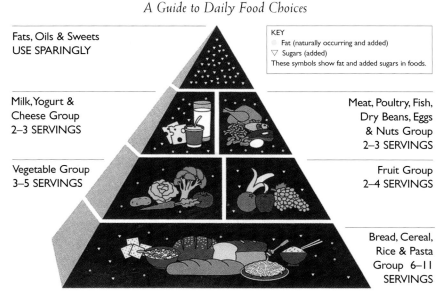

Fats, Oils & Sweets
USE SPARINGLY

KEY
◦ Fat (naturally occurring and added)
▽ Sugars (added)
These symbols show fat and added sugars in foods.

Milk, Yogurt & Cheese Group
2–3 SERVINGS

Meat, Poultry, Fish, Dry Beans, Eggs & Nuts Group
2–3 SERVINGS

Vegetable Group
3–5 SERVINGS

Fruit Group
2–4 SERVINGS

Bread, Cereal, Rice & Pasta Group 6–11 SERVINGS

Source: U.S. Department of Agriculture/U.S. Department of Health and Human Services

SNACK SMART

Keeping these quick snacks close at hand will ensure a convenient and powerful energy boost when you need it the most. They're categorized by food groups from the Food Guide Pyramid.

Breads & Cereals
- Bagels
- Breadsticks
- Dry cereal
- Fat-free or low-fat crackers
- Fig bars
- Gingersnaps
- Granola bars (those that have less than 3 grams of fat per 100 calories)
- Graham crackers
- Pita bread
- Pretzels
- Vanilla wafers
- Whole grain rolls
- Whole wheat bread

Vegetables
- Raw vegetables
- Vegetable juice

Fruits
- Fresh fruit
- Dried fruit
- Juice and frozen juice bars

Meats & Poultry
- Lunch meat (95% to 98% fat-free)
- Water-packed tuna
- Turkey breast

Milk, Yogurt & Cheese
- Fat-free ice cream
- Fat-free or low-fat frozen yogurt
- Frozen fudge pops
- Nonfat or low-fat yogurt
- String cheese or cheese with 5 or fewer grams of fat per ounce
- Fat-free or reduced-fat, plain or chocolate milk

Set Realistic Goals

Ever made lofty New Year's resolutions only to find them deflated by the end of January? Chances are either you weren't committed to the goals that you set or you weren't realistic in terms of what you could achieve. Here's how to set goals for success.

7 steps
to effective
goal setting

. . . .

1. *Make your goals realistic.*

2. *Write goals down so that you can refer to them.*

3. *Specify how you'll accomplish each goal.*

4. *Designate a time frame.*

5. *Review your accomplishments.*

6. *Reward your successes!*

7. *Revise your list by adding new goals.*

Give Goals Priority

Steal some time alone in a comfortable place where you know you won't be interrupted. Reward your commitment to goal setting with a cup of tea or a glass of wine. Grab a pen and a notebook or a journal to record your thoughts.

Brainstorm Changes You'd Like to Make

Peruse the previous pages about a healthful lifestyle. How do the ideas apply to you? Are there areas you'd really like to work on? List the areas on which you want to focus. Keep your objectives short and simple. Do you need to

- block out more time in your schedule for YOU?
- read food labels and experiment with more healthful food products?
- increase the number of fruits and vegetables you eat each day?
- start taking a calcium supplement?
- lose 10 pounds?
- begin an exercise program? Will it be daily? Three times a week?

Narrow Down a List of Goals

Review the list you made. Is it achievable? If so, adopt the list as your official goals. Just remember: The key is to make changes in moderation. If you've written down more goals than you can realistically accomplish right away, decide which ones are most important and which you can currently achieve. Then write just those down as your official goals.

Plan Your Path to Success

Decide which activities you'll choose to help you achieve your goals, and plan how often you will do each activity. Don't be extreme, but be consistent. Pencil the activities and the dates on your calendar, and place a star by each activity once it's accomplished.

Hold Yourself Accountable

Set a time frame by which you'll accomplish your goals, and write the date on

your calendar. Share your goals and time frame with a buddy or two, and ask them to check in with you periodically to see how things are going. The deadline and the buddy system will make you more accountable for accomplishing your goals.

Review, Revise, and Reward

When your goal period is up, review your goals and count your accomplishments. Have some goals become a natural part of your life? If so, check them off your list, and be sure to reward yourself. Are there other goals not completed that you need to work on harder? Or do you need to revise the activity by which you'll accomplish them? Are there other lifestyle changes from your original list you're now ready to add to a new list of goals? Congratulations—you're making progress!

1 Use the Recipes in This Book

Every recipe in the Southern Living® Healthy Hearty Cookbook *helps you meet the healthy eating requirements of the U.S. Dietary Guidelines. Here's how:*

- **The nutrient analysis** adjacent to each recipe in this book shows you how the recipe fits into your healthful eating plan. Each value given is for one serving of the recipe.

- **Food Exchange Values** are included in each nutrient analysis. The chart on page 7 will help you determine how many exchanges you need daily from each food group to help achieve or maintain your desired weight with a balanced diet.

- **Sample the following menus** that are made up from the recipes in this book. Then mix and match other recipes to make new menus your family will enjoy.

Country Summer Supper

Serves 6
Calories per servings: 817
Calories from fat: 26%

Pork Chops 'n' Gravy
(page 115)

Roasted Garlic Mashed Potatoes
(page 182)

Marinated Two-Bean Salad
(page 159)

Whole Wheat Biscuits
(page 49)

Very Berry Sorbet
(page 214)

Family Favorites

Serves 4
Calories per servings: 841
Calories from fat: 26%

Sweet and Sour Pork Strips
(rice included in recipe)
(page 117)

Parsley-Garlic Rolls
(page 60)

Banana Cream Pie
(page 225)

Celebration Brunch

Serves 4
Calories per servings: 646
Calories from fat: 23%

Mexican Souffléed Omelets
(page 84)

Fresh Fruit with Mint Tea Vinaigrette
(page 158)

Blueberry-Oat Streusel Muffins
(page 51)

Banana Smoothie
(page 42)

Bayou Bonanza

Serves 16
Calories per servings: 715
Calories from fat: 24%

Chicken and Shrimp Gumbo
(page 199)

Crusty French Pistou Bread
(page 56)

Frosted Carrot Cake
(page 223)

Company's Coming

Serves 6
Calories per servings: 847
Calories from fat: 19%

Zucchini-Beef Spaghetti
(page 125)

Seven Layer Italian Salad
(page 162)

Rosemary Focaccia
(page 63)

Raspberry-Cherry Cobbler
(page 229)

Dinner on the Deck

Serves 10
Calories per servings: 880
Calories from fat: 24%

Mock Margaritas
(double recipe)
(page 45)

Java Fajitas (2 each)
(page 105)

Caramel-Pineapple
Upside-Down Cake
(page 222)

Picnic on the Grounds

Serves 4
Calories per servings: 512
Calories from fat: 22%

Italian Chicken Sandwiches
(page 202)

Grilled Vegetable Salad
(page 160)

Oatmeal-Raisin Cookies (2 each)
(page 232)

Minted Orange-Lemon Fizz (page 45) and
Shrimp Canapés (page 40)

Appetizers & Beverages

Let your next gathering reflect today's healthy lifestyle. Peruse this chapter for just the right appetizers and beverages to serve hungry guests. Discover lightened versions of those dips and hors d'oeuvres that you can't do without, as well as new recipes that are sure to have everyone clamoring for seconds. And hot or cold, cocktail or "mocktail," choose from beverages to quench a thirst on any occasion.

Quick Fruit Dip

This three-ingredient dip couldn't be easier or more versatile. Change the flavor of the fruit spread to complement the fruit dippers you serve alongside.

per tablespoon:

Calories: 9
Fat: 0.2g
Protein: 0.7g
Carbohydrate: 1.1g
Cholesterol: 1mg
Sodium: 9mg
Exchanges:
   Free (up to 5 tablespoons)

1⅓ cups plain low-fat yogurt
¼ cup low-sugar orange
   marmalade

¼ teaspoon ground cinnamon

Combine all ingredients in a small bowl, stirring until blended.
Cover and chill until ready to serve. Serve with assorted fresh fruit. Yield: 1½ cups.

Dilled Garden Dip

This creamy dip can showcase any fresh herb from your garden. Vary the herb to coincide with your pick of the day.

per tablespoon:

Calories: 11
Fat: 0.1g
Protein: 1.8g
Carbohydrate: 0.5g
Cholesterol: 1mg
Sodium: 58mg
Exchanges:
   Free (up to 4 tablespoons)

2 cups low-fat cottage cheese
2 tablespoons tarragon vinegar
1 to 2 tablespoons fat-free milk
1 tablespoon finely chopped
   green onions

1 tablespoon chopped fresh
   parsley
1½ teaspoons fresh dill or ½
   teaspoon dried dillweed
Dash of freshly ground pepper

Process cottage cheese and vinegar in a blender until smooth, stopping to scrape down sides as needed.
Combine cottage cheese mixture, milk, and remaining ingredients. Cover and chill 2 hours. Serve with raw vegetables or as a condiment on hamburgers. Yield: 2 cups.

Vegetable Salsa

3¼ pounds tomatoes, peeled
12 jalapeño peppers
1 green bell pepper
1 large onion
2 celery ribs
4 garlic cloves

3½ teaspoons salt, divided
2 tablespoons chopped fresh
cilantro
2 (6-ounce) cans tomato paste
¼ cup lime juice
2 tablespoons olive oil

per tablespoon:

Calories: 13
Fat: 0.4g
Protein: 0.4g
Carbohydrate: 2.2g
Cholesterol: 0mg
Sodium: 107mg
Exchanges:
  ½ Vegetable

Chop first 6 ingredients.

Combine chopped vegetables, 1 teaspoon salt, and remaining 4 ingredients in a large Dutch oven; cook mixture over medium-high heat until hot, stirring often. Do not boil.

Pack salsa into hot jars, filling to ½ inch from top of each. Add ½ teaspoon salt to each jar. Remove air bubbles; wipe jar rims. Cover at once with metal lids, and screw on bands.

Process in pressure canner at 10 pounds pressure (240°) for 20 minutes. Store in refrigerator after opening. Yield: 5 pints.

Hot Spinach-Crabmeat Dip

¾ cup fat-free ricotta cheese
¾ cup plus 2 tablespoons fat-free
milk
½ cup nonfat mayonnaise
1 tablespoon dry sherry
1 (10-ounce) package frozen
chopped spinach, thawed
1 (8-ounce) can sliced water
chestnuts, drained and
chopped

6 ounces fresh lump crabmeat,
drained
¾ cup (3 ounces) shredded
reduced-fat Monterey Jack
cheese
½ cup drained finely diced
roasted red pepper in water
¼ cup minced green onions
½ teaspoon hot sauce
Vegetable cooking spray

per tablespoon:

Calories: 12
Fat: 0.3g
Protein: 1.4g
Carbohydrate: 1.1g
Cholesterol: 3mg
Sodium: 62mg
Exchanges:
  Free (up to 4 tablespoons)

Press ricotta cheese through a fine-mesh sieve into a large bowl. Add milk, mayonnaise, and sherry; stir well.

Drain spinach; press between paper towels to remove excess moisture. Add spinach and next 6 ingredients to cheese mixture; stir well.

Spoon mixture into a 1½-quart casserole coated with cooking spray. Cover and bake at 350° for 30 minutes. Uncover and bake 10 more minutes or until hot and bubbly. Serve with toasted pita wedges. Yield: 4¾ cups.

Chicken Nacho Dip

per ¼ cup:

Calories: 69
Fat: 2.1g
Protein: 7.1g
Carbohydrate: 5.0g
Cholesterol: 14mg
Sodium: 189mg
Exchanges:
  ½ Starch
  1 Very Lean Meat

1 (1¼-ounce) package taco seasoning mix
2½ cups shredded cooked chicken breast (skinned before cooking and cooked without salt)
½ cup light beer
1 (4.5-ounce) can chopped green chiles, undrained
½ cup no-salt-added salsa
1 (15-ounce) can black beans, drained

1 tablespoon crushed garlic
½ cup minced fresh cilantro
1½ cups (6 ounces) shredded fat-free Cheddar cheese
1 (16-ounce) carton nonfat sour cream
1½ cups seeded, diced tomato
½ cup minced green onions
¼ cup sliced ripe olives

Reserve 1 teaspoon taco seasoning mix; set aside. Combine remaining taco seasoning mix, chicken, beer, and chiles in a large skillet; bring to a boil. Reduce heat, and simmer, uncovered, 5 minutes or until mixture is thickened. Remove from heat; stir in salsa.

Mash beans and garlic until smooth; stir in cilantro. Spread bean mixture in a 10-inch quiche dish. Spoon chicken mixture evenly over bean mixture; top with cheese. Bake, uncovered, at 375° for 15 minutes or until cheese melts and mixture is thoroughly heated.

Combine sour cream and reserved 1 teaspoon taco seasoning mix; spread over melted cheese. Top with tomato, green onions, and olives. Serve with no-oil baked tortilla chips. Yield: 8 cups.

Hummus

Serve this creamy bean dip with pita chips or vegetables.
Or spread ½ cup of it inside a pita to make a sandwich.

per ¼ cup:

Calories: 98
Fat: 4.6g
Protein: 3.5g
Carbohydrate: 11.5g
Cholesterol: 0mg
Sodium: 193mg
Exchanges:
  1 Starch
  ½ Fat

1 (15-ounce) can chickpeas, drained
¼ cup tahini
2 tablespoons chopped fresh parsley
1 garlic clove

⅓ cup lemon juice
1½ teaspoons ground cumin
¼ teaspoon ground red pepper
2 tablespoons chopped onion
1 tablespoon reduced-sodium soy sauce

Process all ingredients in a food processor until smooth, stopping to scrape down sides. Yield: 2 cups.

Roasted Red Bell
Pepper Spread

Roasted Red Bell Pepper Spread

This recipe yields a lot of spread; the leftovers are
great on pasta, grilled fish, or chicken.

4 large red bell peppers
1 (8-ounce) package sliced fresh
   mushrooms
½ cup chopped purple onion
2 garlic cloves, minced
2 tablespoons olive oil, divided
1 cup grated Parmesan cheese
½ cup Italian-seasoned
   breadcrumbs
¼ cup chopped walnuts

2 tablespoons minced fresh basil
   or 2 teaspoons dried basil
2 teaspoons lemon juice
1 teaspoon Worcestershire sauce
¼ teaspoon salt
¼ teaspoon pepper
¼ teaspoon hot sauce
Garnish: fresh fennel sprigs

per ¼ cup:
Calories: 98
Fat: 6.1g
Protein: 4.8g
Carbohydrate: 6.9g
Cholesterol: 5mg
Sodium: 312mg
Exchanges:
  ½ Starch
  ½ High-Fat Meat

Place bell peppers on an aluminum foil-lined baking sheet.

Broil 5 inches from heat (with electric oven door partially open) 5 to 10
minutes on each side or until bell peppers look blistered.

Place bell peppers in a heavy-duty zip-top plastic bag; seal and let stand
10 minutes to loosen skins. Peel bell peppers; remove and discard seeds.

Sauté mushrooms, onion, and garlic in ½ tablespoon hot oil in a large skillet 10 minutes or until liquid evaporates. Remove from heat, and set aside.

Process bell peppers in a food processor until smooth, stopping to scrape
down sides. Add mushroom mixture, remaining 1½ tablespoons oil,
cheese, and next 8 ingredients; pulse until ground.

Serve with breadsticks, crackers, or assorted fresh vegetables. Garnish, if
desired. Yield: 3 cups.

Pineapple-Apricot Cheese Spread

Brandy-spiked fruit flavors this creamy cheese spread. Slathered on gingersnaps, it makes a tasty snack or even a not-so-sweet dessert.

per appetizer:

Calories: 55
Fat: 2.8g
Protein: 2.1g
Carbohydrate: 7.2g
Cholesterol: 5mg
Sodium: 86mg
Exchanges:
  ½ Starch
  ½ Fat

1 (8-ounce) can crushed pineapple in juice, undrained
½ cup finely chopped dried apricot
¼ cup chopped chutney
¼ cup brandy
½ teaspoon ground ginger
2 cups (8 ounces) reduced-fat shredded Cheddar cheese

2 (8-ounce) packages fat-free cream cheese, softened
¼ cup reduced-calorie margarine, softened
2 tablespoons brandy
Garnish: edible flowers
64 gingersnap cookies

Drain pineapple, reserving 3 tablespoons juice.

Combine pineapple, reserved juice, apricot, and next 3 ingredients in a saucepan; bring to a boil. Reduce heat; simmer, uncovered, 5 to 7 minutes or until mixture is thickened, stirring frequently. Transfer to bowl, and chill thoroughly.

Process cheeses and margarine in a food processor until smooth, scraping sides of bowl occasionally.

Line 2 (2½-cup) molds with cheesecloth dampened with 2 tablespoons brandy. Spread ½ cup cheese mixture in bottom of each mold. Spread ¼ cup pineapple mixture over cheese mixture in each. Repeat layers with ½ cup cheese mixture and half of remaining pineapple mixture in each mold. Spread remaining cheese mixture evenly over each. Cover and chill. Unmold onto serving plates; peel off cheesecloth. Garnish, if desired. To serve, spread 1 tablespoon cheese mixture on each gingersnap. Yield: 64 appetizers.

Spicy Pita Chips

These chips are a great crunchy substitute for potato chips.
Store in an airtight container up to one week.

4 pita bread rounds
Butter-flavored cooking spray
1 teaspoon garlic powder

½ teaspoon sugar
½ teaspoon paprika
¼ teaspoon ground red pepper

Split each bread round into 2 rounds; cut each round into 8 wedges. Coat with cooking spray.

Combine garlic powder and remaining 3 ingredients; sprinkle evenly over wedges. Place wedges on a baking sheet coated with cooking spray.

Bake at 300° for 20 minutes or until lightly browned and crisp. Yield: 64 chips.

per chip:
Calories: 11
Fat: 0.1g
Protein: 0.4g
Carbohydrate: 2.2g
Cholesterol: 0mg
Sodium: 20mg
Exchanges:
  Free (up to 3 chips)

Onion-Parmesan Stuffed Mushrooms

Just a bit of high-flavored goat cheese packs a
powerful punch in these mushrooms.

24 large fresh mushrooms
Olive oil-flavored cooking spray
⅔ cup minced green onions
1 cup soft breadcrumbs
    (homemade)

2 tablespoons freshly grated
    Parmesan cheese
¼ teaspoon salt
1 ounce goat cheese
½ teaspoon freshly ground pepper

Clean mushrooms with damp paper towels. Remove stems. Set mushroom caps aside. Finely chop stems, and set aside.

Coat a large nonstick skillet with cooking spray; place over medium-high heat until hot. Add mushroom caps; sauté 5 minutes. Remove from skillet, and drain on paper towels. Coat skillet with cooking spray, and add reserved mushroom stems and green onions; sauté over medium heat 3 minutes or until tender. Remove from heat. Stir in breadcrumbs, Parmesan cheese, and salt. Set aside.

Crumble goat cheese evenly into mushroom caps. Spoon breadcrumb mixture evenly into mushroom caps over goat cheese, and sprinkle evenly with pepper.

Arrange mushrooms on rack of a broiler pan coated with cooking spray. Broil 5½ inches from heat (with electric oven door partially opened) 2 to 3 minutes or until lightly browned. Yield: 2 dozen.

per mushroom:
Calories: 24
Fat: 0.8g
Protein: 1.5g
Carbohydrate: 3.3g
Cholesterol: 1mg
Sodium: 57mg
Exchanges:
  1 Vegetable

Mexican Pinwheels

per pinwheel:

Calories: 30
Fat: 1.6g
Protein: 1.6g
Carbohydrate: 2.2g
Cholesterol: 4mg
Sodium: 64mg
Exchanges:
    Free (up to 3 pinwheels)

2 cups (8 ounces) shredded reduced-fat Cheddar cheese
½ cup light sour cream
1 (8-ounce) package light cream cheese, softened
1 (4.5-ounce) can chopped green chiles, drained
1 (2¼-ounce) can sliced ripe olives, drained
3 green onions, chopped
1 garlic clove, pressed
¼ teaspoon seasoned salt
6 (8-inch) flour tortillas
Salsa

Stir together first 8 ingredients; spread evenly over tortillas. Roll up tortillas, jellyroll fashion, and wrap separately in plastic wrap. Chill up to 8 hours, or freeze in airtight wrap up to 1 month. (Thaw before slicing.)
Cut each roll into 12 slices. Secure slices with wooden picks, if desired. Serve with salsa. Yield: 6 dozen.

Buffalo Shrimp with Blue Cheese Dip

per serving:

Calories: 154
Fat: 2.9g
Protein: 25.5g
Carbohydrate: 4.8g
Cholesterol: 174mg
Sodium: 433mg
Exchanges:
    ½ Starch
    3 Very Lean Meat

48 unpeeled, large fresh shrimp (about 2 pounds)
¾ cup sweet barbecue sauce
2 to 4 teaspoons hot sauce
¼ teaspoon pepper
1 garlic clove, pressed
¾ cup nonfat cottage cheese
3 tablespoons fat-free milk
2 tablespoons crumbled blue cheese
⅛ teaspoon pepper
Vegetable cooking spray
Garnish: finely chopped fresh chives

Peel shrimp, leaving tails intact; devein, if desired. Place shrimp in a large shallow dish.
Combine barbecue sauce and next 3 ingredients; cover and chill ¼ cup sauce. Pour remaining sauce over shrimp. Cover and chill 30 minutes, turning shrimp often.
Process cottage cheese and next 3 ingredients in a blender until smooth; cover Blue Cheese Dip, and chill.
Remove shrimp from marinade, discarding marinade. Arrange shrimp on a rack coated with cooking spray; place rack in a shallow roasting pan.
Broil shrimp 3 inches from heat (with electric oven door partially open) 3 minutes. Turn shrimp over, and baste with reserved ¼ cup sauce. Broil 3 additional minutes or until done. Serve with chilled Blue Cheese Dip. Garnish dip, if desired. Yield: 8 servings.

Potato Skins with Cheese and Bacon

4 medium baking potatoes, unpeeled (about 2 pounds)

Vegetable cooking spray

¾ cup (3 ounces) shredded reduced-fat sharp Cheddar cheese

4 slices turkey bacon, cooked and crumbled

1 tablespoon finely chopped fresh or frozen chives

¼ cup nonfat sour cream

per potato skin:
Calories: 126
Fat: 5.7g
Protein: 8.1g
Carbohydrate: 9.1g
Cholesterol: 25mg
Sodium: 438mg
Exchanges:
  ½ Starch
  1 Medium-Fat Meat

Bake potatoes at 425° for 1 hour or until done. Cool slightly. Cut each potato in half lengthwise; scoop out pulp, leaving a ¼-inch-thick shell. Reserve pulp for another use.

Place potato shells on a baking sheet. Coat insides of shells with cooking spray. Spoon cheese evenly into shells.

Bake at 425° for 5 minutes or until cheese melts. Sprinkle evenly with turkey bacon and chives. Serve with sour cream. Yield: 8 servings.

Buffalo Shrimp with Blue Cheese Dip, Potato Skins with Cheese and Bacon

Shrimp Canapés

(pictured on page 30)

per canapé:

Calories: 66
Fat: 1.6g
Protein: 4.4g
Carbohydrate: 6.9g
Cholesterol: 22mg
Sodium: 117mg
Exchanges:
  ½ Starch
  ½ Very Lean Meat

12 unpeeled, medium-size fresh shrimp
½ cup dry white wine
½ cup low-sodium canned chicken broth
2 fresh dill sprigs
6 (1-ounce) whole wheat bread slices

¼ cup (2 ounces) light cream cheese, softened
1½ teaspoons minced fresh dill
1 teaspoon dry white wine
Garnish: fresh dill sprigs

Peel shrimp, leaving tails on; devein, if desired.

Bring ½ cup wine, broth, and 2 dill sprigs to a boil in a medium saucepan over medium-high heat. Add shrimp, and cook 3 to 4 minutes or until shrimp turn pink. Drain shrimp; cover and chill.

Cut bread into 12 rounds with a 2-inch cutter. Place rounds on a baking sheet.

Broil 5½ inches from heat (with electric door partially open) 1 minute on each side or until lightly toasted.

Stir together cream cheese, minced dill, and 1 teaspoon wine; spread evenly over 1 side of each bread round. Top each with a shrimp. Garnish, if desired. Yield: 1 dozen.

Green Chile Quesadillas

Two kinds of cheese mingle and melt with chopped green chiles between toasty tortillas that you cut into wedges. Bet you can't eat just one.

per 2 wedges:

Calories: 58
Fat: 2.1g
Protein: 3.6g
Carbohydrate: 6.5g
Cholesterol: 6mg
Sodium: 173mg
Exchanges:
  ½ Starch
  ½ Lean Meat

1 (4.5-ounce) can chopped green chiles
8 (6-inch) corn tortillas
Vegetable cooking spray
1 cup (4 ounces) shredded part-skim mozzarella cheese

½ cup (2 ounces) shredded reduced-fat Cheddar cheese
⅛ to ¼ teaspoon ground red pepper

Drain chiles on paper towels.

Place 4 tortillas on a baking sheet coated with cooking spray. Divide cheeses and chiles evenly among 4 tortillas; spread to within ½ inch of edge. Sprinkle evenly with red pepper, and top with remaining tortillas.

Bake at 375° for 5 minutes or until cheese melts. Cut each into 8 wedges. Yield: 16 (2-wedge) servings.

German Chocolate Café au Lait

½ cup sugar
2 tablespoons unsweetened cocoa
½ cup fat-free milk
2½ cups brewed chocolate
   almond-flavored coffee

½ teaspoon coconut extract
½ teaspoon almond extract

Combine sugar and cocoa in a small saucepan, and stir well. Gradually add milk, and stir well. Place over medium heat; cook until sugar dissolves, stirring frequently.

Remove from heat; stir in coffee and flavorings. Pour into individual cups, and serve immediately. Yield: 3 cups.

Cinnamon Cream Hot Cocoa

A small amount of marshmallow cream adds a lot of body to this cocoa.

3 cups fat-free milk
2 (3-inch) sticks cinnamon
¼ cup unsweetened cocoa
3 tablespoons sugar

¼ cup marshmallow cream
1½ teaspoons vanilla extract
¼ teaspoon almond extract
Garnish: cinnamon sticks

Place milk and 2 cinnamon sticks in a medium saucepan. Bring to a boil over medium heat, stirring occasionally. Remove from heat, and let cool 10 minutes. Remove and discard cinnamon sticks.

Combine cocoa and sugar; stir well. Add to milk mixture, and stir well. Stir in marshmallow cream. Cook over medium heat, stirring constantly with a wire whisk, until thoroughly heated. Remove from heat; stir in flavorings. Pour into individual mugs, and serve immediately. Garnish, if desired. Yield: 3 cups.

Hot Cranberry Cocktail

per 1 cup:

Calories: 122
Fat: 0.2g
Protein: 0.4g
Carbohydrate: 30.6g
Cholesterol: 0mg
Sodium: 6mg
Exchanges:
  2 Fruit

1 tablespoon whole cloves
2 teaspoons whole allspice
1 (32-ounce) bottle cranberry
  juice cocktail
3 cups unsweetened pineapple
  juice
1 cup water

Tie cloves and allspice in a cheesecloth bag. Combine cranberry juice, pineapple juice, water, and spice bag in a Dutch oven; bring to a boil. Cover, reduce heat, and simmer 5 minutes. Discard spice bag. Yield: 8 cups.

Strawberry-Banana Shakes

per 1 cup:

Calories: 136
Fat: 0.3g
Protein: 5.2g
Carbohydrate: 29.5g
Cholesterol: 1mg
Sodium: 78mg
Exchanges:
  ½ Starch
  1 Fruit
  ½ Skim Milk

1 large banana, peeled and cut
  into ½-inch-thick slices
1 teaspoon lemon juice
1½ cups strawberry nonfat frozen
  yogurt
1 cup frozen unsweetened
  strawberries
1 cup fat-free milk
1 teaspoon vanilla extract

Combine banana and lemon juice; toss gently to coat. Place banana slices on a baking sheet. Cover and freeze 1 hour or until firm.
Process banana, yogurt, and remaining 3 ingredients in a blender until smooth, stopping twice to scrape down sides. Serve immediately. Yield: 4 cups.

Banana Smoothie

*Chocolate or strawberry ice cream makes a tasty
substitute for vanilla ice cream.*

per ½ cup:

Calories: 123
Fat: 0.2g
Protein: 3.4g
Carbohydrate: 27.0g
Cholesterol: 1mg
Sodium: 52mg
Exchanges:
  1½ Starch

1 medium banana, peeled and cut
  into ½-inch-thick slices
1 cup fat-free vanilla ice
  cream
1 cup fat-free milk
2 tablespoons sugar

Process all ingredients in a blender until smooth, stopping once to scrape down sides. Pour smoothie into glasses, and serve immediately. Yield: 2 cups.

Strawberry-Banana Shakes

Bellini Spritzers

6 ripe peaches (2 pounds)
1 (750-milliliter) bottle
     champagne, chilled

1 (23-ounce) bottle sparkling
     mineral water, chilled

Peel and halve peaches. Process in a blender or food processor until smooth.

Combine 3 cups peach puree, champagne, and mineral water in a large pitcher. Pour into chilled wineglasses; serve immediately. Yield: 9 cups.

Citrus Punch

1 cup water
¼ cup sugar
3 cups unsweetened pineapple
     juice
3 cups water
½ cup lemon juice

1 (6-ounce) can frozen orange
     juice concentrate, thawed and
     undiluted
3 (12-ounce) cans lemon-lime
     carbonated beverage, chilled

Combine 1 cup water and sugar in a small saucepan; cook over low heat, stirring constantly, until sugar dissolves. Remove from heat; cool.

Stir in pineapple juice and next 3 ingredients; cover and chill. Just before serving, stir in carbonated beverage; serve over ice. Yield: 3 quarts.

Piña Colada Slush

Enjoy the flavor and the thickness a banana adds to this tropical beverage. We froze the banana to help make the drink extra thick and slushy.

1 medium banana, peeled and
     sliced
1 tablespoon lemon juice
½ (12-ounce) can frozen
     pineapple juice concentrate
¼ cup instant nonfat dry milk
     powder

¼ cup water
¼ cup light rum
2 tablespoons coconut liqueur
1 teaspoon coconut extract
Crushed ice

Combine banana and lemon juice; toss gently to coat. Place banana slices on a baking sheet. Cover and freeze 1 hour or until firm.

Process banana, frozen pineapple juice concentrate, and next 5 ingredients in a blender until smooth. Add enough crushed ice to reach 4 cups; process until slushy. Pour into glasses, and serve immediately. Yield: 4 cups.

Mock Margaritas

1 (6-ounce) can frozen lemonade concentrate, thawed and undiluted
1 (6-ounce) can frozen limeade concentrate, thawed and undiluted
½ cup sifted powdered sugar
3¼ cups crushed ice
1½ cups club soda, chilled
Garnish: lime slices

per ¾ cup:
Calories: 107
Fat: 0.1g
Protein: 0.1g
Carbohydrate: 28.0g
Cholesterol: 0mg
Sodium: 10mg
Exchanges:
  ½ Starch
  1 Fruit

Combine first 4 ingredients in a large plastic container; stir well. Freeze mixture. Remove from freezer 30 minutes before serving.

Spoon half of mixture into a blender; add half of club soda, and process until smooth. Pour into glasses. Repeat with remaining half of ingredients. Garnish, if desired. Yield: 6 cups.

Minted Orange-Lemon Fizz

(pictured on page 30)

1¼ cups water
⅔ cup sugar
½ cup firmly packed fresh mint leaves
1 tablespoon grated orange rind
¾ cup fresh orange juice
¾ cup lemon juice
2 cups lemon-flavored sparkling water, chilled
Garnish: fresh mint sprigs

per ¾ cup:
Calories: 130
Fat: 0.0g
Protein: 0.4g
Carbohydrate: 34.3g
Cholesterol: 0mg
Sodium: 20mg
Exchanges:
  1 Starch
  1 Fruit

Cook 1¼ cups water and sugar in a small saucepan over medium heat, stirring constantly, until sugar dissolves. Remove pan from heat, and cool completely.

Stir in mint and next 3 ingredients; cover and chill at least 3 hours.

Pour mixture through a wire-mesh strainer into a pitcher, discarding mint and orange rind. Stir in sparkling water, and serve immediately over ice. Garnish, if desired. Yield: 5 cups.

Old-Fashioned Cinnamon Rolls
(page 61)

Breads

Nothing welcomes your family home like the aroma of freshly baked bread. Experience the therapeutic kneading and punching of yeast bread dough or just relish the ease of quick breads. An inviting variety of quick and yeast breads—both savory and sweet—await your selection. You'll increase the amount of grains in your diet, benefit from the low calorie and fat count, and simply enjoy the bounties homemade breads have to offer.

Apricot-Pecan Bread

This bread is surprisingly moist for a low-fat sweet.

2½ cups dried apricots, chopped
1 cup chopped pecans
4 cups all-purpose flour, divided
¼ cup butter or margarine, softened
2 cups sugar

2 large eggs
4 teaspoons baking powder
½ teaspoon baking soda
½ teaspoon salt
1½ cups orange juice
Vegetable cooking spray

Combine chopped apricot and warm water to cover in a large bowl; let stand 30 minutes. Drain apricot. Stir in pecans and ½ cup flour; set aside.

Beat butter at medium speed with an electric mixer 2 minutes; gradually add sugar, beating mixture well. Add eggs, one at a time, beating after each addition.

Combine remaining 3½ cups flour, baking powder, soda, and salt. Add to butter mixture alternately with orange juice, beginning and ending with flour mixture. Stir in apricot mixture.

Spoon batter into two 8½- x 4½-inch loafpans lightly coated with cooking spray and sprinkled with flour; let stand at room temperature 20 minutes.

Bake bread at 350° for 1 hour or until a wooden pick inserted in center comes out clean. Cool in pans on a wire rack 10 to 15 minutes; remove from pans, and cool completely on wire rack. Yield: 2 loaves.

Fruity Banana Bread

⅓ cup margarine, softened
¾ cup sugar
½ cup egg substitute
1¾ cups all-purpose flour
2¾ teaspoons baking powder

1 cup mashed ripe banana
¾ cup coarsely chopped mixed dried fruit
Vegetable cooking spray

Beat margarine at medium speed with an electric mixer until creamy; gradually add sugar, beating well. Add egg substitute, beating until blended.

Combine flour and baking powder; add to butter mixture. Beat at low speed until blended. Stir in mashed banana and dried fruit. Pour batter into an 8½- x 4½-inch loafpan lightly coated with cooking spray.

Bake at 350° for 1 hour or until a wooden pick inserted in center of loaf comes out clean. Cool in pan on a wire rack 10 minutes; remove from pan, and cool completely on a wire rack. Yield: 1 loaf.

Buttermilk Biscuits

Tender, flaky biscuits are the end result when you make
this quick down-home bread.

2 cups all-purpose flour
2 teaspoons baking powder
½ teaspoon baking soda
¼ teaspoon salt
1 tablespoon sugar

¼ cup reduced-calorie margarine
¾ cup plus 1 tablespoon nonfat
 buttermilk
Vegetable cooking spray

Combine first 5 ingredients in a medium bowl; cut in margarine with a pastry blender until mixture resembles coarse meal. Add buttermilk, stirring just until dry ingredients are moistened.

Turn dough out onto a lightly floured surface, and knead 5 or 6 times. Roll dough to ½-inch thickness; cut into rounds with a 2½-inch biscuit cutter. Place rounds on a baking sheet coated with cooking spray. Bake at 425° for 10 to 12 minutes or until biscuits are golden. Yield: 8 biscuits.

per biscuit:
Calories: 163
Fat: 4.1g
Protein: 4.2g
Carbohydrate: 27.3g
Cholesterol: 1mg
Sodium: 282mg
Exchanges:
 1½ Starch
 1 Fat

Whole Wheat Biscuits

1½ cups all-purpose flour
½ cup whole wheat flour
1 tablespoon baking powder
½ teaspoon salt

3 tablespoons reduced-calorie
 margarine
¾ cup fat-free evaporated milk
Vegetable cooking spray

Combine flours, baking powder, and salt; cut in margarine with a pastry blender until mixture is crumbly.

Add milk, stirring just until dry ingredients are moistened. Turn dough out onto a lightly floured surface, and knead about 1 minute.

Shape dough into 12 balls; place balls in an 8-inch square pan coated with cooking spray. Flatten dough slightly. Bake at 450° for 10 to 12 minutes or until golden. Yield: 1 dozen.

per biscuit:
Calories: 105
Fat: 2.2g
Protein: 3.6g
Carbohydrate: 18.2g
Cholesterol: 1mg
Sodium: 144mg
Exchanges:
 1 Starch
 ½ Fat

Almond-Yogurt Scones

per scone:

Calories: 184
Fat: 5.1g
Protein: 5.6g
Carbohydrate: 28.7g
Cholesterol: 1mg
Sodium: 263mg
Exchanges:
  2 Starch
  1 Fat

1 cup all-purpose flour
1 cup sifted cake flour
2 teaspoons baking powder
½ teaspoon baking soda
¼ teaspoon salt
2 tablespoons brown sugar
2 tablespoons margarine
¼ cup chopped almonds, lightly toasted
1 (8-ounce) carton plain nonfat yogurt
Vegetable cooking spray
1 egg white, lightly beaten

Combine first 6 ingredients in a medium bowl; cut in margarine with a pastry blender until mixture resembles coarse meal. Add almonds; toss well. Add yogurt to dry ingredients, stirring just until dry ingredients are moistened.

Turn dough out onto a lightly floured surface, and knead 3 or 4 times. Pat dough into an 8-inch round on a baking sheet coated with cooking spray. Cut round into 8 wedges, cutting to, but not through, bottom of dough. Brush wedges with egg white. Bake at 425° for 10 to 12 minutes or until golden. Yield: 8 scones.

Granola Muffins

per muffin:

Calories: 140
Fat: 3.3g
Protein: 2.5g
Carbohydrate: 25.1g
Cholesterol: 14mg
Sodium: 153mg
Exchanges:
  ½ Starch

1½ cups reduced-fat biscuit and baking mix
1 cup firmly packed brown sugar
1 teaspoon ground cinnamon
1 cup oats and honey granola cereal with almonds (we tested with Quaker 100% Natural Oats & Honey Cereal)
½ cup raisins
1 large egg, lightly beaten
¾ cup fat-free milk
1 tablespoon vegetable oil
Vegetable cooking spray

Combine first 3 ingredients in a bowl; stir in cereal and raisins. Make a well in center of mixture; set aside.

Combine egg, milk, and oil; add to flour mixture, stirring just until dry ingredients are moistened. (Batter will be thin.)

Spoon batter into muffin pans coated with cooking spray, filling three-fourths full.

Bake at 375° for 15 to 20 minutes or until muffins are golden. Remove from pans immediately. Yield: 16 muffins.

Blueberry-Oat Streusel Muffins

⅓ cup regular oats, uncooked
3 tablespoons brown sugar
1 tablespoon all-purpose flour
1 tablespoon reduced-calorie margarine
2 tablespoons chopped almonds
2 cups all-purpose flour
2 teaspoons baking powder
¼ teaspoon baking soda
¼ teaspoon salt
½ cup sugar
2 teaspoons grated lemon rind
1½ cups fresh or frozen blueberries, thawed
¾ cup nonfat buttermilk
¼ cup vegetable oil
1 large egg, lightly beaten
Vegetable cooking spray

per muffin:

Calories: 177
Fat: 6.0g
Protein: 3.5g
Carbohydrate: 27.9g
Cholesterol: 16mg
Sodium: 128mg
Exchanges:
  1 Starch
  1 Fruit
  1 Fat

Process first 3 ingredients in a food processor 5 seconds or until mixture resembles fine meal. Add margarine; pulse 5 times or until mixture resembles coarse meal. Transfer to a small bowl; stir in almonds. Set aside.

Combine 2 cups flour and next 5 ingredients in a large bowl. Add blueberries; toss gently. Make a well in center of mixture. Combine buttermilk, oil, and egg; add to dry ingredients, stirring just until moistened.

Spoon batter into muffin pans coated with cooking spray, filling two-thirds full. Sprinkle evenly with oat mixture. Bake at 400° for 15 to 20 minutes or until muffins are golden. Remove from pans immediately. Yield: 14 muffins.

Blueberry-Oat Streusel Muffins

Ginger Pancakes with
Creamy Maple Topping

Ginger Pancakes with
Creamy Maple Topping

2 cups all-purpose flour
1 tablespoon baking powder
1 teaspoon ground cinnamon
1 teaspoon ground ginger
½ teaspoon ground cloves
1 cup fat-free milk
⅓ cup molasses

2 tablespoons vegetable oil
1 large egg, lightly beaten
2 egg whites
Vegetable cooking spray
Creamy Maple Topping
Garnish: Fresh strawberries

Combine first 5 ingredients in a large bowl; make a well in center of mixture. Combine milk, molasses, oil, egg, and egg whites; add to dry ingredients, stirring just until dry ingredients are moistened.

For each pancake, pour ¼ cup batter onto a hot griddle or skillet coated with cooking spray. Cook pancakes until tops are covered with bubbles and edges look cooked; turn and cook other side. Top each pancake with 2 tablespoons Creamy Maple Topping. Garnish, if desired. Yield: 12 (4-inch) pancakes.

Creamy Maple Topping

1½ cups vanilla nonfat frozen yogurt, softened

¼ teaspoon ground cinnamon

¼ cup plus 2 tablespoons reduced-calorie maple syrup

Combine all ingredients in a small bowl; stir well. Cover and chill. Yield: 1½ cups.

Yogurt Waffles

Treat your family to a breakfast of these crisp homemade waffles—they're a delicious way to start the day.

2 cups all-purpose flour
1 teaspoon baking soda
½ teaspoon baking powder
¼ teaspoon salt
1 tablespoon sugar
1½ cups fat-free milk
¾ cup plain nonfat yogurt

2 tablespoons vegetable oil
3 egg whites
⅛ teaspoon cream of tartar
Vegetable cooking spray
Reduced-calorie maple syrup
    (optional)

per waffle:

Calories: 93
Fat: 2.0g
Protein: 3.6g
Carbohydrate: 14.8g
Cholesterol: 1mg
Sodium: 129mg
Exchanges:
  1 Starch
  ½ Fat

Combine first 5 ingredients in a large bowl; make a well in center of mixture. Combine milk, yogurt, and oil; stir with a wire whisk. Add to dry ingredients, stirring just until dry ingredients are moistened.

Beat egg whites and cream of tartar at high speed with an electric mixer until stiff peaks form; gently fold beaten egg white mixture into batter.

Coat an 8-inch square waffle iron with cooking spray; allow waffle iron to preheat. For each waffle, spoon 1¼ cups batter onto hot waffle iron, spreading batter to edges. Bake 4 to 5 minutes or until steaming stops. Repeat procedure with remaining batter. Cut each waffle into 4 squares. Top with maple syrup, if desired. Yield: 16 (4-inch) waffles.

Jalapeño Cornbread

1 cup cornmeal
2 teaspoons baking powder
¼ teaspoon salt
2 large eggs
3 tablespoons nonfat sour cream
1 (8¾-ounce) can cream-style corn
1 (4¼-ounce) jar pickled, chopped jalapeño peppers, drained (5 tablespoons)
1½ teaspoons vegetable oil
Vegetable cooking spray

Heat an 8-inch cast-iron skillet in a 400° oven for 5 minutes.

Combine first 3 ingredients in a large bowl; make a well in center of mixture. Set aside.

Combine eggs and next 4 ingredients; add mixture to dry ingredients, stirring just until moistened.

Remove skillet from oven, and coat with cooking spray; pour batter into hot skillet. Bake at 400° for 20 minutes or until golden. Cut into wedges Yield: 8 servings.

Note: We tried Jalapeño Cornbread with egg substitute instead of the eggs and were disappointed with the results.

Baked Hush Puppies

These savory pups are pictured on page 64.

1 cup yellow cornmeal
1 cup all-purpose flour
1 tablespoon baking powder
1 teaspoon salt
1 teaspoon sugar
⅛ teaspoon ground red pepper
2 large eggs, lightly beaten
¾ cup milk
¼ cup vegetable oil
½ cup finely chopped onion
Vegetable cooking spray

Combine first 6 ingredients in a large bowl; make a well in center of mixture. Set aside.

Combine eggs and next 3 ingredients, stirring well; add to dry ingredients, stirring just until moistened.

Coat miniature muffin pans with cooking spray. Spoon about 1 tablespoon batter into each muffin cup. (Cups will be about three-fourths full.)

Bake at 425° for 15 minutes or until done. Remove from pans, and serve immediately. Yield: 3 dozen.

Swedish Rye Loaves

This recipe makes two loaves—one for keeping and one for sharing.

2 cups water
¼ cup molasses
¼ cup butter or margarine
2½ cups medium rye flour
⅓ cup firmly packed brown sugar

2 (¼-ounce) envelopes active dry yeast
1 tablespoon salt
3½ to 4 cups all-purpose flour
Vegetable cooking spray

Cook first 3 ingredients in a small saucepan over medium heat until butter melts, stirring often. Cool mixture to 120° to 130°.

Combine rye flour and next 3 ingredients in a large mixing bowl; gradually add molasses mixture, beating at low speed with an electric mixer. Beat 2 more minutes at medium speed. Gradually stir in enough all-purpose flour to make a soft dough.

Turn dough out onto a well-floured surface; knead until smooth and elastic (about 5 minutes). Place in a large bowl coated with cooking spray, turning to coat top.

Cover and let rise in a warm place (85°), free from drafts, 45 minutes or until almost doubled in bulk.

Punch dough down, and divide in half. Shape each portion into a round loaf, and place in two greased 8-inch round cakepans.

Cover and let rise in a warm place, free from drafts, 40 minutes or until almost doubled in bulk.

Bake at 375° for 25 to 30 minutes or until loaves sound hollow when tapped. Remove from pans immediately, and cool on wire racks. Cut each loaf into 8 equal wedges. Yield: 2 loaves.

per wedge:
Calories: 222
Fat: 3.6g
Protein: 5.0g
Carbohydrate: 43.0g
Cholesterol: 8mg
Sodium: 472mg
Exchanges:
  2 Starch
  1 Carbohydrate
  ½ Fat

Crusty French Pistou Bread

Crusty French Pistou Bread

Pistou (pees-TOO) is the French version of pesto, combining
basil, garlic, and olive oil.

3½ to 4½ cups bread flour
2 (¼-ounce) envelopes rapid-rise
    yeast
1 tablespoon sugar
1 to 2 teaspoons salt
⅓ cup olive oil
½ cup minced fresh parsley
1 cup chopped fresh basil

1 cup grated Parmesan cheese
4 garlic cloves, minced
1⅓ cups very warm water
    (120° to 130°)
Vegetable cooking spray
1 tablespoon cornmeal
1 large egg, lightly beaten
1 tablespoon water

Combine 3½ cups flour and next 3 ingredients; add oil and next 4 ingredients; beat at low speed with a heavy-duty electric mixer until blended.
Add warm water; beat at medium speed until blended. Turn dough out
onto a lightly floured surface, and knead until smooth and elastic (5 to 10
minutes), adding remaining flour as needed.
Place dough in a bowl coated with cooking spray, turning to coat top.
Cover and let rise in a warm place (85°), free from drafts, 1 hour or until
doubled in bulk.

Punch dough down; turn out onto a lightly floured surface, and knead lightly 4 or 5 times. Divide dough in half. Shape each portion into a round loaf, and place on a baking sheet lightly coated with cooking spray and sprinkled with cornmeal.

Let rise in a warm place, free from drafts, 45 minutes or until doubled in bulk. Make ½-inch-deep slashes in top of each loaf with a sharp knife. Combine egg and 1 tablespoon water, stirring well; gently brush mixture over loaves.

Place a shallow pan on lower oven rack; fill with boiling water. Place loaves on middle rack. Bake at 400° for 25 to 30 minutes or until loaves sound hollow when tapped. Remove from pans immediately, and cool on wire racks. Cut each loaf into 8 wedges. Yield: 2 loaves.

Wheat-Lover's Bread

2 cups stone-ground whole wheat
   flour
½ teaspoon salt
2 (¼-ounce) envelopes active dry
   yeast
2 cups very warm water
   (120° to 130°)

¼ cup molasses
2 tablespoons vegetable oil
½ cup toasted wheat germ
½ cup unprocessed wheat bran
1½ cups bread flour
Vegetable cooking spray

per ½-inch slice:
Calories: 71
Fat: 1.3g
Protein: 2.5g
Carbohydrate: 13.3g
Cholesterol: 0mg
Sodium: 36mg
Exchanges:
   1 Starch

Combine first 3 ingredients in a large mixing bowl; stir well. Add warm water to flour mixture, beating well at low speed with an electric mixer. Add molasses and oil; beat 2 minutes at medium speed. Gradually add wheat germ, wheat bran, and enough of the 1½ cups bread flour to make a soft dough.

Turn dough out onto a lightly floured surface; knead until smooth and elastic (about 8 to 10 minutes). Place dough in a large bowl coated with cooking spray, turning to coat top. Cover and let rise in a warm place (85°), free from drafts, 35 minutes or until doubled in bulk.

Punch dough down; divide in half. Turn 1 portion of dough out onto lightly floured surface; roll into a 14- x 7-inch rectangle. Roll up, starting at short side, pressing firmly to eliminate air pockets; pinch ends to seal. Place, seam side down, in an 8½- x 4½-inch loafpan coated with cooking spray. Repeat procedure with remaining dough.

Cover; let rise in a warm place, free from drafts, 30 minutes or until doubled in bulk. Bake at 375° for 35 minutes or until loaves sound hollow when tapped. Remove from pans immediately; cool on wire racks. Yield: 1 loaf.

Parmesan-Onion Twist

Treat company to these savory, braided loaves. They'll enjoy the
Italian flavor of the herbs and Parmesan cheese.

per ½-inch slice:

Calories: 65
Fat: 0.9g
Protein: 2.7g
Carbohydrate: 11.3g
Cholesterol: 1mg
Sodium: 28mg
Exchanges:
  1 Starch

¾ cup canned no-salt-added
  chicken broth, undiluted
1 tablespoon vegetable oil
2 cups finely chopped onion
1 teaspoon dried whole basil
1 teaspoon dried whole oregano
6 cups bread flour, divided
2 (¼-ounce) envelopes active dry
  yeast

2 cups very warm fat-free milk
  (120° to 130°)
1 cup freshly grated Parmesan
  cheese
1 tablespoon sugar
Vegetable cooking spray
1 egg white, lightly beaten

Combine broth and oil in a nonstick skillet. Place over medium heat until
hot. Add onion, basil, and oregano; sauté until onion is tender. Combine

Parmesan-Onion Twist

2 cups flour and yeast, stirring well. Add milk to flour mixture, beating at low speed with an electric mixer. Beat 2 minutes at medium speed. Add onion mixture, cheese, and sugar. Stir in enough of the remaining 4 cups flour to make a soft dough.

Turn dough out onto a lightly floured surface; knead until smooth and elastic. Place in a bowl coated with cooking spray, turning to coat top. Cover and let rise in a warm place (85°), free from drafts, 30 minutes or until doubled in bulk.

Punch dough down; divide in half. Divide each half into 3 equal portions. Roll each portion into a 16-inch rope. Braid 3 ropes together on a baking sheet coated with cooking spray, pinching ends to seal; tuck ends under. Repeat procedure with remaining ropes.

Cover and let rise in a warm place, free from drafts, 20 minutes or until doubled in bulk. Brush with egg white. Bake at 350° for 35 minutes or until loaves sound hollow when tapped. (Cover with aluminum foil the last 15 minutes of baking to prevent overbrowning, if necessary.) Yield: 2 loaves.

Cinnamon-Raisin Batter Bread

3 cups all-purpose flour, divided
2 tablespoons sugar
1 teaspoon ground cinnamon
¼ teaspoon salt
¼ teaspoon ground allspice
1 (¼-ounce) envelope active dry yeast
1 cup fat-free milk
¼ cup molasses
2 tablespoons margarine
1 large egg
½ cup raisins
Vegetable cooking spray

per ½-inch slice:
Calories: 126
Fat: 1.8g
Protein 3.3g
Carbohydrate: 24.2g
Cholesterol: 13mg
Sodium: 62mg
Exchanges:
  1½ Starch

Combine 1½ cups flour, sugar, and next 4 ingredients in a large bowl.

Combine milk, molasses, and margarine in a small saucepan; cook over medium heat until margarine melts. Cool to 120° to 130°. Gradually add to flour mixture, beating at low speed with an electric mixer until smooth. Add egg, and beat at low speed until blended. Beat at medium speed 3 minutes. Stir in remaining 1½ cups flour and raisins.

Spoon into a 9- x 5-inch loafpan coated with cooking spray.

Cover and let rise in a warm place (85°), free from drafts, 40 minutes or until doubled in bulk.

Bake at 350° for 35 to 40 minutes or until golden. Remove from pan; cool on a wire rack. Yield: 1 loaf.

Buttermilk Dinner Rolls

2 (¼-ounce) envelopes active dry
  yeast
¼ cup warm water (105° to 115°)
1¾ cups nonfat buttermilk
¼ cup sugar

2 tablespoons margarine, softened
½ teaspoon salt
1 large egg
5 cups bread flour
Vegetable cooking spray

Combine yeast and warm water in a 1-cup liquid measuring cup; let stand 5 minutes. Combine yeast mixture, buttermilk, and next 4 ingredients in a large mixing bowl; beat at medium speed with an electric mixer until well blended. Add 2 cups flour, and beat 2 minutes at medium speed. Gradually stir in enough of the remaining 3 cups flour to make a soft dough.

Turn dough out onto a lightly floured surface, and knead until smooth and elastic (about 8 to 10 minutes). Place dough in a large bowl coated with cooking spray, turning to coat top. Cover and let rise in a warm place (85°), free from drafts, 45 minutes or until doubled in bulk.

Punch dough down; divide in half. Divide each half into 8 equal portions; shape each portion into a ball. Place at least 1 inch apart on large baking sheets coated with cooking spray.

Cover and let rise in a warm place, free from drafts, 30 minutes or until doubled in bulk. Bake at 325° for 18 to 20 minutes or until lightly browned. Remove rolls from baking sheets; let cool on wire racks. Yield: 16 rolls.

Parsley-Garlic Rolls

2 tablespoons reduced-calorie
  margarine, melted
2 garlic cloves, crushed
1 (16-ounce) loaf frozen bread
  dough, thawed

1 tablespoon chopped fresh
  parsley
Vegetable cooking spray

Combine margarine and garlic; set mixture aside.

Cut bread dough crosswise into 6 even portions with kitchen shears; cut portions in half crosswise. Roll each half to ¼-inch thickness on a lightly floured surface; brush with margarine mixture, and sprinkle with parsley.

Roll each piece of dough, jellyroll fashion; place, swirl side down, in muffin pans coated with cooking spray. Cover and let rise in a warm place (85°), free from drafts, 1 hour or until doubled in bulk. Bake at 400° for 10 to 12 minutes. Serve immediately. Yield: 1 dozen.

Old-Fashioned Cinnamon Rolls

Find these yummy cinnamon rolls pictured on page 46.

⅓ cup fat-free milk
⅓ cup reduced-calorie margarine
¼ cup firmly packed brown sugar
1 teaspoon salt
1 (¼-ounce) envelope active dry yeast
½ cup warm water (105° to 115°)
½ cup egg substitute
3½ cups bread flour
¾ cup quick-cooking oats, uncooked

Vegetable cooking spray
¼ cup reduced-calorie margarine, softened
¾ cup firmly packed brown sugar
¼ cup raisins
2 teaspoons ground cinnamon
1 cup sifted powdered sugar
2 tablespoons water

per roll:
Calories: 159
Fat: 3.4g
Protein: 3.6g
Carbohydrate: 29.0g
Cholesterol: 0mg
Sodium: 153mg
Exchanges:
  2 Starch

Combine first 4 ingredients in a saucepan; heat until margarine melts, stirring occasionally. Cool mixture to 105° to 115°.

Combine yeast and warm water; let stand 5 minutes. Combine yeast mixture, milk mixture, egg substitute, 1 cup flour, and oats in a large bowl, stirring well. Gradually stir in enough remaining flour to make a soft dough.

Turn dough out onto a lightly floured surface; knead until smooth and elastic (about 8 minutes). Place dough in a large bowl coated with cooking spray, turning to coat top.

Cover and let rise in a warm place (85°), free from drafts, 1 hour or until doubled in bulk.

Punch dough down. Cover; let rest 10 minutes. Divide in half; roll each half into a 12-inch square. Spread each with 2 tablespoons margarine.

Combine ¾ cup brown sugar, raisins, and cinnamon; sprinkle over each square. Roll up, jellyroll fashion; pinch seam to seal. Cut each roll into 1-inch slices; place, cut side down, in two 8-inch square pans coated with cooking spray.

Cover and let rise in a warm place, free from drafts, 30 minutes or until almost doubled in bulk.

Bake at 375° for 15 to 20 minutes or until golden. Combine powdered sugar and 2 tablespoons water; drizzle over warm rolls. Yield: 2 dozen.

Puffy Pitas

Puffy Pitas

Serve these pitas alone, with your favorite spread, or stuffed with your choice of sandwich filling. Leftovers freeze nicely in an airtight container.

per pita:

Calories: 226
Fat: 3.5g
Protein: 7.0g
Carbohydrate: 40.7g
Cholesterol: 0mg
Sodium: 221mg
Exchanges:
  2½ Starch
  ½ Fat

6 to 6½ cups bread flour
2 (¼-ounce) envelopes active dry yeast
1½ teaspoons salt

2½ cups hot water (130°)
3 tablespoons olive oil
Vegetable cooking spray

Combine 3 cups flour, yeast, and salt in a large mixing bowl; add hot water and olive oil, and beat mixture at low speed with an electric mixer until blended. Beat mixture at high speed 3 minutes. Stir in 3 cups of remaining flour, 1 cup at a time, using a wooden spoon.

Turn dough out onto a well-floured surface; knead until smooth and elastic (about 10 minutes), adding remaining flour as needed.

Place dough in a bowl coated with cooking spray, turning to coat top. Cover and let rise in a warm place (85°), free from drafts, 45 to 50 minutes or until doubled in bulk.

Punch dough down, and turn out onto a lightly floured surface. Knead dough lightly 4 or 5 times. Divide into 16 portions; shape each portion into a ball. Roll each ball into a 6½-inch circle on a lightly floured surface.

Place each circle on a 7-inch square of heavy-duty aluminum foil lightly coated with cooking spray, and let dough rise in a warm place, uncovered, 30 minutes or until doubled in bulk.

Bake pitas, a few at a time, at 500° on foil on lower oven rack 5 to 7 minutes or until pitas are puffed and lightly browned. Yield: 16 pitas.

Rosemary Focaccia

Serve a wedge of this Italian flatbread with one of the many soups and salads featured in this book.

1 (¼-ounce) envelope active dry yeast
1¼ cups warm water (105° to 115°)
3½ cups all-purpose flour, divided
1 teaspoon salt, divided

¼ cup butter, melted
½ cup chopped fresh rosemary, divided
Vegetable cooking spray
2 tablespoons olive oil
4 garlic cloves, minced

per wedge:
Calories: 202
Fat: 7.3g
Protein: 4.2g
Carbohydrate: 29.8g
Cholesterol: 10mg
Sodium: 236mg
Exchanges:
  2 Starch
  1½ Fat

Combine yeast and warm water in a 2-cup liquid measuring cup; let stand 5 minutes.

Combine yeast mixture, 2 cups flour, and ½ teaspoon salt in a large bowl, stirring well.

Cover and let rise in a warm place (85°), free from drafts, 1 hour or until dough is doubled in bulk.

Punch dough down, and stir in remaining flour, butter, and ¼ cup chopped rosemary.

Turn dough out onto a lightly floured surface, and knead 10 minutes.

Divide dough into thirds; roll each portion into a 9-inch circle on baking sheets coated with cooking spray.

Brush dough evenly with olive oil; sprinkle evenly with remaining ¼ cup rosemary, ½ teaspoon salt, and garlic. Prick dough generously with fork.

Bake at 400° for 20 minutes. Cut each round into 4 wedges. Yield: 12 servings.

Oven-Fried Catfish (page 66), Green Bean Slaw
(page 180), and Baked Hush Puppies (page 54)

Fish & Shellfish

For quick preparation and great-tasting entrées, it's hard to beat fish and shellfish. They're low in fat and loaded with protein, vitamins, and minerals. You'll find healthy suggestions for preparing these entrées, plus recommendations for using herbs, spices, and savory marinades to pump up the flavor. Eating more healthfully has never been easier or tastier!

Amberjack with Tomato-Fennel Sauce

per serving:

Calories: 169
Fat: 2.5g
Protein: 25.8g
Carbohydrate: 10.2g
Cholesterol: 49mg
Sodium: 163mg
Exchanges:
  2 Vegetable
  3 Very Lean Meat

Vegetable cooking spray
1 cup canned no-salt-added
     chicken broth, undiluted
½ cup chopped onion
½ cup chopped fennel bulb
1 teaspoon minced garlic
¼ teaspoon crushed dried fennel
     seeds
1 (14½-ounce) can no-salt-added
     stewed tomatoes

1 (8-ounce) can no-salt-added
     tomato sauce
¼ cup chopped fresh parsley,
     divided
½ teaspoon sugar
½ teaspoon freshly ground
     pepper, divided
¼ teaspoon salt
6 (4-ounce) amberjack fillets
4 cups water

Coat a large nonstick skillet with cooking spray; add chicken broth. Place over medium-high heat until hot. Add onion and next 3 ingredients; cook until vegetables are tender and liquid evaporates. Stir in stewed tomatoes and tomato sauce. Cook, uncovered, over low heat 30 minutes or until mixture is thickened. Stir in 2 tablespoons parsley, sugar, ¼ teaspoon pepper, and salt.

Rinse fillets and pat dry; sprinkle with remaining ¼ teaspoon pepper. Bring water to a boil in a large nonstick skillet over medium heat. Reduce heat, and add fillets; cover and simmer 8 minutes or until fish flakes easily when tested with a fork. Remove fish from liquid, and place on a serving platter; discard liquid. Spoon tomato mixture evenly over fillets, and sprinkle with remaining 2 tablespoons parsley. Yield: 6 servings.

Oven-Fried Catfish

This recipe delivers a crisp, golden crust (see photo on page 64).

per serving:

Calories: 247
Fat: 8.7g
Protein: 25.5g
Carbohydrate: 14.0g
Cholesterol: 77mg
Sodium: 673mg
Exchanges:
  1 Starch
  3 Lean Meat

¾ cup crushed cornflakes cereal
¾ teaspoon celery salt
¼ teaspoon onion powder
¼ teaspoon paprika

Dash of pepper
4 (6-ounce) skinless farm-raised
     catfish fillets, halved
Vegetable cooking spray

Combine first 5 ingredients; set aside. Spray all sides of fish with cooking spray; coat with cornflake mixture. Arrange fillets in a single layer on a baking sheet coated with cooking spray. Spray tops of fillets with cooking spray.

Bake, uncovered, at 350° for 30 minutes or until fish flakes easily when tested with a fork. Yield: 4 servings.

Poached Flounder with Greek Sauce

A white wine poaching liquid imparts delicate flavor to this flounder. It's just right for savoring with the Greek-inspired sauce served on the side.

2 tablespoons chopped onion
2 fresh parsley sprigs
½ bay leaf
⅛ teaspoon salt
4 whole peppercorns

½ cup dry white wine
½ cup water
4 (4-ounce) skinned flounder fillets or other lean white fish
Greek Sauce

per serving:
Calories: 138
Fat: 2.6g
Protein: 21.5g
Carbohydrate: 6.2g
Cholesterol: 59mg
Sodium: 279mg
Exchanges:
 ½ Starch
 3 Very Lean Meat

Combine first 7 ingredients in an 11- x 7-inch baking dish. Cover with heavy-duty plastic wrap; fold back a small corner of wrap for steam to escape.

Microwave at HIGH 4 to 5 minutes or until boiling. Uncover and arrange fillets in liquid with thickest portion to outside of dish.

Cover and microwave at HIGH 3 to 4 minutes, giving dish a half-turn after 2 minutes. Cook until fish turns opaque. Let stand, covered, 3 to 5 minutes. Fish is done if it flakes easily when tested with a fork.

Remove fish to a serving dish. Strain poaching liquid, reserving 2 tablespoons liquid to use in sauce. Serve with Greek Sauce. Yield: 4 servings.

Greek Sauce

¼ cup reduced-fat mayonnaise
¼ cup plain low-fat yogurt
¼ cup minced fresh parsley
2 tablespoons lemon juice

⅛ teaspoon freshly ground pepper
⅛ teaspoon garlic powder
2 tablespoons reserved poaching liquid

Combine all ingredients in a small bowl; stir well. Yield: ¾ cup.

Hot Spicy Grouper

per serving:

Calories: 155
Fat: 5.9g
Protein: 22.5g
Carbohydrate: 2.1g
Cholesterol: 42mg
Sodium: 393mg
Exchanges:
  3 Very Lean Meat
  1 Fat

4 (4-ounce) grouper or snapper
     fillets
¼ cup lemon juice
2 tablespoons water
2 tablespoons hot sauce
1 tablespoon vegetable oil
2 teaspoons grated fresh ginger

½ teaspoon salt
Vegetable cooking spray
1 tablespoon sesame seeds,
     toasted
1 tablespoon chopped fresh
     parsley

Place grouper in a shallow dish; set aside.

Combine lemon juice and next 5 ingredients; divide in half. Cover and chill 1 portion. Pour remaining portion over fish, turning to coat. Cover with aluminum foil.

Chill fillets 1 hour, turning fish occasionally.

Remove fish from marinade, discarding marinade.

Arrange fish in a single layer in a grill basket coated with cooking spray. Grill, covered with grill lid, over high heat (400° to 500°) 5 minutes on each side or until fish flakes easily when tested with a fork, basting with remaining marinade.

Transfer fish to a serving plate; sprinkle with sesame seeds and parsley. Yield: 4 servings.

Steamed Orange Roughy with Herbs

This unbelievably simple recipe has so much flavor you won't need to reach for the salt shaker.

per serving:

Calories: 79
Fat: 0.8g
Protein: 16.7g
Carbohydrate: 0.0g
Cholesterol: 23mg
Sodium: 72mg
Exchanges:
  2½ Very Lean Meat

½ cup fresh parsley sprigs
½ cup fresh chives
½ cup fresh thyme sprigs
½ cup rosemary sprigs

2 (8-ounce) orange roughy
     fillets
Fresh lemon slices

Arrange half of herbs in bottom of a steaming basket. Top with fillets and remaining herbs.

Cover and steam fillets 7 minutes or until fish flakes easily when tested with a fork. Serve with fresh lemon slices. Yield: 4 servings.

Note: Any mild-flavored fish can be substituted in this recipe. Try cod, grouper, snapper, or farm-raised catfish. And don't limit yourself to the herbs we suggest; use any fresh herb you have available.

Steamed Orange Roughy with Herbs

Pesto-Crusted Orange Roughy

Try this flavorful herbed crust on any mild-flavored fish,
such as cod, catfish, snapper, or grouper.

2 tablespoons pesto
½ cup fine, dry breadcrumbs
  (commercial)

¼ teaspoon pepper
4 (4-ounce) orange roughy fillets
Vegetable cooking spray

Combine pesto, breadcrumbs, and pepper in a shallow dish. Dredge fillets in breadcrumb mixture, and place in an 11- x 7-inch baking dish coated with cooking spray. Coat fillets with cooking spray.

Bake at 400° for 15 minutes or until fish flakes easily when tested with a fork. Yield: 4 servings.

Fillets of Salmon with Tomato and Chives

6 (4-ounce) salmon fillets
¼ teaspoon salt
¼ teaspoon freshly ground
  pepper
4 cups water
Olive oil-flavored vegetable
  cooking spray
1 tablespoon minced shallot
½ teaspoon minced garlic

¼ cup dry white wine
1 cup seeded, diced tomato
2 tablespoons chopped fresh
  chives
2 tablespoons fresh lemon juice
¼ teaspoon salt
⅛ teaspoon ground white pepper
Garnish: fresh chives

Sprinkle fillets with ¼ teaspoon salt and ¼ teaspoon pepper. Bring 4 cups of water just to a boil in a large nonstick skillet over medium heat. Reduce heat, and add fillets; cover and simmer 4 to 5 minutes or until fish flakes easily when tested with a fork. Remove fillets from skillet, using a slotted spatula, and place on a serving platter. Set aside, and keep warm.

Coat a small nonstick skillet with cooking spray; place over medium-high heat until hot. Add shallot and garlic; sauté 1 minute. Add wine, and cook until reduced by half. Stir in tomato and next 4 ingredients. Spoon sauce evenly over salmon fillets. Garnish, if desired. Serve immediately. Yield: 6 servings.

Peppered Snapper with Creamy Dill Sauce

Just add a vegetable and some bread to these peppery fillets
served over rice, and your meal is complete.

4 (4-ounce) snapper fillets
2 teaspoons olive oil, divided
2 tablespoons coarsely ground
   pepper

Vegetable cooking spray
2 cups hot cooked rice (cooked
   without salt or fat)
Creamy Dill Sauce

per serving:
Calories: 381
Fat: 10.1g
Protein: 36.8g
Carbohydrate: 32.7g
Cholesterol: 76mg
Sodium: 438mg
Exchanges:
  2 Starch
  4 Lean Meat

Brush snapper on both sides with 1 teaspoon olive oil; sprinkle with pepper, and gently press into fish. Cover and let stand 15 minutes.

Coat a large nonstick skillet with cooking spray; add remaining 1 teaspoon olive oil, and place over medium heat. Cook fillets on both sides 3 to 5 minutes or until fish flakes easily when tested with a fork. Remove from heat; keep warm.

Spoon rice evenly onto serving plates; top each with a fillet and ¼ cup Creamy Dill Sauce. Serve immediately. Yield: 4 servings.

Creamy Dill Sauce

1 (10-ounce) container
   refrigerated reduced-calorie
   Alfredo sauce

2 tablespoons dry white wine
1 teaspoon dried dillweed

Combine all ingredients in a small heavy saucepan; cook, stirring constantly, over medium heat until thoroughly heated. Remove from heat; keep warm. Yield: 1 cup.

Swordfish-Shiitake Skewers

When the fish is done, grill radicchio leaves just until limp to serve on the side. If desired, tuna fillets may be substituted for swordfish, and white mushrooms may be used in place of shiitakes.

per serving:

Calories: 192
Fat: 6.3g
Protein: 25.5g
Carbohydrate: 13.6g
Cholesterol: 44mg
Sodium: 311mg
Exchanges:
  3 Vegetable
  3 Very Lean Meat
  ½ Fat

¼ cup lemon juice
1 tablespoon fresh thyme
1 tablespoon olive oil
¼ teaspoon salt
¼ teaspoon freshly ground pepper
¾ pound swordfish fillets, cut into 1-inch pieces

½ pound fresh shiitake mushrooms
2 lemons, thinly sliced
¼ pound radicchio leaves, separated

Whisk together first 5 ingredients in a shallow dish.

Thread fish, mushrooms, and lemon slices folded in half onto skewers; add to lemon juice mixture, turning to coat. Cover and chill 1 hour.

Remove kabobs from marinade, discarding marinade.

Grill kabobs, covered with grill lid, over medium-high heat (350° to 400°) 10 minutes or until fish is done, turning occasionally.

Grill radicchio leaves, without grill lid, until slightly limp. Serve with kabobs. Yield: 3 servings.

Grilled Trout

You can substitute any fresh herb for the tarragon in this simple, but classic recipe.

per serving:

Calories: 233
Fat: 11.6g
Protein: 29.9g
Carbohydrate: 0.7g
Cholesterol: 83mg
Sodium: 185mg
Exchanges:
  4 Very Lean Meat
  2 Fat

¼ cup olive oil
¼ cup fresh tarragon
¼ cup lemon juice
½ teaspoon salt

2 (2-pound) dressed trout
4 fresh tarragon sprigs
1 lemon, sliced
Vegetable cooking spray

Combine olive oil and tarragon in a saucepan. Cook over very low heat 20 minutes; pour mixture through a wire-mesh strainer, discarding solids.

Whisk together oil mixture, lemon juice, and salt. Brush half of mixture inside each trout. Place 2 tarragon sprigs and 2 lemon slices inside each trout.

Place trout in a large baking dish. Pour remaining oil mixture over trout. Cover and chill 2 hours.

Place trout in a grill basket coated with cooking spray. Grill, covered with grill lid, over high heat (400° to 500°) 5 minutes on each side. Yield: 4 servings.

Trout Fillets with Capers

The pungency of capers adds loads of flavor and no fat to this dish. But if you're watching your sodium intake, you may want to reduce or to omit the capers because of their high sodium content.

½ cup all-purpose flour
¼ teaspoon salt
½ teaspoon pepper
1 teaspoon paprika

4 (6-ounce) trout fillets
1 tablespoon olive oil
¼ cup fresh lemon juice
¼ cup capers, undrained

Combine first 4 ingredients in a shallow dish; dredge fillets in mixture.
Pour olive oil in a large nonstick skillet; place over medium heat. Add fillets, and cook 3 minutes; turn fillets, and cook 1 additional minute. Add lemon juice and capers; cover and remove from heat. Let stand 3 to 5 minutes or until fish flakes easily when tested with a fork.
Transfer fillets to a serving platter; spoon sauce over fillets. Serve immediately. Yield: 4 servings.

per serving:
Calories: 297
Fat: 9.4g
Protein: 37.2g
Carbohydrate: 14.3g
Cholesterol: 97mg
Sodium: 863mg
Exchanges:
  1 Starch
  5 Very Lean Meat
  1 Fat

Oriental Grilled Tuna

6 (4-ounce) tuna steaks (¾-inch thick)
½ cup low-sodium soy sauce
½ cup water
¼ cup firmly packed brown sugar
2 tablespoons lemon juice
2 tablespoons peeled, minced ginger

2 tablespoons minced green onions
1 tablespoon grated lemon rind
2 teaspoons minced garlic
¼ teaspoon crushed red pepper
Vegetable cooking spray
Garnish: green onion curls

Place tuna steaks in a shallow dish. Combine soy sauce and next 8 ingredients in a medium bowl; pour over tuna steaks. Cover and marinate in refrigerator 30 minutes, turning once.
Remove tuna steaks from marinade, reserving marinade. Coat food rack with cooking spray; place on grill over medium-high heat (350° to 400°).
Place tuna on rack; grill, covered with grill lid, 4 to 6 minutes on each side or until fish flakes easily when tested with a fork, basting occasionally with reserved marinade. Transfer tuna to serving plates. Garnish, if desired. Yield: 6 servings.

per serving:
Calories: 179
Fat: 5.9g
Protein: 26.9g
Carbohydrate: 2.6g
Cholesterol: 44mg
Sodium: 176mg
Exchanges:
  4 Very Lean Meat
  1 Fat

Seared Tuna Steaks on Mixed Greens with Lemon-Basil Vinaigrette

Here's a high-flavor one-dish meal you can have on the table minutes after walking through the door. Just stir up the vinaigrette and grill the tuna the night before. Cover and chill until ready to serve it.

4 (4-ounce) tuna steaks
1 tablespoon reduced-sodium
 Cajun seasoning

Vegetable cooking spray
8 cups mixed salad greens
Lemon-Basil Vinaigrette

Sprinkle tuna steaks evenly with seasoning.

Coat food rack with cooking spray; place on grill over medium-high heat (350° to 400°). Place tuna on rack. Grill, covered with grill lid, 5 minutes on each side or until done. Cover and chill tuna steaks at least 8 hours.

Combine greens and half of vinaigrette; arrange on 4 plates. Top each with a tuna steak; drizzle with remaining vinaigrette. Yield: 4 servings.

Lemon-Basil Vinaigrette

2 lemons, peeled, sectioned, and
 finely chopped
2 tablespoons white wine vinegar
1 tablespoon vegetable oil

1 tablespoon finely chopped fresh
 basil
¼ teaspoon cracked black pepper
¼ teaspoon hot sauce

Combine all ingredients in a jar. Cover tightly, and shake vigorously. Yield: ½ cup.

Crawfish Fettuccine

If you prefer, you can use shrimp instead of crawfish in this recipe.

2 pounds crawfish meat
2 teaspoons Cajun seasoning
1 (12-ounce) package fettuccine
2 (½-ounce) envelopes butter-
 flavored granules
1 teaspoon chicken bouillon
 granules
¾ cup water
2 medium onions, chopped
1 green bell pepper, chopped
3 garlic cloves, pressed

½ teaspoon dried basil
½ teaspoon dried thyme
1 tablespoon cornstarch
1 (12-ounce) can fat-free
 evaporated milk
½ (16-ounce) loaf reduced-fat
 process cheese spread, cubed
¼ cup chopped fresh parsley
3 tablespoons freshly grated
 Parmesan cheese
Garnish: chopped fresh parsley

Combine crawfish and Cajun seasoning; cover and chill 30 minutes.

Cook fettuccine according to package directions; drain and keep warm.

Meanwhile, combine butter granules, bouillon granules, and water in a deep skillet or Dutch oven; cook over medium heat until granules dissolve.

Add onion, bell pepper, and garlic; cook over medium-high heat, stirring constantly, 10 minutes or until tender. Stir in crawfish mixture, basil, and thyme; cook 5 minutes.

Combine cornstarch and milk, stirring well; stir into crawfish mixture. Add cheese spread, stirring well. Bring to a boil over medium heat; boil 1 minute, stirring constantly.

Stir in fettuccine and ¼ cup chopped parsley. Sprinkle servings evenly with Parmesan cheese. Garnish, if desired. Serve immediately. Yield: 8 servings.

Crawfish Fettuccine

Clams in Lemon White Sauce

Savor the rich lemon-garlic wine broth along with the steamed clams.
A simple tossed salad and French bread for dunking in the
sauce are all you need to serve on the side.

per serving:

Calories: 265
Fat: 9.7g
Protein: 18.6g
Carbohydrate: 28.3g
Cholesterol: 37mg
Sodium: 537mg
Exchanges:
  2 Starch
  2 Lean Meat
  1 Fat

4 pounds littleneck clams
3 tablespoons cornmeal
1 cup chopped onion
2 tablespoons chopped shallot
1½ cups dry white wine
2 tablespoons reduced-calorie
   margarine
2 tablespoons all-purpose flour
1 cup low-fat milk

2 teaspoons grated lemon rind
¼ cup fresh lemon juice
2 garlic cloves, minced
2 tablespoons minced fresh
   parsley
2 tablespoons minced green
   onions
¼ teaspoon salt
¼ teaspoon ground white pepper

Scrub clams thoroughly, discarding any that are cracked or open. Place clams in a large bowl; cover with cold water, and sprinkle with cornmeal. Let stand 30 minutes. Drain and rinse clams; set aside. Discard cornmeal.

Combine clams, chopped onion, shallot, and wine in a large Dutch oven. Bring to a boil; cover, reduce heat, and simmer 6 minutes or until most clams are open. Remove clams to a serving bowl as they open; keep warm. Discard any clams that don't open. Bring remaining liquid to a boil; cook over high heat until reduced to 1 cup. Pour clam liquid through a sieve, and set aside.

Melt margarine in a heavy saucepan over low heat; add flour, stirring until smooth. Cook 1 minute, stirring constantly. Gradually add milk, reserved 1 cup clam liquid, lemon rind, lemon juice, and garlic. Cook over medium heat, stirring constantly, until mixture is thickened and bubbly. Remove from heat; stir in parsley and remaining 3 ingredients. Pour sauce over clams. Serve immediately. Yield: 2 servings.

Cheesy Crabmeat Bake

Artichoke hearts and a cream sauce laced with Swiss cheese ensure that this crabmeat casserole will be a memorable meal.

Vegetable cooking spray
1 tablespoon reduced-calorie margarine
1¼ cups canned no-salt-added chicken broth, undiluted and divided
½ pound fresh mushrooms, quartered
1 pound fresh lump crabmeat, drained
¼ teaspoon salt
¼ teaspoon ground white pepper
¼ cup plus 2 tablespoons all-purpose flour
¾ cup low-fat milk, divided

½ cup nonfat sour cream
¼ cup (1 ounce) finely shredded reduced-fat Swiss cheese
1 tablespoon lemon juice
1 teaspoon minced garlic
1 (14-ounce) can artichoke hearts, drained and quartered
2 tablespoons fine, dry breadcrumbs (commercial)
2 tablespoons freshly grated Parmesan cheese
2 teaspoons reduced-calorie margarine, melted
½ teaspoon paprika

per serving:
Calories: 212
Fat: 5.6g
Protein: 22.0g
Carbohydrate: 17.5g
Cholesterol: 77mg
Sodium: 447mg
Exchanges:
  1 Starch
  2½ Lean Meat

Coat a nonstick skillet with cooking spray; add 1 tablespoon margarine. Place over medium-high heat until margarine melts. Add ½ cup broth and mushrooms; cook over high heat until liquid evaporates. Remove from heat; stir in crabmeat, salt, and pepper.

Combine flour and ¼ cup milk. Combine remaining milk and remaining broth in a saucepan; add flour mixture. Cook over medium heat, stirring constantly, until thickened. Remove from heat; stir in sour cream and next 3 ingredients. Stir in crabmeat mixture and artichoke. Spoon into a shallow 2-quart baking dish coated with cooking spray.

Combine breadcrumbs and remaining 3 ingredients. Sprinkle over crabmeat mixture. Bake, uncovered, at 400° for 15 minutes or until lightly browned. Yield: 6 servings.

Lobster with Light Curry Sauce

per serving:

Calories: 274
Fat: 7.9g
Protein: 38.0g
Carbohydrate: 11.6g
Cholesterol: 165mg
Sodium: 581mg
Exchanges:
  1 Starch
  5 Very Lean Meat
  ½ Fat

2 (8-ounce) fresh or frozen lobster tails, thawed
Vegetable cooking spray
1 tablespoon margarine
2 teaspoons curry powder
1 tablespoon peeled, minced fresh ginger
1 teaspoon minced garlic
½ cup fat-free evaporated milk
½ cup clam juice
¼ cup dry white wine
¼ cup ruby port wine
1 tablespoon balsamic vinegar
¼ teaspoon freshly ground pepper
¼ teaspoon crushed red pepper
Garnish: sliced green onions

Cut lobster tails in half lengthwise, cutting through upper and lower hard shells with an electric knife. Coat a large nonstick skillet with cooking spray; place over medium-high heat until hot. Add lobster tail halves, cut side down. Cook 4 minutes on each side or until lobster is done. Remove lobster from skillet, and keep warm.

Add margarine and curry powder to skillet; heat over medium-high heat until margarine melts. Cook 30 seconds over medium-high heat, stirring constantly. Add ginger and garlic; sauté until tender. Add milk and next 6 ingredients; stir well. Cook over medium-high heat, stirring constantly, 10 to 12 minutes until mixture is reduced to ½ cup.

Spoon ¼ cup curry mixture onto individual plates. Place 2 lobster tail halves, cut side down, on each plate. Garnish, if desired. Yield: 2 servings.

Seared Scallops with Tomato-Mango Salsa

per serving:

Calories: 246
Fat: 11.2g
Protein: 17.0g
Carbohydrate: 21.7g
Cholesterol: 30mg
Sodium: 782mg
Exchanges:
  1 Vegetable
  1 Fruit
  2 Very Lean Meat
  2 Fat

1 medium tomato, finely chopped
¾ cup finely chopped mango
3 tablespoons finely chopped purple onion
2 tablespoons finely chopped fresh basil
2 tablespoons red wine vinegar
1 tablespoon capers
1 tablespoon olive oil
12 sea scallops
¼ teaspoon salt
¼ teaspoon pepper
¼ avocado, sliced
Garnish: fresh basil sprigs

Combine first 6 ingredients. Cover and chill salsa at least 30 minutes.

Heat olive oil in a skillet over medium-high heat until hot. Add scallops; cook 3 minutes or until scallops are opaque, turning once. Remove scallops from skillet; sprinkle with salt and pepper.

Arrange scallops, salsa, and avocado slices evenly on plates. Garnish, if desired. Yield: 2 servings.

**Seared Scallops with
Tomato-Mango Salsa**

Grilled Sweet-and-Sour Shrimp

Grilled shrimp replaces the batter-dipped variety in this Asian entrée.

per serving:

Calories: 330
Fat: 6.4g
Protein: 32.7g
Carbohydrate: 37.3g
Cholesterol: 230mg
Sodium: 271mg
Exchanges:
  1 Vegetable
  2 Fruit
  4 Very Lean Meat

2 pounds unpeeled, large fresh shrimp
1 (33.3-ounce) jar peach nectar
4 teaspoons dark sesame oil, divided
¾ cup sliced green onions, divided
1 tablespoon minced fresh ginger
¼ cup fresh lime juice
2 tablespoons minced fresh cilantro
2 papayas, peeled and cubed
4 plum tomatoes, seeded and diced
¼ cup minced fresh cilantro
2 teaspoons grated lime rind
2 tablespoons fresh lime juice
1 teaspoon chile garlic paste

Peel shrimp, and devein, if desired.

Bring nectar to a boil in a medium saucepan, and boil 45 minutes or until reduced to 1 cup.

Whisk in 2 teaspoons oil, ¼ cup green onions, ginger, ¼ cup lime juice, and 2 tablespoons cilantro. Pour half of mixture into a shallow dish or large heavy-duty zip-top plastic bag; add shrimp, tossing to coat. Cover or seal; chill 1 hour, stirring occasionally. Set aside remaining half of peach mixture.

Combine remaining 2 teaspoons oil, remaining ½ cup green onions, papaya, and remaining 5 ingredients, tossing gently; set salsa aside.

Remove shrimp from marinade, discarding marinade.

Grill shrimp in a grill basket, covered with grill lid, over medium-high heat (350° to 400°) 5 minutes or until shrimp turn pink. Divide papaya salsa evenly among six individual serving plates, and top with shrimp. Drizzle with reserved peach mixture. Yield: 6 servings.

Shrimp with Peanut Sauce

per serving:

Calories: 146
Fat: 4.5g
Protein: 22.6g
Carbohydrate: 3.0g
Cholesterol: 156mg
Sodium: 231mg
Exchanges:
  3 Very Lean Meat

2 tablespoons sliced green onions
2 garlic cloves, minced
Vegetable cooking spray
¾ cup no-salt-added chicken broth
3 tablespoons creamy peanut butter
1 tablespoon reduced-sodium soy sauce
1 tablespoon lemon juice
1 teaspoon chili powder
1 teaspoon brown sugar
½ teaspoon ground ginger
1 pound unpeeled, large fresh shrimp

Cook green onions and garlic in a skillet coated with cooking spray over medium heat, stirring constantly, about 3 minutes. Add chicken broth and next 6 ingredients, stirring until smooth. Reduce heat, and simmer 10 minutes, stirring often. Remove from heat, and cool.

Peel shrimp, leaving tails intact; devein, if desired. Place shrimp in sauce; turn to coat. Cover and chill 1 hour.

Remove shrimp from sauce, discarding sauce. Thread shrimp onto skewers. Broil 6 inches from heat (with electric oven door partially opened) 5 minutes on each side or until shrimp turn pink. Yield: 4 servings.

Sautéed Shrimp and Linguine

Shrimp, pasta, and fresh tomatoes mingle to
make this a filling one-dish meal.

8 ounces linguine, uncooked
2 pounds unpeeled, medium-size
   fresh shrimp
1 small onion, chopped
2 garlic cloves, minced
1 tablespoon hot sesame oil
6 plum tomatoes, peeled and
   chopped
1 teaspoon dried oregano
½ teaspoon salt
½ teaspoon dried basil
½ teaspoon freshly ground
   pepper
¼ cup chopped fresh parsley
¼ cup kalamata olives, sliced
¼ cup lemon juice
2 ounces crumbled feta cheese

per serving:
Calories: 449
Fat: 10.6g
Protein: 33.9g
Carbohydrate: 54.1g
Cholesterol: 185mg
Sodium: 708mg
Exchanges:
  3½ Starch
  ½ Vegetable
  3 Very Lean Meat
  1 Fat

Cook linguine according to package directions; drain and keep warm.

Peel shrimp, and devein, if desired.

Cook onion and garlic in oil in a large skillet until tender, stirring often. Stir in tomato and next 4 ingredients; cook 3 minutes, stirring constantly. Add shrimp, and cook 3 minutes or until shrimp turn pink, stirring occasionally.

Stir in parsley, olives, and lemon juice; cook just until thoroughly heated. Serve over linguine; sprinkle with cheese. Yield: 4 servings.

Portobello-Potato Pancake
(page 88)

Meatless Main Dishes

Discover the hearty and incredible-tasting meatless entrées we've gathered to help you cut back on meat portions. You're sure to get the appropriate amount of nutrients in these recipes—we've included egg, cheese, legume, and pasta dishes that are loaded in protein. There are recipes for every taste, and best of all, they're good for you.

Vegetable Cheese Strata

This hearty dish is perfect as the main course
to a brunch menu.

Vegetable cooking spray
1 teaspoon reduced-calorie
   margarine
2 tablespoons minced shallot
1 teaspoon minced garlic
1 cup sliced fresh mushrooms
1 cup diced zucchini
1 cup diced green bell pepper
2½ cups fat-free milk

2 eggs, beaten
4 egg whites, lightly beaten
¼ teaspoon freshly ground pepper
⅛ teaspoon salt
6 cups cubed French bread
½ cup (2 ounces) shredded
   reduced-fat Cheddar cheese
¼ cup grated Parmesan cheese

Coat a large nonstick skillet with cooking spray. Add margarine, and place
over medium-high heat until melted. Add shallot and garlic; sauté until
tender. Add mushrooms; sauté 5 minutes. Add zucchini and green pepper;
sauté 5 minutes or until crisp-tender. Remove from heat, and set aside.
Combine milk, eggs, egg whites, pepper, and salt in a large bowl. Stir in
vegetable mixture, bread cubes, and cheeses. Pour mixture into a 13- x 9-
inch baking dish coated with cooking spray. Bake, uncovered, at 325° for
50 to 60 minutes or until lightly browned. Let stand 5 minutes. Cut into
rectangles. Serve immediately. Yield: 8 servings.

Mexican Souffléed Omelets

6 egg whites
¼ teaspoon cream of tartar
4 egg yolks
2 tablespoons all-purpose flour
½ cup (2 ounces) shredded
   reduced-fat Cheddar cheese
1 tablespoon grated Parmesan
   cheese
¼ teaspoon salt
¼ teaspoon freshly ground pepper

Vegetable cooking spray
2 teaspoons reduced-calorie
   margarine, divided
¼ cup peeled, seeded, and
   chopped tomato
¼ cup canned chopped green
   chiles
2 tablespoons sliced ripe olives
2 tablespoons sliced green onions
½ cup nonfat sour cream

Beat egg whites and cream of tartar at high speed with an electric mixer
until stiff peaks form. Combine egg yolks and flour in a large bowl, and
beat until thick and pale. Fold one-third of beaten egg whites into egg

yolk mixture; fold in remaining egg whites. Fold in Cheddar cheese and next 3 ingredients.

Coat a 10-inch ovenproof skillet with cooking spray; add 1 teaspoon margarine. Place over medium heat until margarine melts. Pour half of egg mixture into skillet, smoothing top. Cook 3 to 4 minutes or until browned on bottom. Transfer skillet to oven; bake at 350° for 10 minutes or until puffed and golden.

Cut a ¼-inch-deep slit down center of omelet, and top with half each of tomato, chiles, olives, green onions, and sour cream. Loosen omelet with spatula, and carefully fold in half. Slide omelet onto a serving platter, and cut in half. Repeat procedure with remaining 1 teaspoon margarine, egg mixture, and toppings. Yield: 4 servings.

Mexican Souffléed Omelets

Eggplant Parmesan

per serving:

Calories: 193
Fat: 4.8g
Protein: 11.4g
Carbohydrate: 27.7g
Cholesterol: 12mg
Sodium: 499mg
Exchanges:
  1½ Starch
  1 Vegetable
  1 Lean Meat

2 tablespoons all-purpose flour
1 (1-pound) eggplant
⅓ cup egg substitute
2 tablespoons fat-free milk
⅔ cup fine, dry breadcrumbs
   (commercial)
½ teaspoon dried Italian
   seasoning

Vegetable cooking spray
Marinara Sauce
1 cup (4 ounces) shredded part-
   skim mozzarella cheese
2 tablespoons Parmesan cheese

Place flour in a large zip-top plastic bag; set aside. Peel and cut eggplant into 12 (½-inch-thick) slices. Place slices in plastic bag; shake to coat.
Combine egg substitute and milk; set aside. Combine breadcrumbs and Italian seasoning. Dip each eggplant slice into egg mixture, and dredge lightly in breadcrumb mixture. Place slices on a baking sheet coated with cooking spray. Bake at 400° for 12 to 14 minutes or until lightly browned.
Coat a 13- x 9-inch baking dish with cooking spray. Layer half of eggplant slices in dish, overlapping slightly; spoon half of hot Marinara Sauce over eggplant. Repeat with remaining eggplant and sauce.
Sprinkle with cheeses, and bake 5 minutes or until cheeses melt. Yield: 6 servings.

Marinara Sauce

Vegetable cooking spray
¾ cup chopped onion
½ cup coarsely grated carrot
3 garlic cloves, minced
1 (28-ounce) can tomatoes with
   basil, undrained and chopped

1 teaspoon dried Italian seasoning
1 bay leaf
1½ teaspoons red wine vinegar

Coat a Dutch oven with cooking spray; place over medium-high heat until hot. Add onion, carrot, and garlic; sauté until tender. Add tomatoes, Italian seasoning, and bay leaf; bring to a boil. Reduce heat, and cook 30 minutes, stirring occasionally.
Remove and discard bay leaf. Process sauce in a blender or food processor about 5 seconds (mixture will not be smooth). Return sauce to pan; add vinegar, and cook 5 minutes. Yield: 3 cups.

Veggie Pizza

Savor this hearty pizza that's loaded with fresh veggies and cooked
on a whole-grain crust—you won't miss the meat.

1 medium zucchini thinly sliced
1 yellow squash, thinly sliced
1 cup sliced fresh mushrooms
½ cup chopped onion
½ cup chopped green bell pepper
Vegetable cooking spray
1 (8-ounce) can no-salt-added
  tomato sauce
1½ teaspoons dried Italian
  seasoning

¼ teaspoon salt
Whole Wheat Crust
½ cup freshly grated Parmesan
  cheese
2 cups (8 ounces) shredded part-
  skim mozzarella cheese
4 Roma tomatoes, sliced

per serving:
Calories: 466
Fat: 16.7g
Protein: 25.9g
Carbohydrate: 54.3g
Cholesterol: 41mg
Sodium: 624mg
Exchanges:
  3 Starch
  1 Vegetable
  2 High-Fat Meat

Cook first 5 ingredients in a large nonstick skillet coated with cooking
spray, covered, over medium-high heat 8 to 10 minutes or until crisp-
tender. Drain and set aside.

Combine tomato sauce, Italian seasoning, and salt; spread mixture evenly
over Whole Wheat Crust, and layer with cooked vegetables, cheeses, and
sliced tomatoes.

Bake at 450° for 20 minutes or until cheese melts and crust is browned
around edges. Yield: 4 servings.

Whole Wheat Crust

½ cup warm water (105° to 115°)
1 tablespoon sugar
1 tablespoon olive oil
1½ teaspoons active dry yeast

¾ cup whole wheat flour
¾ cup all-purpose flour
Vegetable cooking spray

Combine first 4 ingredients in a bowl; gradually add flours, mixing well
after each addition.

Turn dough out onto a lightly floured surface, and knead until smooth and
elastic. Place in a bowl coated with cooking spray. Cover and let rise in a
warm place (85°), free from drafts, 1 hour or until doubled in bulk.

Punch dough down, and pat evenly into a 12-inch pizza pan coated with
cooking spray.

Bake at 450° for 5 minutes. Yield: one 12-inch pizza crust.

Spinach-and-Cheese Calzones

per serving:

Calories: 312
Fat: 6.8g
Protein: 22.2g
Carbohydrate: 42.1g
Cholesterol: 18mg
Sodium: 816mg
Exchanges:
  2 Starch
  2 Lean Meat

½ cup chopped onion
1 tablespoon garlic powder
½ teaspoon salt
1 (10-ounce) package frozen chopped spinach, thawed and well drained
½ (6-ounce) package Canadian bacon, chopped
1 teaspoon dried Italian seasoning
1 (15-ounce) carton fat-free ricotta cheese

1 cup (4 ounces) shredded reduced-fat mozzarella cheese
¼ cup freshly grated Parmesan cheese
1 (16-ounce) loaf frozen bread dough, thawed
Vegetable cooking spray
1 (27½-ounce) jar light pasta sauce

Combine first 5 ingredients in a large skillet; cook over medium-high heat, stirring constantly, until bacon is browned. Remove from heat.

Combine Italian seasoning and next 3 ingredients; stir into spinach mixture.

Divide dough into 8 portions; roll each portion into a 6-inch circle on a lightly floured surface.

Spoon about ½ cup spinach mixture onto each circle; lightly brush edges of dough with water. Fold in half, pressing edges to seal. Place calzones on a baking sheet coated with cooking spray, and coat tops with cooking spray.

Bake at 375° for 15 to 20 minutes or until golden. Serve with warm pasta sauce. Yield: 8 servings.

Portobello-Potato Pancake

This crispy hash-brown patty topped with cheese, nuts, and meaty-tasting mushrooms (pictured on page 82) will satisfy both meat- and potato-lovers.

per serving:

Calories: 296
Fat: 9.5g
Protein: 11.7g
Carbohydrate: 43.7g
Cholesterol: 10mg
Sodium: 737mg
Exchanges:
  2½ Starch
  1 Vegetable
  2 Fat

1 (26-ounce) bag frozen shredded hash brown potatoes, thawed
1 small onion, thinly sliced
½ teaspoon salt
½ teaspoon freshly ground pepper
Olive oil-flavored vegetable cooking spray
2 teaspoons olive oil, divided

6 ounces fresh portobello mushrooms, thinly sliced
1 (14-ounce) can artichoke hearts, drained and chopped
½ cup (2 ounces) freshly grated Asiago cheese, divided
2 tablespoons coarsely chopped walnuts
Garnish: fresh rosemary sprigs

Combine first 4 ingredients in a large bowl, stirring well. Coat a 12-inch nonstick skillet with cooking spray. Add 1 teaspoon oil; place over medium heat until hot. Spoon potato mixture into skillet; press to smooth top. Cook 8 minutes or until potato is crisp and browned on bottom. Invert potato pancake onto a baking sheet.

Coat skillet with cooking spray; add remaining 1 teaspoon oil. Place over medium heat until hot. Return pancake to skillet, uncooked side down, 8 minutes or until crisp and browned. Invert pancake onto baking sheet coated with cooking spray; set aside, and keep warm.

Coat skillet with cooking spray; place over medium-high heat until hot. Add mushrooms, and sauté 2 minutes or until tender. Remove from heat, and stir in artichoke hearts.

Sprinkle pancake with ¼ cup cheese. Top with mushroom mixture. Sprinkle with walnuts; top with remaining ¼ cup cheese. Bake at 350° for 12 minutes. Cut into 8 wedges. Garnish, if desired. Yield: 4 servings.

Onion-Stuffed Potatoes

6 (10-ounce) baking potatoes
1 cup canned no-salt-added
   chicken broth, undiluted
1 cup finely chopped onion
1 teaspoon minced garlic
1 cup nonfat sour cream
½ cup fat-free evaporated milk
½ teaspoon freshly ground pepper
½ cup (2 ounces) shredded
   reduced-fat Cheddar cheese
¼ cup plus 1 tablespoon grated
   Parmesan cheese, divided
2 tablespoons fine, dry
   breadcrumbs (commercial)
½ teaspoon paprika
¼ teaspoon minced garlic
1 teaspoon reduced-calorie
   margarine, melted

per serving:
Calories: 335
Fat: 4.5g
Protein: 16.5g
Carbohydrate: 57.0g
Cholesterol: 12mg
Sodium: 276mg
Exchanges:
  4 Starch
  1 Medium-Fat Meat

Wash potatoes; bake at 400° for 1 hour or until done. Let cool to touch.

Cut a 1-inch lengthwise strip from top of each potato; carefully scoop out pulp, leaving shells intact. Mash pulp in a large bowl, and set aside.

Combine broth, onion, and 1 teaspoon garlic in a small saucepan. Bring to a boil. Reduce heat, and simmer, uncovered, until all liquid is evaporated.

Combine potato pulp, onion mixture, sour cream, milk, and pepper; stir well. Stir in Cheddar cheese and ¼ cup Parmesan cheese. Spoon potato mixture evenly into shells.

Combine remaining 1 tablespoon Parmesan cheese, breadcrumbs, and remaining 3 ingredients; stir well. Sprinkle potatoes evenly with breadcrumb mixture; bake, uncovered, at 375° for 20 minutes. Yield: 6 servings.

Macaroni and Cheese

Macaroni and Cheese

*This family favorite easily fits into a healthful lifestyle
with the use of reduced-fat cheeses.*

1 (12-ounce) carton 1% low-fat
    cottage cheese
1 (8-ounce) carton reduced-fat
    sour cream
4 cups cooked elbow macaroni
    (cooked without salt or fat)
2 cups (8 ounces) shredded
    reduced-fat sharp Cheddar
    cheese
½ cup fat-free milk

1 green onion, chopped
¾ teaspoon salt
½ teaspoon pepper
1 large egg
Butter-flavored cooking spray
¼ cup fine, dry breadcrumbs
    (commercial)
¼ teaspoon paprika
Garnish: fresh oregano sprigs

per serving:
Calories: 373
Fat: 14.1g
Protein: 25.9g
Carbohydrate: 34.9g
Cholesterol: 79mg
Sodium: 874mg
Exchanges:
  2 Starch
  3 Medium-Fat Meat

Process cottage cheese and sour cream in a blender until smooth.
Combine cottage cheese mixture, macaroni, and next 6 ingredients; spoon into a 2-quart casserole coated with cooking spray. Sprinkle with breadcrumbs and paprika; coat with cooking spray. Cover and bake at 350° for 30 minutes. Uncover; bake 5 minutes. Garnish, if desired. Yield: 6 servings.

Vegetable-Cheese Enchiladas

8 (6-inch) corn tortillas
1 medium zucchini, cut into
    ½-inch cubes
1 cup (4 ounces) shredded
    reduced-fat Monterey Jack
    cheese, divided
1 cup cooked brown rice (cooked
    without salt or fat)

¼ cup chopped green onions
⅓ cup low-fat sour cream
¼ teaspoon salt
¼ teaspoon pepper
Vegetable cooking spray
2 (10-ounce) cans chopped
    tomatoes and green chiles,
    undrained

per serving:
Calories: 343
Fat: 9.9g
Protein: 14.1g
Carbohydrate: 47.3g
Cholesterol: 26mg
Sodium: 1031mg
Exchanges:
  3 Starch
  1 High-Fat Meat

Wrap tortillas in aluminum foil, and bake at 350° for 7 minutes.
Cook zucchini in boiling water to cover 2 minutes; drain and pat dry.
Combine zucchini, half of cheese, and next 5 ingredients. Spoon mixture evenly down center of each tortilla; fold opposite sides over filling, and roll up tortillas. Place, seam side down, in an 11- x 7-inch baking dish coated with cooking spray. Pour chopped tomatoes and green chiles over tortillas.
Bake at 350° for 15 minutes; sprinkle with remaining cheese, and bake 5 more minutes. Yield: 4 servings.

Lentil Burgers

Even beef-lovers will like this vegetable burger recipe.

per serving:

Calories: 316
Fat: 8.4g
Protein: 12.9g
Carbohydrate: 47.5g
Cholesterol: 41mg
Sodium: 359mg
Exchanges:
  3 Starch
  ½ Lean Meat
  1 Fat

1 cup dried lentils
2½ cups water
¼ cup ketchup
¼ teaspoon garlic powder
1 small onion, chopped
1 cup quick-cooking oats, uncooked
1 large egg
½ teaspoon salt
1 tablespoon whole wheat flour
2 tablespoons vegetable oil
8 hamburger buns
Tomato slices
Lettuce leaves
Pickle slices

Combine lentils and water in a saucepan; bring to a boil over medium-high heat. Cover, reduce heat, and simmer 25 minutes. Cook, uncovered, 10 minutes or until water is absorbed and lentils are tender.

Stir ketchup and next 5 ingredients into lentils.

Shape into 8 patties; sprinkle with flour. Cover and chill 1 hour.

Pour 1 tablespoon oil in a skillet. Fry 4 patties over medium-high heat 1 to 2 minutes on each side or until golden. Drain on paper towels. Repeat procedure with remaining 1 tablespoon oil and remaining 4 patties.

Place a patty on bottom half of each bun. Top with tomato, lettuce and pickles; add top half of bun. Yield: 8 servings.

Note: You can freeze cooked lentil patties in an airtight container. Bake thawed patties, uncovered, at 350° for 12 minutes or until thoroughly heated.

Grilled Polenta with Black Bean Salsa

per serving:

Calories: 296
Fat: 1.9g
Protein: 12.3g
Carbohydrate: 55.9g
Cholesterol: 0mg
Sodium: 263mg
Exchanges:
  4 Starch

4 cups reduced-sodium, fat-free chicken broth
1 cup yellow cornmeal
Vegetable cooking spray
Black Bean Salsa

Bring broth to a boil in a heavy saucepan; add cornmeal, stirring constantly. Reduce heat; cook 20 minutes or until thickened, stirring often.

Spread cornmeal mixture into a 9-inch square pan coated with cooking spray; chill until firm. Cut polenta into four squares; cut each square in half diagonally. Coat a grill basket with cooking spray; arrange polenta triangles in basket. Grill, covered with grill lid, over high heat (400° to 500°) 5 minutes on each side or until polenta begins to brown.

Serve with Black Bean Salsa. Yield: 4 servings.

Black Bean Salsa

2 cups canned black beans,
   drained and rinsed
¾ cup finely chopped tomato
½ cup finely chopped onion
½ cup finely chopped red bell
   pepper

¼ cup chopped fresh cilantro
1 teaspoon finely chopped
   jalapeño pepper
⅓ cup red wine vinegar

Combine all ingredients in a large bowl, and toss gently. Cover and chill.
Serve with polenta. Yield: 4 cups.

**Grilled Polenta with Black
Bean Salsa and Steamed
Garden Vegetables (page 186)**

Roasted Chiles Rellenos
With Tomatillo Sauce

8 Anaheim chile peppers
10 tomatillos, husked
1 small onion, sliced
2 garlic cloves, minced
¼ teaspoon salt
¼ teaspoon pepper
¼ teaspoon ground cumin
2 tablespoons chopped fresh
   cilantro
¾ cup canned black beans,
   drained and rinsed

1 cup (4 ounces) shredded
   reduced-fat Monterey Jack
   cheese
1 egg white
¼ cup egg substitute
¾ cup all-purpose flour
1 teaspoon vegetable oil
Vegetable cooking spray

Place chile peppers, tomatillos, and onion on food rack of grill. Grill, covered with grill lid, over high heat (400° to 500°) about 5 minutes on each side or until peppers look blistered and tomatillos and onion are lightly browned.

Place peppers immediately in a heavy-duty zip-top plastic bag; seal and chill at least 8 hours.

Place grilled vegetables in an airtight container; chill at least 8 hours.

Peel peppers, and remove seeds; set aside.

Process tomatillos, onion, garlic, and next 3 ingredients in a blender until smooth. Stir in cilantro; set tomatillo sauce aside.

Combine black beans and cheese; spoon into peppers (some peppers may split). Set aside.

Beat egg white at high speed with an electric mixer until stiff peaks form; gradually beat in egg substitute. Set aside.

Coat stuffed peppers with flour; dip in egg white mixture, and lightly recoat peppers with flour. Add oil to a large nonstick skillet coated with cooking spray. Cook chiles in hot oil on both sides until lightly browned.

Serve immediately with tomatillo sauce. Yield: 4 servings.

Note: Instead of grilling 8 Anaheim chile peppers, substitute 3 (4-ounce) cans whole green chiles, drained.

Spicy Pinto Bean Burritos

Use hot salsa rather than mild for maximum flavor—and more bite—in these burritos.

6 (9-inch) flour tortillas
Vegetable cooking spray
1 teaspoon extra-virgin olive oil
½ cup chopped onion
1 jalapeño pepper, seeded and
 minced
1 teaspoon minced garlic
2 cups canned pinto beans,
 drained, rinsed, and mashed
½ cup fat-free cream cheese,
 softened

¼ cup nonfat mayonnaise
½ cup chopped green onions
¼ cup plus 2 tablespoons no-salt-
 added salsa
½ cup (2 ounces) shredded
 reduced-fat Cheddar cheese
3 cups finely shredded lettuce
1 cup seeded, chopped tomato
½ cup chopped green bell pepper
2 tablespoons chopped fresh
 cilantro

per burrito:
Calories: 345
Fat: 7.2g
Protein: 16.3g
Carbohydrate: 53.7g
Cholesterol: 10mg
Sodium: 747mg
Exchanges:
 3½ Starch
 1 Medium-Fat Meat

Place a damp paper towel in center of a sheet of aluminum foil. Stack tortillas on paper towel. Cover stack with another damp paper towel; seal foil. Bake at 250° for 10 minutes.

Coat a nonstick skillet with cooking spray; add olive oil. Place over medium heat until hot. Add ½ cup onion; sauté 4 minutes. Add jalapeño and garlic; sauté 1 minute. Add pinto beans; cook 3 minutes or until thoroughly heated, stirring frequently. Combine cream cheese and mayonnaise; stir well.

Spoon about ¼ cup bean mixture down one side of each tortilla. Top evenly with cream cheese mixture, green onions, and salsa. Roll up tortillas; arrange seam side down in a 13- x 9-inch baking dish coated with cooking spray. Cover and bake at 350° for 20 minutes. Sprinkle with Cheddar cheese; bake, uncovered, 5 minutes or until cheese melts. Place ½ cup lettuce and 1 burrito on each plate. Top burritos evenly with tomato, green pepper, and cilantro. Yield: 6 burritos.

Cannelloni

per serving:

Calories: 346
Fat: 7.4g
Protein: 19.2g
Carbohydrate: 51.2g
Cholesterol: 10mg
Sodium: 770mg
Exchanges:
  2½ Starch
  2 Vegetable
  1 High-Fat Meat

1 (10-ounce) package frozen chopped spinach, thawed
Vegetable cooking spray
¾ cup diced fresh mushrooms
¼ cup diced onion
3 garlic cloves, minced
¼ cup egg substitute
2 tablespoons freshly grated Parmesan cheese
½ teaspoon dried oregano
¼ teaspoon dried basil
8 cooked manicotti shells (cooked without salt or fat)
2 cups low-fat spaghetti sauce, divided
Parmesan Sauce
2 tablespoons chopped fresh parsley

Place thawed spinach between paper towels, and squeeze until barely moist; set aside.

Coat a large nonstick skillet with cooking spray; place over medium heat until hot. Add mushrooms, onion, and garlic; sauté 2 minutes. Add spinach; sauté until mushrooms are tender and liquid evaporates. Remove mixture from heat, and cool slightly. Stir in egg substitute, Parmesan cheese, oregano, and basil. Stuff each manicotti shell with an equal amount of the spinach mixture.

Spread 1 cup spaghetti sauce in a 13- x 9-inch baking dish. Place stuffed shells on spaghetti sauce. Spread remaining spaghetti sauce over shells. Spoon Parmesan Sauce down center of casserole. Cover and bake at 375° for 30 minutes or until thoroughly heated. Sprinkle with parsley. Yield: 4 servings.

Parmesan Sauce

2 tablespoons instant nonfat dry milk powder
1 cup fat-free milk
1½ tablespoons reduced-calorie margarine
2 tablespoons all-purpose flour
⅓ cup freshly grated Parmesan cheese
¼ teaspoon ground nutmeg
¼ teaspoon ground white pepper

Combine first 2 ingredients; set aside. Melt margarine in a saucepan over medium heat; add flour, and cook 1 minute, stirring constantly. Gradually add milk, and cook until thickened, stirring constantly with a wire whisk. Add Parmesan cheese, nutmeg, and pepper; cook until cheese melts, stirring constantly. Yield: 1 cup plus 1 tablespoon.

Spinach-Bean Lasagna

Take a break from traditional lasagna by serving this healthy substitute. Chopped kidney beans replace meat in the sauce, and spinach teams with three kinds of cheese for a great-tasting filling.

2 (15-ounce) cans kidney beans, rinsed and drained
1¾ cups water
1 (27.5-ounce) jar reduced-fat, reduced-sodium pasta sauce
1 (10-ounce) package frozen chopped spinach, thawed and well drained
1 (15-ounce) container part-skim ricotta cheese
¼ cup egg substitute, thawed
Vegetable cooking spray
10 lasagna noodles, uncooked
1 cup (4 ounces) shredded part-skim mozzarella cheese
¼ cup grated Parmesan cheese

per serving:
Calories: 436
Fat: 10.8g
Protein: 24.8g
Carbohydrate: 62.2g
Cholesterol: 27mg
Sodium: 364mg
Exchanges:
  4 Starch
  2 Medium-Fat Meat

Pulse beans in a food processor 2 or 3 times; gradually add water, and process until beans are coarsely chopped.

Combine bean mixture and pasta sauce in a saucepan; bring to a boil. Reduce heat, and simmer, stirring occasionally, 10 minutes; set aside.

Combine spinach, ricotta cheese, and egg substitute; set aside.

Coat a 13- x 9-inch baking dish with cooking spray, and spread a thin layer of sauce on bottom of dish.

Arrange 5 noodles over sauce. Spread half of spinach mixture over noodles; top with mozzarella. Spoon half of sauce over cheese. Repeat layers.

Cover and chill 24 hours. Remove from refrigerator, and let stand at room temperature 30 minutes.

Bake, uncovered, and bake at 350° for 1 hour. Uncover and sprinkle with Parmesan cheese; bake 15 more minutes. Yield: 8 servings.

Artichoke Veal Chop (page 108)

Meats

Yes, you can enjoy meat when following a low-fat eating plan, and we've made it easy for you. The key is to purchase lean cuts and to follow low-fat cooking methods. We've included a delicious variety of beef, veal, lamb, and pork recipes. Whether serving these dishes to company or to family, everyone will agree that satisfying taste is delivered in these healthful dishes.

Eye-of-Round Roast with Caramelized Onion Sauce

1 (3-pound) beef eye-of-round roast
½ cup dry white wine
¼ cup white wine vinegar
1 tablespoon minced fresh parsley
1 teaspoon dried whole thyme
1 teaspoon dried whole rosemary, crushed
¼ teaspoon ground red pepper

1 garlic clove, minced
Vegetable cooking spray
2 cups water
2 large onions, thinly sliced and separated into rings
1 cup fat-free milk
1 tablespoon cornstarch
2 tablespoons Dijon mustard

Trim fat from roast. Place roast in a shallow dish. Combine wine and next 6 ingredients, stirring well. Pour mixture over roast. Cover and marinate in refrigerator 8 to 10 hours, turning occasionally.

Remove roast from marinade, reserving marinade; bring marinade to a boil, and set aside. Place roast on rack of a broiler pan coated with cooking spray. Insert meat thermometer into thickest part of roast. Pour water into broiler pan. Cover with aluminum foil, and bake at 450° for 20 minutes. Uncover and bake 55 additional minutes or until meat thermometer registers 150° (medium-rare), basting roast frequently with marinade.

Let roast stand 15 minutes; cut diagonally across grain into thin slices.

Coat a Dutch oven with cooking spray; place over medium-high heat until hot. Add onions; cook 15 minutes or until onions start to brown, stirring frequently. Combine milk, cornstarch, and mustard, stirring until smooth. Gradually add milk mixture to onions, stirring constantly until thickened and bubbly. (Mixture will first appear curdled but will smooth out as it cooks.) Serve with roast. Yield: 12 servings.

Sirloin Steaks with Thyme Pesto

2 tablespoons pine nuts
2 (12-ounce) boneless beef top loin steaks, trimmed
¾ teaspoon salt, divided
½ teaspoon coarsely ground pepper
⅓ cup fresh thyme leaves

½ cup chopped fresh parsley
1 garlic clove, chopped, or ½ teaspoon minced bottled garlic
¼ cup freshly grated Parmesan cheese
2 tablespoons olive oil or canola oil

Bake pine nuts in a shallow pan at 350°, stirring occasionally, 5 minutes or until toasted; cool.

Coat steaks evenly with ½ teaspoon salt and pepper.

Grill steaks, covered with grill lid, over medium-high heat (350° to 400°) 7 minutes on each side or to desired degree of doneness. Keep warm.

Process pine nuts, remaining ¼ teaspoon salt, thyme, and remaining 4 ingredients in a blender until smooth. Serve pesto with steaks. Yield: 6 servings.

Beef Stroganoff

Indulge in this creamy, rich-tasting stroganoff. But don't worry; our version splurges on flavor not fat.

1 pound lean boneless beef sirloin steak
Vegetable cooking spray
3 cups sliced fresh mushrooms
¾ cup chopped onion
2 garlic cloves, crushed
¾ cup hot water
1 teaspoon beef-flavored bouillon granules
½ cup Burgundy or other dry red wine
2 tablespoons all-purpose flour

1 tablespoon margarine
2 teaspoons low-sodium Worcestershire sauce
1 teaspoon dry mustard
½ teaspoon dried whole thyme
¼ teaspoon pepper
1 (8-ounce) container nonfat sour cream
3 cups cooked medium egg noodles (cooked without salt or fat)
2 tablespoons sliced green onions

per serving:
Calories: 312
Fat: 9.0g
Protein: 26.6g
Carbohydrate: 28.9g
Cholesterol: 81mg
Sodium: 263mg
Exchanges:
 2 Starch
 3 Lean Meat

Partially freeze steak; trim fat from steak. Slice steak diagonally across grain into 2- x ¼-inch strips.

Coat a large nonstick skillet with cooking spray, and place over medium-high heat until hot. Add steak, mushrooms, chopped onion, and crushed garlic; cook 15 minutes or until steak and vegetables are tender. Drain and wipe drippings from skillet with a paper towel. Set steak mixture aside, and keep warm.

Combine water and bouillon granules in skillet. Combine wine and flour; stir well, and add to broth. Stir in margarine and next 4 ingredients. Cook over medium heat, stirring constantly with a wire whisk, until thickened and bubbly. Add reserved steak mixture. Cook over medium heat until thoroughly heated. Remove from heat, and stir in sour cream. To serve, spoon steak mixture over noodles, and sprinkle with green onions. Yield: 6 servings.

American Steakhouse Beef

1 (1½-pound) boneless beef top
    sirloin steak, trimmed
⅓ cup low-sodium soy sauce
⅓ cup unsweetened pineapple
    juice
⅓ cup dry sherry
¼ cup cider vinegar

Place steak in a large, shallow dish. Combine soy sauce and remaining 3 ingredients; pour over steak. Cover and chill 4 hours, turning steak occasionally. Drain, discarding marinade.

Grill over high heat (400° to 500°) 10 to 15 minutes on each side or to desired degree of doneness. To serve, slice across the grain into thin slices. Yield: 6 servings.

Beef Tenderloin Steaks with Peperonata

Guests will savor the tasty combination of these tender steaks served with peperonata, a tangy Italian mixture of sweet peppers, onion, and garlic.

1 large egg
1 tablespoon water
¼ cup Italian-seasoned
    breadcrumbs
¼ cup grated Parmesan cheese
1 tablespoon minced fresh
    rosemary or dried rosemary
¼ teaspoon salt
¼ teaspoon freshly ground
    pepper
6 (4-ounce) beef tenderloin steaks
3 garlic cloves, halved
2 teaspoons olive oil
Peperonata
Garnish: fresh rosemary sprigs

Stir together egg and water.

Stir together breadcrumbs and next 4 ingredients.

Rub steaks with garlic. Dip steaks in egg mixture; coat with crumb mixture.

Cook steaks in hot oil in a cast-iron skillet over medium-high heat 2 minutes. Turn steaks; bake in skillet at 450° for 3 to 5 minutes or to desired degree of doneness. Serve with Peperonata. Garnish, if desired. Yield: 6 servings.

Beef Tenderloin Steaks with Peperonata

Peperonata

2 large onions
1 red bell pepper
1 green bell pepper
3 garlic cloves
1 tablespoon minced fresh
   rosemary or dried rosemary

2 teaspoons olive oil
¾ teaspoons salt
½ teaspoon freshly ground
   pepper
2 tablespoons red wine vinegar

Slice onions, and separate into rings. Cut bell peppers into thin strips, and mince garlic.

Sauté onion rings, bell pepper strips, garlic, and rosemary in hot oil in a large skillet until crisp-tender. Stir in salt, pepper, and vinegar. Yield: 3 cups.

Beef and Cauliflower over Rice

1 pound boneless beef top round steak
3 tablespoons reduced-sodium soy sauce
   Vegetable cooking spray
3 cups cauliflower flowerets
¾ cup coarsely chopped red bell pepper
2 garlic cloves, minced
1 tablespoon cornstarch
⅓ teaspoon beef-flavored bouillon granules
½ to 1 teaspoon dried crushed red pepper
½ teaspoon sugar
1 cup water
1 cup sliced green onions
2 cups hot cooked rice (cooked without salt or fat)

Trim fat from steak; slice diagonally across grain into thin strips. Place in a shallow dish. Sprinkle with soy sauce, stirring gently to coat; cover and chill 30 minutes.

Coat a Dutch oven with cooking spray; place over medium heat until hot. Add meat, and cook, stirring until browned. Reduce heat; cover and cook 10 minutes. Stir in cauliflower, red bell pepper, and garlic; cover and cook 5 minutes.

Combine cornstarch and next 4 ingredients in a small bowl, stirring until smooth; stir into meat mixture. Add green onions; bring to a boil. Cook, stirring constantly, 1 minute. Serve over rice. Yield: 4 servings.

Tropical Flank Steak

1 (1-pound) lean flank steak
1 cup canned papaya nectar
2 teaspoons ground ginger
1 teaspoon coconut extract
1 teaspoon cracked black pepper
1 teaspoon crushed white peppercorns
1 teaspoon crushed green peppercorns
   Vegetable cooking spray
1 fresh papaya, peeled, sliced, and cut into decorative shapes
   Garnish: edible flowers

Trim fat from steak. Combine papaya nectar, ginger, and coconut extract in a large heavy-duty zip-top plastic bag; seal bag, and shake well. Add steak to bag; seal bag, and shake until steak is well coated. Marinate steak in refrigerator 8 hours, turning bag occasionally.

Remove steak from marinade, reserving marinade. Bring marinade to a boil in a small saucepan; set aside.

Combine pepper and peppercorns, and press onto both sides of steak. Coat a food rack with cooking spray; place on grill over medium-high heat (350° to 400°). Place steak on rack; grill, covered, 6 minutes on each side or to desired degree of doneness, brushing steak frequently with reserved marinade.

Remove steak from grill, and let stand 10 minutes; cut diagonally across grain into thin slices. Serve with papaya slices. Garnish, if desired. Yield: 4 servings.

Java Fajitas

Brewed coffee gives these fajitas their unique flavor.

⅓ cup tomato paste
1¼ cups strongly brewed coffee
½ cup Worcestershire sauce
1 tablespoon sugar
2 teaspoons ground red pepper
1 teaspoon ground black pepper
3 tablespoons fresh lime juice

1 tablespoon vegetable oil
2 (1½-pound) flank steaks
24 (10-inch) flour tortillas
Pico de Gallo
Garnishes: fresh cilantro sprigs, lime wedges, serrano chile peppers, avocado slices

per fajita:
Calories: 276
Fat: 9.0g
Protein: 15.7g
Carbohydrate: 31.5g
Cholesterol: 28mg
Sodium: 449mg
Exchanges:
 2 Starch
 1 Medium-Fat Meat
 1 Fat

Combine first 8 ingredients in a shallow dish or large heavy-duty zip-top plastic bag; add steaks. Cover or seal; chill 8 hours, turning occasionally.

Remove steaks from marinade, reserving marinade.

Grill steaks, covered with grill lid, over high heat (400° to 500°) about 6 minutes on each side or to desired degree of doneness.

Cut steaks diagonally across grain into thin slices; keep warm.

Bring reserved marinade to a boil in a skillet; boil 10 to 15 minutes or until reduced to 1 cup.

Place steak down center of tortillas; drizzle with reduced marinade, and top with Pico de Gallo. Roll up, and serve immediately. Garnish, if desired. Yield: 24 fajitas.

Pico de Gallo

2 medium tomatoes, chopped
½ onion, chopped
3 serrano chile peppers, chopped
½ cup fresh cilantro, chopped

¼ teaspoon salt
¼ teaspoon ground white pepper
2 tablespoons lemon juice

Combine all ingredients in a medium bowl. Cover and chill at least 3 hours. Yield: 3 cups.

Grilled Flank Steak
With Black Bean-and-Corn Salsa

This jazzy salsa is packed with fresh ingredients,
giving extra punch to grilled steak.

1 pound flank steak
½ cup dry red wine
3 garlic cloves, pressed
2 tablespoons chopped shallot
2 tablespoons Worcestershire
    sauce
¼ cup lemon juice
1½ teaspoons pepper
½ teaspoon garlic powder
½ teaspoon pepper
Black Bean-and-Corn Salsa
½ avocado, peeled and sliced

Place steak in a large shallow dish or heavy-duty zip-top plastic bag, and set aside.

Combine wine, garlic, shallot, Worcestershire sauce, lemon juice, and 1½ teaspoons pepper; pour over steak. Cover dish or seal bag, and refrigerate 8 hours, turning steak occasionally.

Drain steak, discarding marinade. Sprinkle with garlic powder and ½ teaspoon pepper.

Grill, without grill lid, over high heat (400° to 500°) 7 minutes on each side or until meat is desired degree of doneness. Slice steak diagonally across grain into thin slices, and serve steak with Black Bean-and-Corn Salsa and avocado slices. Yield: 4 servings.

Black Bean-and-Corn Salsa

1½ cups fresh corn, cut from cob
1 cup canned black beans, rinsed
1 red bell pepper, chopped
1 jalapeño pepper, seeded and
    finely chopped
1 garlic clove, pressed
2 tablespoons lime juice
2 teaspoons chopped fresh
    cilantro
¼ teaspoon salt
¼ teaspoon pepper

Cook corn in a small amount of boiling water 4 minutes or until corn is crisp-tender; drain and cool.

Combine corn and remaining ingredients. Yield: 4 cups.

Note: 1½ cups frozen whole kernel corn may be substituted for fresh corn, if desired.

Steak Kabobs

1½ pounds beef sirloin tip, trimmed
¼ cup low-sodium soy sauce
2 tablespoons brown sugar
½ teaspoon ground ginger
2 teaspoons dry sherry
1½ teaspoons vegetable oil
1 (15¼-ounce) can unsweetened pineapple chunks
6 cups hot cooked rice (cooked without salt or fat)

per serving:
Calories: 460
Fat: 8.8g
Protein: 30.4g
Carbohydrate: 61.5g
Cholesterol: 76mg
Sodium: 380mg
Exchanges:
  3 Starch
  1 Fruit
  3 Lean Meat

Cut meat into ½-inch cubes; place in a shallow dish or a heavy-duty zip-top plastic bag, and set aside. Combine soy sauce and next 4 ingredients; pour over meat, and cover or seal. Chill 3 to 8 hours. Drain meat, discarding marinade.

Alternate meat and pineapple on 14-inch skewers. Grill over medium-high heat (350° to 400°) 8 minutes or until desired degree of doneness, turning often. Serve with rice. Yield: 6 servings.

Gingersnap Meat Loaf

Vegetable cooking spray
½ cup finely chopped onion
½ cup finely chopped celery
2 pounds ground round
½ cup soft breadcrumbs (homemade)
½ cup finely crushed gingersnaps
½ cup egg substitute
3 tablespoons cider vinegar
1½ teaspoons prepared mustard
¼ cup canned no-salt-added beef broth, undiluted
2 tablespoons all-purpose flour
¼ teaspoon salt
¼ teaspoon ground ginger
¾ cup fat-free milk
¼ cup nonfat sour cream

per serving:
Calories: 186
Fat: 4.9g
Protein: 23.9g
Carbohydrate: 9.7g
Cholesterol: 54mg
Sodium: 181mg
Exchanges:
  1 Starch
  3 Very Lean Meat

Coat a large nonstick skillet with cooking spray; place over medium-high heat until hot. Add onion and celery; sauté until tender.

Combine sautéed vegetables, ground round, and next 5 ingredients in a large bowl; stir well. Shape mixture into a 9- x 5-inch loaf; place on a rack in a roasting pan coated with cooking spray. Bake at 350° for 1 hour and 15 minutes.

Combine beef broth, flour, salt, and ginger in a small saucepan; stir until smooth. Gradually add milk, stirring constantly. Cook over medium heat, stirring constantly, until thickened. Remove from heat, and add sour cream, stirring just until blended. Spoon evenly over meat loaf. Yield: 10 servings.

Veal Parmesan with Fresh Tomato Salsa

A tangy, chunky fresh salsa replaces the familiar marinara-type
sauce that traditionally tops this veal dish.

2 cups peeled, seeded, and
   chopped plum tomato
1 cup thinly sliced arugula
½ cup sliced green onions
2 tablespoons minced fresh
   basil
2 tablespoons red wine vinegar
1 tablespoon olive oil
¼ teaspoon garlic powder
¼ teaspoon pepper

8 (6-ounce) lean veal loin chops
   (¾-inch thick)
1 cup crushed toasted whole grain
   wheat flake cereal
¼ cup grated Parmesan cheese
2 egg whites, lightly beaten
Vegetable cooking spray
½ cup (2 ounces) shredded part-
   skim mozzarella cheese

Combine first 8 ingredients in a small bowl. Cover and set tomato mixture
aside.

Trim fat from veal chops. Combine cereal and Parmesan cheese in a shallow bowl. Dip chops in egg whites, and dredge in cereal mixture. Place
chops in a 13- x 9-inch baking dish coated with cooking spray. Cover and
chill 1 hour.

Bake chops, uncovered, at 375° for 30 to 35 minutes or until tender.
Sprinkle with mozzarella cheese; bake an additional 5 minutes or until
cheese melts. Transfer to a serving platter; spoon tomato mixture evenly
over chops. Yield: 8 servings.

Artichoke Veal Chops

A rainbow of peppers adds pizzazz to these veal chops;
they're pictured on page 98.

4 (6-ounce) lean veal loin chops
   (¾-inch thick)
½ teaspoon cracked pepper
½ teaspoon green peppercorns,
   crushed
Vegetable cooking spray
⅓ cup sliced green bell pepper
¼ cup sliced orange bell pepper
¼ cup sliced red bell pepper
¼ cup sliced yellow bell pepper

¼ cup dry vermouth
2 tablespoons canned no-salt-
   added chicken broth,
   undiluted
¼ teaspoon dried whole thyme
2 garlic cloves, minced
1 (14-ounce) can artichoke hearts,
   drained and quartered
2 tablespoons chopped fresh
   parsley

Trim fat from veal chops. Combine cracked pepper and crushed peppercorns in a small bowl; rub mixture over chops.

Coat a large nonstick skillet with cooking spray; place over medium-high heat until hot. Add chops, and cook 3 to 4 minutes on each side or until browned. Remove chops from skillet. Drain chops, and pat dry with paper towels. Wipe drippings from skillet with a paper towel. Place chops in an 11- x 7-inch baking dish coated with cooking spray; set aside.

Place green pepper and next 7 ingredients in skillet. Bring to a boil; reduce heat, and simmer 5 minutes. Stir in artichoke hearts. Spoon artichoke mixture over veal chops. Cover and bake at 350° for 25 minutes or until veal is tender. Transfer veal and vegetable mixture to a serving platter; sprinkle with chopped fresh parsley. Yield: 4 servings.

Parslied Leg of Lamb

1 cup chopped fresh parsley
½ cup chopped green onions
2 teaspoons grated orange rind
¼ cup plus 2 tablespoons
    unsweetened orange juice
1 tablespoon chopped hazelnuts

½ teaspoon pepper
1 (3½-pound) lean boneless leg
    of lamb
Vegetable cooking spray
Garnishes: fresh orange slices,
    fresh parsley sprigs

per serving:
Calories: 155
Fat: 6.5g
Protein: 21.5g
Carbohydrate: 1.4g
Cholesterol: 67mg
Sodium: 53mg
Exchanges:
 3 Lean Meat

Process first 6 ingredients in a blender or food processor until mixture forms a paste.

Trim fat from lamb, and place lamb in a shallow dish. Rub parsley mixture over lamb. Cover and marinate in refrigerator 8 hours.

Place lamb on a rack in a roasting pan coated with cooking spray. Insert meat thermometer into thickest part of roast, if desired. Bake, uncovered, at 325° for 1 hour and 45 minutes or until meat thermometer registers 150° (medium-rare) to 160° (medium). Transfer lamb to a serving platter. Let stand 15 minutes. Garnish, if desired. Yield: 14 servings.

Tangy Lamb Chops Véronique

"Véronique" refers to the grapes that highlight this dish.

per serving:

Calories: 254
Fat: 8.4g
Protein: 26.4g
Carbohydrate: 17.5g
Cholesterol: 75mg
Sodium: 280mg
Exchanges:
  1 Fruit
  4 Lean Meat

½ cup fine, dry breadcrumbs (commercial)
2 teaspoons dried whole dillweed
½ teaspoon garlic powder
¼ teaspoon pepper
8 (3-ounce) lean lamb loin chops (¾-inch thick)
3 tablespoons hot-sweet mustard

3 tablespoons cider vinegar or balsamic vinegar
Vegetable cooking spray
½ cup seedless green grapes, quartered
½ cup seedless red grapes, quartered

Combine first 4 ingredients in a shallow bowl; stir well.

Trim fat from lamb chops. Combine mustard and vinegar; brush mustard mixture evenly over chops. Dredge chops in breadcrumb mixture.

Coat a large nonstick skillet with cooking spray; place over medium heat until hot. Add chops; cover and cook 4 minutes on each side or until browned. Uncover and cook 5 minutes on each side or to desired degree of doneness. Transfer chops to a serving platter, and sprinkle evenly with grapes. Yield: 4 servings.

Barbecued Pork Loin Roast

per serving:

Calories: 183
Fat: 4.3g
Protein: 25.7g
Carbohydrate: 9.4g
Cholesterol: 82mg
Sodium: 329mg
Exchanges:
  1 Starch
  3 Very Lean Meat

1 (2¼-pound) boneless pork loin roast, trimmed
¾ cup no-salt-added ketchup
¾ cup finely chopped onion
1 garlic clove, minced, or ⅛ teaspoon granulated garlic
1 tablespoon honey
1½ teaspoons unsweetened cocoa

1½ teaspoons brown sugar
2¼ teaspoons lemon juice
1½ teaspoons liquid smoke
1 teaspoon salt
⅛ teaspoon pepper
Dash of mace
Vegetable cooking spray

Butterfly roast by making a lengthwise cut in center, cutting to within ½ inch of other side, and open roast. Place in a shallow dish; set aside.

Combine ketchup and next 10 ingredients; spread half of marinade mixture on roast, reserving remaining marinade. Cover roast, and chill 8 hours. Cover and chill reserved marinade.

Remove roast from marinade, and discard marinade. Lightly coat a food rack with cooking spray; place rack over medium-high heat (350° to 400°).

Place roast on rack, and grill, turning once, 20 minutes or until meat thermometer inserted in thickest portion of roast registers 160°. Remove roast from grill, and wrap in heavy-duty plastic wrap.

Cook reserved marinade in a heavy saucepan over medium-low heat 15 minutes, stirring often. Cut meat into thin slices, and serve with sauce. Yield: 9 servings.

Grilled Pork Tenderloin with Molasses Sauce

½ cup molasses
2 tablespoons chopped fresh
   rosemary
2 tablespoons Dijon mustard
1 tablespoon olive oil
½ teaspoon salt
½ teaspoon freshly ground pepper
2 (¾-pound) pork tenderloins,
   trimmed

1 small onion, chopped
2 garlic cloves, chopped
1 tablespoon olive oil
1 cup dry white wine
1 cup chicken broth
1 teaspoon cornstarch
1 tablespoon water
½ teaspoon salt
Garnish: fresh rosemary sprigs

per serving:
Calories: 286
Fat: 8.1g
Protein: 25.1g
Carbohydrate: 20.9g
Cholesterol: 74mg
Sodium: 742mg
Exchanges:
   1½ Starch
   3 Lean Meat

Stir together first 6 ingredients. Set aside half of mixture; cover and chill. Place pork in a shallow dish or heavy-duty zip-top plastic bag; pour remaining molasses mixture over pork. Cover or seal; chill 8 hours, turning occasionally.

Remove pork from marinade, and discard marinade.

Grill, covered with grill lid, over medium heat (300° to 350°) about 25 minutes or until a meat thermometer inserted into thickest portion registers 160°, turning occasionally.

Sauté onion and garlic in 1 tablespoon hot oil in a saucepan until tender. Add wine and broth; cook over medium-high heat, stirring occasionally, until mixture is reduced by three-fourths.

Stir in reserved molasses mixture, and simmer 5 minutes. Pour through a wire-mesh strainer into a bowl, discarding onion and garlic; return to pan. Stir together cornstarch and water. Stir into wine mixture.

Bring to a boil over medium heat, stirring constantly. Boil, stirring constantly 1 minute.

Stir in ½ teaspoon salt. Serve sauce with sliced pork. Garnish, if desired. Yield: 5 servings.

Peachy Pork Medaillons

per serving:

Calories: 231
Fat: 4.6g
Protein: 26.7g
Carbohydrate: 20.7g
Cholesterol: 83mg
Sodium: 94mg
Exchanges:
  1½ Fruit
  4 Very Lean Meat

2 (¾-pound) pork tenderloins
Vegetable cooking spray
½ cup peach nectar
¼ cup dry white wine
1 teaspoon peeled, minced ginger
¼ teaspoon pepper

1 teaspoon cornstarch
1 tablespoon water
⅓ cup mango chutney
2 cups peeled, sliced fresh peaches
½ cup sliced green onions
Garnish: green onion curls

Partially freeze tenderloins; trim fat from tenderloins. Cut tenderloins diagonally across grain into ¼-inch-thick slices.

Coat a large nonstick skillet with cooking spray. Place over medium-high heat until hot. Add half of pork, and cook 3 minutes on each side or until pork is lightly browned. Remove pork from skillet. Drain; set aside, and keep warm. Repeat procedure with remaining pork slices. Wipe drippings from skillet with a paper towel.

Combine peach nectar and next 3 ingredients in skillet. Return pork to skillet. Bring to a boil; cover, reduce heat, and simmer 4 to 5 minutes or until pork is tender.

Peachy Pork Medaillons

Transfer pork to a serving platter, using a slotted spoon. Set aside, and keep warm. Combine cornstarch and water; stir until smooth. Add cornstarch mixture and chutney to peach nectar mixture, stirring well. Add peaches and sliced green onions. Bring to a boil; reduce heat, and simmer, stirring constantly, until thickened. Spoon peach mixture over pork. Garnish, if desired. Yield: 6 servings.

Pork Tenderloin with Fruit Stuffing And Shiitake Sauce

1½ cups vegetable broth, divided
1 cup chopped mixed dried fruit
½ cup minced shallot, divided
½ teaspoon minced garlic
3 tablespoons olive oil, divided
¼ cup Italian-seasoned breadcrumbs
1 (1-pound) pork tenderloin, trimmed
¼ teaspoon salt
¼ teaspoon pepper
4 to 6 fresh sage leaves
8 ounces shiitake mushrooms, thinly sliced
¼ cup dry red wine
⅛ teaspoon salt
⅛ teaspoon pepper

per serving:
Calories: 355
Fat: 14.0g
Protein: 22.0g
Carbohydrate: 33.3g
Cholesterol: 58mg
Sodium: 862mg
Exchanges:
 1 Starch
 1 Fruit
 3 Medium-Fat Meat

Bring ½ cup broth to a boil in a small saucepan over high heat; remove from heat, and add dried fruit. Let stand 20 minutes.

Sauté ¼ cup shallot and garlic in 1 tablespoon hot oil in a large skillet until tender. Stir in fruit mixture and breadcrumbs; set aside.

Cut tenderloin in half lengthwise, cutting to within 1 inch of opposite side. Open halves; press flat. Place between two sheets of heavy-duty plastic wrap, and flatten to ½-inch thickness, using a meat mallet or a rolling pin. Sprinkle both sides evenly with ¼ teaspoon salt and ¼ teaspoon pepper.

Spoon stuffing mixture down center of tenderloin; top with sage leaves. Close tenderloin, securing with string at 1-inch intervals. Wipe skillet clean with a paper towel.

Brown tenderloin on all sides in 1 tablespoon hot olive oil in skillet over medium-high heat (about 2 minutes on each side). Transfer to a lightly greased broiler pan.

Bake tenderloin at 350° for 35 minutes or until done.

Wipe skillet clean; sauté remaining ¼ cup shallot in remaining 1 tablespoon hot oil until tender. Add mushrooms, and sauté 5 minutes.

Add remaining 1 cup broth and wine; cook until liquid is reduced by half. Stir in ⅛ teaspoon salt and ⅛ teaspoon pepper. Serve with tenderloin slices. Yield: 4 servings.

Spinach-and-Bacon Stuffed
Pork Tenderloin

A small helping of crumbled bacon delivers big
taste to this stuffed tenderloin.

per serving:

Calories: 227
Fat: 7.6g
Protein: 29.4g
Carbohydrate: 6.0g
Cholesterol: 88mg
Sodium: 504mg
Exchanges:
  1 Vegetable
  4 Lean Meat

½ cup finely chopped onion
1 garlic clove, minced
Vegetable cooking spray
1 cup sliced fresh mushrooms
1 (10-ounce) package frozen
   chopped spinach, thawed and
   drained
4 slices bacon, cooked and
   crumbled
1 tablespoon Dijon mustard
¼ teaspoon salt

¼ teaspoon pepper
2 (¾-pound) pork tenderloins,
   trimmed
2 tablespoons Dijon mustard
2 teaspoons dried rosemary,
   crushed
1 teaspoon dried oregano
1 teaspoon dried thyme
1 teaspoon pepper
¼ teaspoon salt
½ cup dry white wine

Cook onion and garlic in a large nonstick skillet coated with cooking spray over medium heat, stirring constantly, until vegetables are tender. Add mushrooms; cook, stirring constantly, 3 minutes. Stir in spinach and next 4 ingredients; set aside.

Slice each pork tenderloin lengthwise down center, cutting to, but not through, bottom. Place between sheets of heavy-duty plastic wrap; pound into a 12- x 8-inch rectangle.

Spoon half of spinach mixture over 1 tenderloin; spread to within ½ inch of sides. Roll tenderloin, jellyroll fashion, starting with short side. Tie with heavy string at 1½-inch intervals. Repeat procedure with remaining tenderloin and spinach mixture.

Combine 2 tablespoons mustard and next 5 ingredients; spread evenly over tenderloins. Place seam side down in a shallow baking pan coated with cooking spray. Add wine to pan.

Bake, uncovered, at 325° for 45 minutes. Let stand 10 minutes; remove strings. Cut into ½-inch slices. Yield: 6 servings.

Fruit-Topped Pork Chops

1 tablespoon reduced-calorie margarine
¼ cup chopped celery
2 tablespoons chopped onion
1 cup herb-seasoned stuffing mix
3 (0.9-ounce) packages mixed dried fruit
2 tablespoons raisins
6 (4-ounce) lean, boneless center-cut loin pork chops (¾-inch thick)
¼ teaspoon salt
¼ teaspoon pepper
¼ cup all-purpose flour
Vegetable cooking spray
½ cup dry white wine

per serving:
Calories: 293
Fat: 9.7g
Protein: 26.9g
Carbohydrate: 23.6g
Cholesterol: 71mg
Sodium: 367mg
Exchanges:
 1½ Starch
 3 Lean Meat

Melt margarine in a large skillet; add celery and onion. Cook, stirring constantly, until tender. Add stuffing mix, mixed dried fruit, and raisins; toss gently. Set aside.

Sprinkle pork chops with salt and pepper; dredge in flour. Set aside.

Coat a large nonstick skillet with cooking spray; add chops, and brown on both sides over medium heat.

Arrange chops in an 11- x 7-inch baking dish coated with cooking spray; top each with fruit mixture. Add wine to dish. Cover and bake at 350° for 40 to 45 minutes or until done. Yield: 6 servings.

Pork Chops 'n' Gravy

Vegetable cooking spray
6 (4-ounce) boneless pork chops, trimmed
1 cup finely chopped onion
3 garlic cloves, minced
½ cup water
⅓ cup all-purpose flour
1 (14½-ounce) can fat-free chicken broth
1 teaspoon browning-and-seasoning sauce
¼ teaspoon pepper

per serving:
Calories: 227
Fat: 8.2g
Protein: 26.2g
Carbohydrate: 9.3g
Cholesterol: 71mg
Sodium: 79mg
Exchanges:
 ½ Starch
 3 Lean Meat

Coat a large nonstick skillet with cooking spray; place over medium-high heat until hot. Add chops, and cook until browned on both sides. Remove chops from skillet; drain and set aside.

Wipe drippings from skillet with a paper towel. Sauté onion and garlic in skillet coated with cooking spray until tender. Add chops and ½ cup water; bring to a boil.

Whisk together flour, chicken broth, browning sauce, and pepper until smooth. Add to skillet, stirring well.

Cover and cook over low heat 30 to 45 minutes or until pork chops are tender, stirring occasionally. Yield: 6 servings.

Pork-and-Pepper Skillet

Pork-and-Pepper Skillet

per serving:

Calories: 215

Fat: 9.4g

Protein: 25.8g

Carbohydrate: 5.6g

Cholesterol: 71mg

Sodium: 224mg

Exchanges:

1 Vegetable

3 Lean Meat

8 (2-ounce) boneless center-cut pork loin chops

1 teaspoon chopped fresh or ¼ teaspoon dried thyme

½ teaspoon pepper

¼ teaspoon salt

Vegetable cooking spray

1 teaspoon olive oil

1 small onion, cut into thin strips

2 medium-size red bell peppers, cut into thin strips

1 garlic clove, pressed

1 tablespoon red wine vinegar

Garnish: fresh thyme sprigs

Rub both sides of pork chops with thyme, pepper, and salt. Cook pork in a large nonstick skillet coated with cooking spray over medium-high heat

2 minutes on each side. Add oil; cover, reduce heat, and cook 3 minutes. Remove pork from skillet.

Sauté onion, bell pepper, and garlic in skillet until crisp-tender. Return pork to skillet, and cook 2 minutes. Cover, reduce heat, and cook 9 minutes or until pork is done. Drizzle with vinegar. Garnish, if desired. Yield: 4 servings.

Sweet-and-Sour Pork Strips

Bring the flair of the Orient to your table with this classic sweet-and-sour specialty.

1 pound lean boneless pork loin
Vegetable cooking spray
1 (8-ounce) can no-salt-added
    tomato sauce
¼ cup rice wine vinegar
2 tablespoons brown sugar
2 teaspoons low-sodium soy sauce
¼ teaspoon minced garlic
⅛ teaspoon ground red pepper
1 (20-ounce) can pineapple
    chunks in juice

1 medium-size green bell pepper,
    seeded and cut into 1-inch
    pieces
¼ cup chopped green onions
2 tablespoons cornstarch
2 cups cooked long-grain rice
    (cooked without salt or fat)
Garnish: bell pepper triangles

per serving:
Calories: 445
Fat: 11.8g
Protein: 25.3g
Carbohydrate: 57.9g
Cholesterol: 73mg
Sodium: 140mg
Exchanges:
  3 Starch
  1 Fruit
  2 Lean Meat
  1 Fat

Partially freeze pork; trim fat from pork. Slice pork diagonally across grain into thin slices; slice into 1-inch-wide strips. Coat a nonstick skillet with cooking spray; place over medium-high heat until hot. Add pork; cook 8 minutes or until browned, stirring frequently. Remove from skillet. Drain and pat dry. Wipe drippings from skillet with a paper towel.

Combine pork, tomato sauce, and next 5 ingredients in skillet; bring to a boil. Cover, reduce heat, and simmer 15 minutes or until pork is tender. Drain pineapple, reserving juice. Add enough water to juice to make 1 cup liquid. Set aside. Add pineapple, green bell pepper pieces, and green onions to skillet; cover and simmer 5 to 7 minutes or until vegetables are crisp-tender.

Combine cornstarch and reserved pineapple juice mixture; stir into pork mixture. Cook, stirring constantly, until thickened. Spoon pork mixture over rice. Garnish, if desired. Yield: 4 servings.

Orange-Baked Ham

Orange-Baked Ham

Use any leftover ham in the kabob recipe on the next page. This ham can
also be refrigerated up to 3 to 5 days or frozen up to 3 months.

per slice:

Calories: 104
Fat: 3.2g
Protein: 12.1g
Carbohydrate: 6.0g
Cholesterol: 30mg
Sodium: 683mg
Exchanges:
  1 ½ Starch
  2 Very Lean Meat

1 (2-pound) lean cooked ham
½ cup frozen orange concentrate,
     thawed
¼ cup water
3 tablespoons brown sugar
2 teaspoons white wine vinegar

1 teaspoon dry mustard
½ teaspoon grated orange rind
¼ teaspoon ground ginger
Vegetable cooking spray
Whole cloves
Garnish: orange slices

Make ¼-inch-deep cuts in ham in a diamond design.

Combine juice concentrate and next 6 ingredients in a shallow dish or
large heavy-duty zip-top plastic bag; add ham. Cover or seal bag, and chill
at least 8 hours, turning ham occasionally.

Remove ham from marinade, reserving ½ cup marinade.

Place ham on a rack coated with vegetable cooking spray in a roasting pan; stud with cloves, and brush with reserved marinade.

Cover and bake at 325° for 1½ hours or until meat thermometer inserted in thickest portion registers 140°, basting occasionally with marinade. Remove cloves from ham before slicing. Garnish, if desired. Yield: 16 (2-ounce) slices.

Mustard-Honey-Glazed Ham Kabobs

3 tablespoons Dijon mustard
¼ cup honey
¼ cup orange juice
1 teaspoon minced ginger
1 garlic clove, pressed
2 medium-sized red bell peppers
¾ pound lean cooked ham
1 (6-ounce) package frozen snow pea pods, thawed
1 (20-ounce) can pineapple chunks in juice, drained
Vegetable cooking spray
2 cups cooked long-grain rice (cooked without salt or fat)

per serving:
Calories: 387
Fat: 5.8g
Protein: 20.6g
Carbohydrate: 62.2g
Cholesterol: 45mg
Sodium: 1363mg
Exchanges:
  3½ Starch
  2 Vegetable
  1 Medium-Fat Meat

Combine first 5 ingredients.

Cut bell peppers into 32 (1-inch) pieces and ham into 24 (1-inch) cubes.

Wrap 1 snow pea around each pineapple chunk.

Thread 4 pineapple chunks, 4 bell pepper pieces, and 3 ham cubes alternately onto each of 8 (12-inch) skewers. Place on a rack coated with cooking spray in a broiler pan. Brush with mustard mixture.

Broil 5½ inches from heat (with electric oven door partially open) 3 minutes. Turn and brush with remaining mustard mixture; broil 3 to 4 more minutes or until thoroughly heated. Serve over rice. Yield: 4 servings.

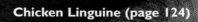
Chicken Linguine (page 124)

Pasta

Pasta is not only good, it's good for you. It's loaded with complex carbohydrates, plus it's naturally low in fat and sodium. Pasta is also easy to cook, and mixes well with other ingredients. You'll find creative blends of seasonings and healthful food in the toppings and the stuffings included in the following recipes. So enjoy the "pastabilities" with these main-dish and side-dish delicacies.

Fettuccine Primavera

Enjoy the bounty of vegetables with each bite of this creamy pasta classic.

per serving:

Calories: 339
Fat: 2.1g
Protein: 23.3g
Carbohydrate: 57.1g
Cholesterol: 6mg
Sodium: 509mg
Exchanges:
  3 Starch
  3 Vegetable
  1 Very Lean Meat

1 small onion, chopped
Vegetable cooking spray
1 (10-ounce) package frozen snow
  pea pods, thawed
1 red bell pepper, cut into thin
  strips

1 cup fresh broccoli flowerets
½ cup sliced fresh mushrooms
Alfredo Sauce
1 (12-ounce) package fettuccine
  cooked without salt or fat

Cook onion in a large nonstick skillet coated with cooking spray over medium heat, stirring constantly, until tender. Add snow peas and next 3 ingredients; cook, stirring constantly, until vegetables are crisp-tender. **Stir** in Alfredo Sauce; add cooked fettuccine, and toss gently. Serve immediately. Yield: 6 servings.

Alfredo Sauce

2 cups nonfat cottage cheese
3 tablespoons grated Parmesan
  cheese
2 tablespoons butter-flavored
  granules
½ cup fat-free evaporated milk

½ teaspoon chicken-flavored
  bouillon granules
½ teaspoon dried basil
¼ teaspoon ground black pepper
Dash of ground red pepper

Process all ingredients in a blender until smooth, stopping once to scrape down sides.
Pour into a small saucepan; cook sauce over low heat, stirring constantly, until thoroughly heated. Yield: 2¾ cups.

Ham-and-Asparagus Fettuccine

The leftover ham and fresh asparagus in this recipe offer a quick and refreshing makeover for the Alfredo Sauce on the opposite page. Bottled Alfredo sauce will speed you up even more when time is tight.

1 pound fresh asparagus
2 cups chopped, reduced-fat, low-salt lean ham
Vegetable cooking spray
Alfredo Sauce (recipe at left)
1 (12-ounce) package fettuccine, cooked without salt or fat

Snap off tough ends of asparagus. Remove scales from stalks with a knife or vegetable peeler, if desired. Cut diagonally into ½-inch slices.

Cook asparagus in a small amount of boiling water 3 minutes. Drain well, and set aside.

Cook ham over medium heat in a large nonstick skillet coated with cooking spray, stirring constantly, until thoroughly heated. Stir in Alfredo Sauce; add cooked fettuccine and asparagus, and toss gently before serving. Yield: 6 servings.

per serving:
Calories: 370
Fat: 4.6g
Protein: 30.4g
Carbohydrate: 52.0g
Cholesterol: 33mg
Sodium: 917mg
Exchanges:
3 Starch
1 Vegetable
3 Very Lean Meat

Fettuccine and Shrimp with Dried Tomato Pesto

8 ounces fettuccine, uncooked
1½ pounds unpeeled, medium-size fresh shrimp
2 garlic cloves, minced
2 teaspoons olive oil
¼ cup dry white wine
1 cup Dried Tomato Pesto (see page 208)
¼ cup freshly grated Parmesan cheese
Garnish: fresh basil sprigs

Cook fettuccine according to package directions, omitting salt or fat. Drain and keep warm.

Meanwhile, peel shrimp, and devein, if desired.

Cook garlic in olive oil in a large skillet over medium heat, stirring constantly, until tender; add shrimp, and cook, stirring constantly, about 1 minute. Add wine, and cook, stirring constantly, until shrimp turn pink.

Stir in Dried Tomato Pesto; cook until thoroughly heated. Spoon over fettuccine, and sprinkle with cheese. Garnish, if desired. Yield: 4 servings.

per serving:
Calories: 458
Fat: 14.1g
Protein: 32.3g
Carbohydrate: 50.6g
Cholesterol: 144mg
Sodium: 622mg
Exchanges:
3½ Starch
3 Lean Meat
1 Fat

Chicken Linguine

Add a green salad and bread, and your meal is complete.
See this dish pictured on page 120.

See this dish pictured on page 120.

per serving:
Calories: 289
Fat: 6.1g
Protein: 18.7g
Carbohydrate: 37.7g
Cholesterol: 31mg
Sodium: 167mg
Exchanges:
   2½ Starch
   1½ Lean Meat

1 pound sliced fresh mushrooms
½ cup dry sherry
2 tablespoons reduced-calorie margarine, melted and divided
4 (4-ounce) skinned, boned chicken breast halves
Vegetable cooking spray
½ cup chopped onion
¼ cup plus 2 tablespoons all-purpose flour
3 cups canned no-salt-added chicken broth, undiluted and divided

1 (8-ounce) carton nonfat sour cream
1 (16-ounce) package linguine, uncooked
½ cup (2 ounces) shredded reduced-fat Monterey Jack cheese
¼ cup plus 2 tablespoons freshly grated Parmesan cheese, divided
⅛ teaspoon freshly ground pepper
¼ cup fine, dry breadcrumbs (commercial)

Sauté mushrooms in sherry and 1 tablespoon margarine in a nonstick skillet over high heat 5 minutes.

Place chicken in a saucepan; add water to cover. Bring to a boil; cover, reduce heat, and simmer 20 minutes. Drain; let cool, and shred.

Coat a saucepan with cooking spray; place over medium heat until hot. Add onion, and sauté until tender. Combine flour and ½ cup broth. Add remaining 2½ cups broth and the flour mixture to onion. Cook over medium heat until thickened. Remove from heat; stir in sour cream.

Cook linguine according to package directions, omitting salt and fat; drain. Combine mushroom mixture, chicken, sour cream mixture, Monterey Jack cheese, ¼ cup Parmesan cheese, and pepper. Stir in linguine. Spoon into a 13- x 9-inch baking dish coated with cooking spray.

Combine breadcrumbs, remaining Parmesan cheese, and remaining 1 tablespoon of margarine; sprinkle over chicken. Bake, uncovered, at 350° for 30 minutes. Yield: 12 servings.

Zucchini-Beef Spaghetti

Vegetable cooking spray
1 pound ground round
2 cups sliced fresh mushrooms
2 cups thinly sliced zucchini
1 cup chopped onion
½ teaspoon salt
¼ teaspoon crushed red pepper
4 garlic cloves, minced
1 (14½-ounce) can no-salt-added whole tomatoes, undrained and chopped
1 cup water
1 (6-ounce) can no-salt-added tomato paste
1 teaspoon dried whole oregano
6 cups hot cooked spaghetti (cooked without salt or fat)
½ cup finely shredded zucchini
2 tablespoons grated Parmesan cheese
Garnish: fresh oregano sprigs

per serving:
Calories: 359
Fat: 5.4g
Protein: 26.7g
Carbohydrate: 51.0g
Cholesterol: 45mg
Sodium: 295mg
Exchanges:
   2½ Starch
   2 Vegetable
   2 Lean Meat

Coat a large nonstick skillet with cooking spray; place over medium heat until hot. Brown ground round, stirring until it crumbles. Drain and pat dry with paper towels. Wipe drippings from skillet with a paper towel.

Coat skillet with cooking spray; place over medium-high heat until hot. Add mushrooms and next 5 ingredients; sauté 5 minutes, stirring frequently. Stir in beef, tomatoes, and next 3 ingredients. Bring to a boil; cover, reduce heat, and simmer 10 to 15 minutes. Serve over spaghetti; top with zucchini and cheese. Garnish, if desired. Yield: 6 servings.

Zucchini-Beef Spaghetti

Spaghetti with Peanut Sauce

per serving:

Calories: 400
Fat: 13.0g
Protein: 14.8g
Carbohydrate: 59.3g
Cholesterol: 0mg
Sodium: 577mg
Exchanges:
  3 Starch
  3 Vegetable
  2 Fat

8 ounces spaghetti, uncooked
12 green onions
3 yellow squash
1 red bell pepper
1 tablespoon dark sesame oil
1 tablespoon minced garlic
¼ cup creamy peanut
    butter
¼ cup reduced-sodium soy
    sauce
3 tablespoons lime juice
1 tablespoon sugar
1 teaspoon dried crushed red
    pepper

Cook spaghetti according to package directions, omitting salt and fat; drain and keep warm.

Meanwhile, cut white portion of green onions into 2-inch pieces; reserve green tops for another use. Cut squash in half lengthwise; cut halves into slices. Remove and discard seeds from red bell pepper, and cut red bell pepper into thin strips.

Cook vegetables in a saucepan in boiling water to cover 3 minutes; drain vegetables, and set aside.

Pour oil into a large skillet; place over medium heat until hot. Add minced garlic, and cook 1 minute, stirring constantly. Add peanut butter, stirring until smooth. Stir in soy sauce and remaining 3 ingredients.

Add vegetables to skillet, and toss gently to coat; remove vegetables from skillet with a slotted spoon.

Add spaghetti to sauce in skillet, tossing to coat; transfer to a serving platter, and top with vegetables. Serve immediately. Yield: 4 servings.

Salmon-Pesto Vermicelli

per serving:

Calories: 265
Fat: 7.0g
Protein: 20.3g
Carbohydrate: 28.5g
Cholesterol: 49mg
Sodium: 146mg
Exchanges:
2 Starch
2 Lean Meat

1 cup firmly packed fresh basil
    leaves
¼ cup oil-free Italian dressing
2 tablespoons water
3 garlic cloves, crushed
1 (1-pound) salmon fillet
¼ teaspoon cracked pepper
Vegetable cooking spray
4 cups hot cooked vermicelli
    (cooked without salt or fat)
6 lemon wedges (optional)

Process first 4 ingredients in a food processor 2 minutes, scraping sides of bowl occasionally. Set aside.

Sprinkle fish with pepper, and place, skin side down, on a broiler pan coated with cooking spray. Broil 6 inches from heat (with electric oven door partially opened) 5 minutes. Turn fish over carefully, and broil 4 minutes or until fish flakes easily when tested with a fork. Remove from pan; cool. Remove and discard skin; break fish into bite-size pieces.

Combine fish, basil mixture, and hot cooked vermicelli in a large bowl; toss gently. Serve with lemon wedges, if desired. Yield: 6 servings.

Vegetable Stir-Fry Pasta

We serve this stir-fry over pasta rather than the typical rice.
Pasta's protein turns it into a one-dish meal;
smaller servings can be a side dish.

8 ounces angel hair pasta,
   uncooked
¾ cup vegetable broth, divided
⅓ cup reduced-sodium soy
   sauce
3 tablespoons dry white wine
1 tablespoon cornstarch
2 teaspoons minced fresh ginger
1 teaspoon garlic powder

2 carrots
2 celery ribs
1 onion
1 red bell pepper
4 small yellow squash
8 mushrooms
3 green onions
1 teaspoon olive oil
2 cups broccoli flowerets

per serving:
Calories: 326
Fat: 3.0g
Protein: 12.7g
Carbohydrate: 64.2g
Cholesterol: 0mg
Sodium: 699mg
Exchanges:
  3 Starch
  3 Vegetable
  ½ Fat

Cook pasta according to package directions, omitting salt and fat; drain and keep warm.

Meanwhile, combine ½ cup broth and next 5 ingredients, stirring well; set broth mixture aside.

Cut carrots, celery, onion, and bell pepper into thin slices; cut squash in half lengthwise, and cut into thin slices. Slice mushrooms and green onions.

Pour oil around top of a wok or a large nonstick skillet, coating sides; heat at medium-high (325°). Add carrot, celery, onion, and bell pepper; stir-fry 5 minutes.

Stir in remaining ¼ cup broth, squash, mushrooms, green onions, and broccoli; stir-fry 5 additional minutes or until tender.

Stir in broth mixture; boil 1 minute. Serve over pasta. Yield: 4 servings.

Hearty Lasagna

Hearty Lasagna

Four types of cheese and a hearty tomato sauce make up
the layers of this incredible-tasting lasagna.

¾ pound ground round
1 cup chopped onion
3 garlic cloves, minced
1½ tablespoons dried parsley
flakes
1 (14½-ounce) can diced
tomatoes, undrained
1 (14½-ounce) can Italian-style
stewed tomatoes, undrained
and chopped
1 (8-ounce) can tomato sauce
1 (6-ounce) can tomato paste
2 teaspoons dried oregano
1 teaspoon dried basil

¼ teaspoon salt
¼ teaspoon pepper
2 cups nonfat cottage cheese
½ cup shredded Parmesan cheese
1 (15-ounce) container nonfat
ricotta cheese
1 egg white
Vegetable cooking spray
12 lasagna noodles, cooked
without salt or fat
2 cups (8 ounces) shredded
provolone cheese or part-skim
mozzarella cheese
Garnish: fresh oregano sprigs

per serving:
Calories: 380
Fat: 11.1g
Protein: 27.4g
Carbohydrate: 45.3g
Cholesterol: 34mg
Sodium: 859mg
Exchanges:
3 Starch
3 Medium-Fat Meat

Cook meat, onion, and garlic in a Dutch oven over medium heat until meat is browned, stirring until it crumbles. Drain and set aside. Wipe pan with a paper towel, and return meat mixture to pan; add parsley and next 8 ingredients.

Bring to a boil. Cover, reduce heat, and simmer 15 minutes. Uncover and simmer 20 minutes. Set aside.

Combine cottage cheese and next 3 ingredients; set aside.

Spread ¾ cup tomato mixture in a 13- x 9-inch baking dish coated with cooking spray. Arrange 4 cooked noodles over mixture; top with half of cottage cheese mixture, 2¼ cups tomato mixture, and ⅔ cup provolone cheese. Repeat layers, ending with noodles. Top with remaining tomato mixture.

Cover and bake at 350° for 1 hour. Uncover and sprinkle with remaining provolone cheese; bake 10 additional minutes. Let stand 10 minutes. Garnish, if desired. Yield: 9 servings.

Vegetable Lasagna

Chopped spinach, chunky vegetables, and fresh herbs layer
this lasagna with enough flavor and nutrients to be a meal in itself.
Just add crusty French bread on the side.

Vegetable cooking spray
1 cup chopped onion
½ cup chopped green bell pepper
2 garlic cloves, minced
1½ cups peeled, chopped tomato
1½ cups sliced fresh mushrooms
2 cups no-salt-added tomato sauce
1 cup shredded carrot
¼ cup no-salt-added beef broth, undiluted
1 (6-ounce) can no-salt-added tomato paste
2½ tablespoons chopped fresh basil
1 tablespoon chopped fresh oregano

½ teaspoon dried Italian seasoning
½ teaspoon pepper
1 (10-ounce) package frozen chopped spinach, thawed
1 (15-ounce) carton light ricotta cheese
½ cup nonfat cottage cheese
1 cup (4 ounces) shredded part-skim mozzarella cheese, divided
9 cooked lasagna noodles (cooked without salt or fat)
2 tablespoons grated Parmesan cheese

Coat a Dutch oven with cooking spray; place over medium heat until hot.
Add onion, green pepper, and garlic; sauté until tender. Add tomato and
next 9 ingredients. Bring to a boil. Cover, reduce heat, and simmer 20 minutes. Add spinach; simmer 5 minutes.

Process ricotta and cottage cheeses in a food processor; stir in ½ cup mozzarella cheese. Spoon 1 cup vegetable mixture into a 13- x 9-inch baking
dish coated with cooking spray. Layer with 3 noodles, one-third of remaining vegetable mixture, and half of cheese mixture. Repeat layers once. Top
with remaining noodles and vegetable mixture. Cover and bake at 350° for
25 minutes. Uncover and sprinkle with remaining ½ cup mozzarella cheese
and Parmesan cheese. Bake 10 minutes. Yield: 8 servings.

Mediterranean Ravioli

Refrigerated ravioli and commercial tomato sauce speed up
preparation of this trendy Mediterranean-inspired one-dish meal.

Vegetable cooking spray
2 teaspoons olive oil
½ pound eggplant, peeled and cut
    into ½-inch cubes
1 cup chopped onion
2 garlic cloves, minced
1 (15-ounce) container
    refrigerated light chunky
    tomato sauce

2 tablespoons sliced ripe olives
1 tablespoon balsamic vinegar
1 teaspoon dried thyme
1 (9-ounce) package refrigerated,
    light cheese-filled ravioli,
    uncooked
3 tablespoons grated Parmesan
    cheese

per serving:
Calories: 288
Fat: 7.9g
Protein: 14.1g
Carbohydrate: 40.0g
Cholesterol: 44mg
Sodium: 771mg
Exchanges:
  2 Starch
  2 Vegetable
  1 High-Fat Meat

Coat a large nonstick skillet with cooking spray. Add olive oil; place over
medium-high heat.

Add eggplant, onion, and garlic; cook, stirring constantly, 5 minutes or
until tender. Stir in tomato sauce and next 3 ingredients; remove from heat.

Cook ravioli according to package directions, omitting salt or fat; drain.
Rinse and drain. Toss with vegetables; place in a 1½-quart shallow baking
dish coated with cooking spray. Sprinkle with cheese.

Bake at 350° for 30 minutes. Yield: 4 servings.

Easy Cheesy Manicotti

To stuff manicotti, fill a heavy-duty zip-top plastic bag with cheese mixture. Seal
bag, and snip a corner from the bottom. Squeeze the mixture into the shell.

½ cup freshly grated Parmesan
    cheese, divided
2 cups low-fat cottage cheese
½ cup part-skim ricotta cheese
2 tablespoons chopped fresh
    parsley
½ teaspoon dried Italian seasoning

¼ teaspoon garlic powder
1 large egg, lightly beaten
12 cooked manicotti shells
    (cooked without salt or fat)
1 (15½-ounce) jar no-salt-added
    spaghett sauce

per serving:
Calories: 408
Fat: 7.5g
Protein: 25.7g
Carbohydrate: 57.4g
Cholesterol: 53mg
Sodium: 518mg
Exchanges:
  4 Starch
  2 Lean Meat

Combine ⅓ cup Parmesan cheese, cottage cheese, and next 5 ingredients;
stuff each shell with ¼ cup cheese mixture. Arrange shells in a 13- x 9-
inch baking dish. Pour spaghetti sauce over shells. Cover and bake at 375°
for 25 minutes or until heated. Sprinkle with remaining Parmesan cheese
before serving. Yield: 6 servings.

Stuffed Zucchini with Pasta

Stuffed zucchini slices are gracefully secured by fresh whole chives and served over a hot bed of fettuccine in this elegant presentation.

5 large zucchini
1 cup soft breadcrumbs (homemade)
1¼ cups diced onion, divided
4 garlic cloves, minced and divided
1 tablespoon olive oil
4 (15-ounce) cans diced tomatoes, undrained and divided
1 cup dry red wine, divided
1¼ teaspoons salt, divided
¾ teaspoon freshly ground pepper, divided
16 ounces fettuccine, uncooked
2 teaspoons olive oil
½ cup freshly grated Parmesan cheese, divided
¼ cup chopped fresh basil
1 bunch fresh chives

Cut zucchini lengthwise into ¼-inch-thick slices. Cook zucchini in boiling water 1 minute; drain. Plunge zucchini into ice water to stop the cooking process; drain and set aside.

Bake breadcrumbs in a shallow pan at 350° for 5 minutes or until toasted, stirring occasionally.

Sauté ½ cup onion and half of garlic in 1 tablespoon hot oil in a large skillet until tender. Add 2 cans tomatoes, ½ cup wine, 1 teaspoon salt, and ¼ teaspoon pepper; cook 15 minutes, stirring often. Cool slightly.

Process tomato mixture in a blender or food processor until smooth. Pour sauce into a small saucepan; set aside.

Cook fettuccine according to package directions, omitting salt and fat; keep warm.

Meanwhile, sauté remaining ¾ cup onion and remaining garlic in 2 teaspoons hot oil in skillet until tender. Add remaining 2 cans tomatoes, remaining ½ cup wine, remaining ¼ teaspoon salt, and remaining ½ teaspoon pepper; cook until very thick, stirring often. Remove from heat.

Stir in breadcrumbs, ¼ cup cheese, and basil. Shape into 24 (1½- to 2-inch-tall) mounds; wrap 1 zucchini slice around each mound, and tie each with a chive. Place in a lightly greased 8-inch square baking dish. Sprinkle with remaining ¼ cup cheese.

Bake, covered, at 350° for 3 to 4 minutes or until thoroughly heated.

Cook sauce over medium heat until thoroughly heated, stirring often. Chop remaining chives, and toss with fettuccine. Serve zucchini over fettuccine, and top with sauce. Yield: 8 servings.

Confetti Pasta

4 ounces spinach fettuccine, uncooked
4 ounces plain fettuccine, uncooked
4 ounces lean cooked ham, diced
1 garlic clove, pressed
Vegetable cooking spray
½ cup frozen English peas, thawed
1 cup fat-free milk
½ cup low-fat cottage cheese
1 tablespoon cornstarch
½ cup shredded Parmesan cheese, divided
¼ teaspoon salt
⅛ teaspoon pepper
⅛ teaspoon ground nutmeg

per serving:
Calories: 114
Fat: 2.8g
Protein: 9.7g
Carbohydrate: 12.1g
Cholesterol: 13mg
Sodium: 423mg
Exchanges:
  1 Starch
  1 Lean Meat

Cook fettuccine according to package directions, omitting salt and fat. Drain and keep warm.

Meanwhile, sauté diced ham and garlic in a nonstick skillet coated with vegetable cooking spray 2 minutes. Stir in English peas; sauté 2 minutes. Remove from skillet.

Process milk, cottage cheese, and cornstarch in a blender or food processor until smooth; pour into skillet. Add ¼ cup Parmesan cheese, salt, pepper, and ground nutmeg. Cook over medium heat, stirring occasionally, until cheese melts. Stir in ham mixture.

Pour mixture over hot cooked fettuccine, tossing to coat well. Sprinkle with remaining ¼ cup Parmesan cheese. Serve immediately. Yield: 8 servings.

Asian Pesto Vermicelli

Fish sauce, along with fresh ginger and jalapeño, delivers a kick to this potent pasta side dish. An extract of anchovies, fish sauce is sometimes labeled nam pla or nuoc nam. Look for it in the Oriental foods section of your supermarket.

½ cup condensed chicken broth, undiluted
2 tablespoons reduced-sodium soy sauce
2 tablespoons fish sauce
1 tablespoon grated fresh ginger
1 jalapeño pepper, seeded and chopped
¼ cup finely chopped fresh basil
¼ cup finely chopped fresh cilantro
¼ cup finely chopped fresh mint leaves
12 ounces vermicelli, cooked without salt or fat

per serving:
Calories: 234
Fat: 0.9g
Protein: 8.0g
Carbohydrate: 46.7g
Cholesterol: 0mg
Sodium: 272mg
Exchanges:
  3 Starch

Combine first 8 ingredients; pour over hot cooked vermicelli, and toss gently. Serve immediately. Yield: 6 servings.

Linguine with Mushrooms and Pine Nuts

1½ ounces dried tomatoes
½ cup hot water
6½ ounces linguine, uncooked and broken in half
1 cup canned no-salt-added chicken broth, undiluted
3½ ounces fresh shiitake mushrooms, thinly sliced
½ cup chopped shallot
1 teaspoon minced garlic
2 teaspoons dried whole basil
½ teaspoon freshly ground pepper
½ cup drained roasted red peppers in water, cut into thin strips
¼ cup pine nuts, toasted
2 tablespoons grated Parmesan cheese
2 tablespoons chopped fresh parsley
Garnish: fresh basil sprig

Combine tomatoes and water in a small bowl; cover and let stand 15 minutes. Drain tomatoes, and slice thinly; set aside.

Cook linguine according to package directions, omitting salt and fat. Drain and set aside.

Place chicken broth in a large nonstick skillet; bring to a boil. Add mushrooms, shallot, and garlic; cook, uncovered, over medium heat 5 minutes. Add tomatoes, basil, and ground pepper. Cook, covered, 10 minutes. Add linguine, pepper strips, pine nuts, and cheese; stir well. Cover and cook 5 more minutes or until thoroughly heated. Sprinkle with fresh parsley and serve immediately. Garnish, if desired. Yield: 10 servings.

Linguine with Red Pepper Sauce

8 ounces linguine, uncooked
Vegetable cooking spray
2 tablespoons olive oil
6 cups chopped red bell pepper
3 garlic cloves, crushed
½ cup balsamic vinegar or red wine vinegar
⅔ cup chopped fresh basil
½ teaspoon salt
¼ teaspoon pepper

Cook linguine according to package directions, omitting salt or fat; drain and keep warm. Coat a nonstick skillet with cooking spray; add olive oil, red bell pepper, and garlic. Cook over low heat, stirring occasionally, 30 minutes.

Process sauce, vinegar, and remaining 3 ingredients in a blender or a food processor until smooth. Spoon over hot cooked linguine, and serve immediately. Yield: 8 servings.

Linguine with Mushrooms and Pine Nuts

Whole Wheat Rotini with Pesto

3 tablespoon olive oil
1½ tablespoons water
½ teaspoon ground nutmeg
½ teaspoon salt
4 garlic cloves, minced
¾ cup chopped fresh basil

¾ cup chopped fresh parsley
1 cup grated Parmesan cheese
8 cups cooked whole wheat rotini
 (corkscrew pasta) or elbow
 macaroni (cooked without salt
 or fat)

Process first 8 ingredients in a blender 1 to 1½ minutes or until blended, stopping to scrape down sides as needed.

Combine cooked rotini and pesto mixture in a large bowl, and toss gently; serve rotini at room temperature. Yield: 16 servings.

per serving:

Calories: 143
Fat: 4.5g
Protein: 5.5g
Carbohydrate: 19.7g
Cholesterol: 4mg
Sodium: 169mg
Exchanges:
 1½ Starch
 1 Fat

Grilled Vegetable Pasta

Grilled Vegetable Pasta

Throw these vegetables on the grill alongside chicken breasts or fish fllets for a quick and easy dinner. Larger portions of the pasta can even be a meatless entrée. Tip: To hold the onions together on the grill, insert a wooden pick through each slice.

per serving:

Calories: 253
Fat: 7.9g
Protein: 9.8g
Carbohydrate: 36.4g
Cholesterol: 6mg
Sodium: 359mg
Exchanges:
  2 Starch
  1 Vegetable
  1½ Fat

8 ounces penne, uncooked
4 tomatoes, cut into 1-inch slices
1 onion, cut into slices
1 zucchini, cut in half lengthwise
1 yellow squash, cut in half lengthwise

2 garlic cloves, minced
2 tablespoons olive oil
½ teaspoon salt
¼ teaspoon freshly ground pepper
¼ cup chopped fresh basil
½ cup freshly grated Parmesan cheese

Cook penne pasta according to package directions, omitting salt and fat drain and keep warm.

Toss together tomato and next 7 ingredients in a large bowl. Grill, covered with grill lid, over medium-high heat (350° to 400°), turning occasionally, 6 minutes or until tender.

Cut zucchini and squash halves into thin slices, and place in a large bowl. Add remaining grilled vegetables, penne, and basil, tossing gently; sprinkle with cheese. Yield: 6 servings.

Spinach and Noodle Bake

8 ounces medium egg noodles, uncooked
½ cup chopped onion
¼ cup canned no-salt-added chicken broth, undiluted
1 teaspoon minced garlic
1 (10-ounce) package frozen chopped spinach, thawed and drained
1 (4-ounce) can sliced mushrooms, drained
1 cup (4 ounces) shredded reduced-fat Swiss cheese

1 (8-ounce) carton nonfat sour cream
½ cup frozen egg substitute, thawed
½ cup fat-free evaporated milk
¼ teaspoon salt
¼ teaspoon sweet Hungarian paprika
¼ teaspoon ground red pepper
¼ teaspoon black pepper
Vegetable cooking spray

per serving:
Calories: 139
Fat: 2.6g
Protein: 10.0g
Carbohydrate: 18.5g
Cholesterol: 24mg
Sodium: 168mg
Exchanges:
   1 Starch
   1 Lean Meat

Cook noodles according to package directions, omitting salt and fat. Drain and set aside.

Combine onion, chicken broth, and garlic in a large saucepan; stir well. Cook over medium heat, stirring constantly, until onion is tender. Add noodles, spinach, and mushrooms; stir well.

Combine cheese and next 7 ingredients in a medium bowl; stir well. Add cheese mixture to noodle mixture, stirring well. Spoon into an 11- x 7-inch baking dish coated with cooking spray. Cover and bake at 350° for 30 minutes or until thoroughly heated. Yield: 12 servings.

Basil-Stuffed Chicken with Tomato-Basil Pasta (page 145)

Poultry

Poultry is the ticket for ease and versatility—plus, it's high in protein and low in total fat. You'll find recipes for every poultry-lover that are sure to whet the appetite. Included are favorites that have all the flavor but little of the fat of traditional recipes, as well as new ideas that the whole family will enjoy. Give this collection a try—no one will ever guess how light these luscious entrées really are.

Lemon-Roasted Chicken

Always roast chicken with the skin on. It keeps the chicken moist, and the fat in the skin won't be absorbed into the meat. Just be sure to remove the skin before serving.

1½ teaspoons salt
2 teaspoons freshly ground pepper
2 to 3 teaspoons dried rosemary, crushed

1 (3-pound) broiler-fryer
1 medium lemon, cut in half

Combine first 3 ingredients; set aside.

Loosen skin from chicken breast by running fingers between the skin and meat; rub 1 teaspoon seasoning mixture under skin. Rub remaining seasoning mixture over outside of chicken. Place chicken in a heavy-duty zip-top plastic bag; seal and store in refrigerator 8 hours.

Remove chicken from bag. Insert lemon halves in cavity; tie ends of legs together with string. Lift wingtips up and over back, and tuck under bird. Place chicken, breast side down, in a lightly greased shallow pan.

Bake at 450°, turning over every 15 minutes, for 50 minutes or until a meat thermometer inserted into meaty part of thigh registers 180°. Let chicken stand 10 minutes. Remove skin before serving. Yield: 4 servings.

Chicken Fricassee

1 (3-pound) broiler-fryer, cut up and skinned
½ teaspoon freshly ground black pepper
¼ teaspoon salt
1 teaspoon dried whole thyme
Vegetable cooking spray
1 teaspoon vegetable oil
12 small boiling onions
3 cups canned no-salt-added chicken broth, undiluted and divided

1 cup dry white wine
1 pound small fresh mushrooms, sliced
2 teaspoons minced garlic
¼ cup all-purpose flour
1 cup nonfat sour cream
¼ teaspoon ground white pepper
⅛ teaspoon salt
1 tablespoon minced parsley

Sprinkle chicken with ½ teaspoon pepper, ¼ teaspoon salt, and thyme. Coat a Dutch oven with cooking spray; add oil. Place over medium heat until hot. Add chicken and onions; cook until chicken is browned on all sides. Remove chicken, and set aside.

Add 2¾ cups chicken broth and wine to pan; bring to a boil. Cover, reduce heat and simmer 15 minutes. Return chicken to pan; cover and simmer 10 minutes.

Coat a large nonstick skillet with cooking spray; place over medium-high heat until hot. Add mushrooms, and sauté until tender. Add garlic, and sauté 1 minute.

Combine remaining ¼ cup broth and flour, stirring with a wire whisk until smooth. Gradually add to chicken mixture, stirring well. Stir in mushroom mixture, sour cream, white pepper, and ⅛ teaspoon salt. Cook over low heat 5 minutes or until thoroughly heated, stirring frequently. Sprinkle with parsley. Yield: 6 servings.

Oven-Fried Chicken

The crisp oven-fried coating of this chicken will satisfy the
most ardent of fried chicken lovers.

¼ cup fine, dry breadcrumbs
  (commercial)
1 teaspoon paprika
½ teaspoon dried whole thyme
¼ teaspoon freshly ground black
  pepper
1 (3-pound) broiler-fryer, cut up
  and skinned
Vegetable cooking spray

1½ tablespoons reduced-calorie
  margarine
1 cup fat-free evaporated milk
½ cup canned no-salt-added
  chicken broth, undiluted
2 tablespoons all-purpose flour
¼ teaspoon salt
⅛ teaspoon ground white pepper

per serving:
Calories: 208
Fat: 5.6g
Protein: 27.4g
Carbohydrate: 10.4g
Cholesterol: 78mg
Sodium: 289mg
Exchanges:
  ½ Starch
  4 Very Lean Meat

Combine first 4 ingredients in a shallow dish, stirring well. Dredge chicken pieces in crumb mixture, coating each piece well. Place on a baking sheet coated with cooking spray. Bake at 375° for 45 minutes or until chicken is done.

Melt margarine in a small saucepan over medium heat. Combine milk, broth, and flour; stir until smooth. Gradually add to margarine, stirring constantly Cook over medium heat, stirring constantly, until mixture is thickened and bubbly. Stir in salt and white pepper. Serve with chicken. Yield: 6 servings.

Arroz con Pollo

Arroz con pollo (ah-ROHS con POH-yoh), meaning
"rice with chicken," is a Spanish and Mexican dish.

per serving:

Calories: 360
Fat: 7.7g
Protein: 29.4g
Carbohydrate: 39.1g
Cholesterol: 108mg
Sodium: 452mg
Exchanges:
  3 Starch
  3 Lean Meat

2 pounds chicken thighs, skinned
3 cups water
½ teaspoon black peppercorns
3 bay leaves
2 cups coarsely chopped onion
1½ cups chopped green bell
   pepper
3 garlic cloves, finely chopped

1 tablespoon vegetable oil
1½ cups long-grain rice, uncooked
½ cup dry white wine
1 tablespoon paprika
1 teaspoon salt
¼ teaspoon pepper
⅛ teaspoon saffron or ground
   turmeric

Combine chicken and next 3 ingredients in a large Dutch oven. Bring to
a boil; cover, reduce heat, and simmer 30 minutes. Remove from heat;
remove chicken from broth, and set aside.

Pour broth through a wire-mesh strainer into a bowl, discarding solids.
Add enough water to broth to equal 3 cups, and set aside.

Cook onion, bell pepper, and garlic in oil in Dutch oven over medium-
high heat, stirring often, 6 minutes or until lightly browned. Add broth,
rice, and remaining 5 ingredients. Bring to a boil; cover, reduce heat, and
simmer 20 minutes. Uncover and stir in chicken; cook 6 more minutes or
until heated. Yield: 7 servings.

Honey-Barbecued Chicken Breasts

per serving:

Calories: 190
Fat: 3.1g
Protein: 26.5g
Carbohydrate: 11.2g
Cholesterol: 72mg
Sodium: 92mg
Exchanges:
  1 Starch
  3 Very Lean Meat

1 cup reduced-calorie ketchup
3 tablespoons lemon juice
2 tablespoons low-sodium
   Worcestershire sauce
2 tablespoons honey
1 tablespoon peeled, minced
   ginger

1 teaspoon minced garlic
Vegetable cooking spray
6 (6-ounce) bone-in chicken
   breast halves, skinned

Combine first 6 ingredients in a saucepan. Bring to a boil, stirring frequently; reduce heat, and simmer 2 minutes. Remove from heat; set aside.

Coat food rack with cooking spray; place on grill over medium-high heat
(350° to 400°). Place chicken on rack; grill, covered, 5 minutes, turning
frequently. Brush chicken with ketchup mixture. Grill 12 more minutes or
until done, turning and basting frequently. Yield: 6 servings.

Honey-Barbecued Chicken Breast and
Nutty Pineapple Slaw (page 164)

Lime-Roasted Chicken Breasts

Fresh limes and basil impart such great flavor that
this chicken needs very little salt.

4 (6-ounce) bone-in chicken
    breast halves
½ teaspoon salt
½ teaspoon pepper
2 limes

3 tablespoons olive oil, divided
2½ teaspoons white wine vinegar
2 limes
1 tablespoon chopped fresh basil

Rub chicken with salt and pepper; place in a shallow dish; set aside.
Grate rind, and squeeze juice from 2 limes.
Combine grated lime rind, lime juice, 2 tablespoons oil, and vinegar; pour over chicken. Cover and chill 2½ hours, turning occasionally.
Bake at 375° in a roasting pan 40 minutes or until done. Remove skin from chicken. Peel 2 limes; cut into thin slices. Heat remaining 1 tablespoon oil in a skillet. Add lime slices and basil; cook, stirring gently, 1 minute or until fruit just begins to soften. Spoon over chicken. Yield: 4 servings.

Chicken Cordon Bleu

4 (4-ounce) skinned and boned
    chicken breast halves
3 tablespoons chopped fresh
    parsley
1 teaspoon dried Italian
    seasoning, divided
4 (1-ounce) slices part-skim
    mozzarella cheese

4 (1-ounce) reduced-fat, low-
    sodium, honey-flavored ham
    slices
1 tablespoon fat-free mayonnaise
1 teaspoon warm water
⅓ cup soft breadcrumbs
    (homemade)
Vegetable cooking spray

Place each piece of chicken between 2 sheets of heavy-duty plastic wrap; flatten to ¼-inch thickness, using a meat mallet or rolling pin. Sprinkle with parsley and ¼ teaspoon Italian seasoning. Place a cheese slice and a ham slice on each chicken breast. Roll up from short side; secure with wooden picks.
Combine mayonnaise and water; brush on chicken, covering all sides. Combine breadcrumbs and remaining ¾ teaspoon Italian seasoning; dredge chicken rolls in mixture. Place on a baking sheet coated with cooking spray. Bake at 425° for 15 minutes or until chicken is done. Remove wooden picks. Yield: 4 servings.

Basil-Stuffed Chicken with Tomato-Basil Pasta

These pretty chicken pinwheels (pictured on page 138) can be grilled ahead of time and microwaved just before serving.

4 (4-ounce) skinned and boned chicken breast halves
¼ teaspoon salt
¼ teaspoon garlic powder

2 bunches fresh basil (about 20 large basil leaves)
Tomato-Basil Pasta
Garnish: fresh basil sprigs

Place each piece of chicken between 2 sheets of heavy-duty plastic wrap; flatten to ¼-inch thickness, using a meat mallet or rolling pin.

Sprinkle chicken breasts evenly with salt and garlic powder.

Arrange basil leaves in a single layer over chicken breasts. Starting at short end, roll up 2 chicken breasts. Place each roll on top of a remaining chicken breast, and roll up, forming two larger rolls. Secure chicken with wooden picks.

Grill, covered with grill lid, over medium-high heat (350° to 400°) 18 to 20 minutes, turning once. Wrap in aluminum foil, and chill at least 8 hours.

Remove chicken rolls from refrigerator, and unwrap. Place chicken rolls on a microwave-safe plate, and cover with wax paper.

Microwave at MEDIUM-HIGH (70% power) 1½ minutes, turning once. Remove wooden picks.

Cut each chicken roll into thin slices. Serve with Tomato-Basil Pasta. Garnish, if desired. Yield: 4 servings.

Tomato-Basil Pasta

1 tablespoon reduced-calorie margarine
2 garlic cloves, minced
¼ cup lemon juice
¼ cup dry white wine

¼ cup chopped fresh basil
1 cup peeled, seeded, and finely chopped tomato
8 ounces thin spaghetti, cooked without salt or fat

Melt margarine in a large saucepan over medium heat; add minced garlic, and cook 1 minute, stirring constantly. Add lemon juice and remaining 4 ingredients; toss gently. Yield: 4 servings.

Spicy Chicken with
Black Bean Puree

Spicy Chicken with Black Bean Puree

per serving:

Calories: 399
Fat: 5.1g
Protein: 41.5g
Carbohydrate: 48.0g
Cholesterol: 66mg
Sodium: 668mg
Exchanges:
  3 Starch
  1 Vegetable
  4 Very Lean Meat

2 (4-ounce) skinned and boned
   chicken breast halves
2 teaspoons fajita seasoning
1 teaspoon olive oil
½ cup chopped onion
2 garlic cloves, minced
1 (15-ounce) can black beans,
   undrained
1 (10-ounce) can diced tomatoes
   and green chiles

¼ teaspoon ground red
   pepper
½ teaspoon ground cumin
2 tablespoons chopped fresh
   cilantro
1 tablespoon lime juice
Shredded reduced-fat Monterey
   Jack cheese (optional)

Rub chicken with fajita seasoning.

Cook chicken in hot oil in a nonstick skillet over medium-high heat
3 minutes on each side or until done. Remove chicken from skillet, reserving drippings in skillet; keep chicken warm.

Sauté onion and garlic in reserved drippings until tender.

Drain beans, reserving 2 tablespoons liquid; rinse and drain beans again.

Process onion mixture, beans, reserved liquid, tomatoes, and next 4 ingredients in a blender or food processor until smooth, stopping once to scrape down sides.

Pour mixture into a small saucepan, and cook over medium heat, stirring constantly, until thoroughly heated. Sprinkle with cheese, if desired. Serve with chicken. Yield: 2 servings.

Sesame-Crusted Chicken With Pineapple Salsa

A sassy pineapple salsa dresses up this simple dish and adds unexpected flavor.

½ cup sesame seeds
2 tablespoons minced fresh
   ginger
2 teaspoons vegetable oil

4 (4-ounce) skinned and boned
   chicken breast halves
½ teaspoon salt
Pineapple Salsa

per serving:
Calories: 356
Fat: 15.5g
Protein: 39.2g
Carbohydrate: 15.5g
Cholesterol: 96mg
Sodium: 385mg
Exchanges:
  1 Fruit
  5½ Lean Meat

Bake sesame seeds in a shallow pan at 350° for 5 minutes or until toasted, stirring frequently; cool.

Combine sesame seeds, ginger, and oil, stirring well.

Sprinkle chicken with salt; coat with sesame seed mixture, and place on a lightly greased rack in a broiler pan.

Bake at 400° for 20 to 25 minutes or until tender. Top evenly with Pineapple Salsa, and serve immediately. Yield: 4 servings.

Pineapple Salsa

1 (15¼-ounce) can pineapple
   tidbits, drained
½ cup chopped red bell pepper
1 teaspoon grated fresh ginger

1 tablespoon fresh lime juice
Pinch of ground cloves
¼ cup chopped fresh cilantro
¼ teaspoon hot sauce

Combine all ingredients in a medium bowl; cover and chill 15 minutes. Yield: 1½ cups.

Chicken à la King

per serving:

Calories: 254

Fat: 4.0g

Protein: 28.0g

Carbohydrate: 26.4g

Cholesterol: 53mg

Sodium: 573mg

Exchanges:

  2 Starch

  3 Very Lean Meat

1 tablespoon reduced-calorie margarine

3 (4-ounce) skinned and boned chicken breast halves, cut into bite-size pieces

¼ cup chopped onion

¼ cup sliced mushrooms

¼ cup all-purpose flour

2 cups fat-free milk

¼ cup frozen English peas, thawed

1 (2-ounce) jar diced pimento, drained

½ teaspoon salt

½ teaspoon pepper

4 slices wheat bread, trimmed and toasted

¼ teaspoon paprika

Melt margarine in a large nonstick skillet over medium heat. Add chicken and onion; cook, stirring constantly, 3 to 5 minutes or until chicken is browned. Add mushrooms; cook 1 minute.

Chicken à la King

Stir in flour, and cook 1 minute, stirring constantly. Gradually add milk and next 4 ingredients; cook over medium heat, stirring constantly, until mixture is thickened and bubbly.

Cut each slice of bread into 4 triangles. Serve chicken mixture with 4 toast triangles; sprinkle with paprika. Yield: 4 servings.

Chicken-and-Black Bean Quesadillas

The ubiquitous Tex-Mex appetizer becomes a hearty meal
with main-dish ingredients.

1 tablespoon fajita seasoning
2 (4-ounce) skinned and boned
    chicken breast halves, cut into
    thin strips
Vegetable cooking spray
½ onion, cut into strips
½ green bell pepper, cut into
    strips
2 garlic cloves, minced

1 to 2 jalapeño peppers, minced
1 (15-ounce) can black beans,
    rinsed and drained
½ cup chopped fresh cilantro
4 (10-inch) flour tortillas
1½ cups (6 ounces) shredded
    reduced-fat Monterey Jack
    cheese

per serving:
Calories: 465
Fat: 13.2g
Protein: 36.5g
Carbohydrate: 49.2g
Cholesterol: 63mg
Sodium: 777mg
Exchanges:
  3½ Starch
  4 Lean Meat

Rub fajita seasoning on all sides of chicken; cover and chill 30 minutes.

Cook chicken in a large nonstick skillet over medium-high heat, stirring constantly, 4 minutes or until done. Remove from skillet, and keep warm.

Coat skillet with cooking spray; add onion and next 3 ingredients, and cook until tender, stirring often. Stir in black beans and cilantro; cook, stirring constantly, until thoroughly heated.

Coat 1 side of each tortilla with cooking spray; layer chicken, vegetable mixture, and cheese evenly on uncoated side of 2 tortillas. Top with remaining tortillas, coated side up. Cook in skillet over medium heat until lightly browned, turning once. Serve immediately. Yield: 2 servings.

Chicken Divan

per serving:

Calories: 379
Fat: 12.6g
Protein: 45.1g
Carbohydrate: 20.8g
Cholesterol: 104mg
Sodium: 804mg
Exchanges:
  1 Starch
  1 Vegetable
  5½ Lean Meat

2 (10-ounce) packages frozen broccoli spears, thawed and coarsely chopped
3 cups chopped cooked chicken breast (about 1½ pounds skinned and boned chicken breast halves)
1¼ cups fat-free milk
3 tablespoons all-purpose flour
1 (10¾-ounce) can reduced-fat condensed cream of mushroom soup, undiluted
1 teaspoon lemon juice
¼ teaspoon salt
¼ teaspoon pepper
½ cup finely crushed savory herb-flavored melba toast rounds (about 18)
1 tablespoon margarine, melted
½ cup (2 ounces) shredded reduced-fat sharp Cheddar cheese

Place broccoli in a 13- x 9-inch baking dish. Top evenly with chicken.
Combine milk and flour in a large heavy saucepan, stirring with a wire whisk until smooth. Stir in soup and next 3 ingredients. Bring mixture to a boil over medium heat, stirring constantly. Cook, stirring often, 5 minutes or until thickened and bubbly. Pour evenly over chicken.
Combine crushed melba toast and margarine; sprinkle over soup mixture.
Bake at 350° for 20 minutes. Sprinkle with cheese, and bake 5 additional minutes. Yield: 6 servings.

Old-Fashioned Chicken and Dumplings

per serving:

Calories: 283
Fat: 8.5g
Protein: 20.6g
Carbohydrate: 26.8g
Cholesterol: 50mg
Sodium: 613mg
Exchanges:
  2 Starch
  2 Medium-Fat Meat

1 (3½-pound) broiler-fryer, cut up and skinned
1 celery rib, cut into thirds
1 medium onion, quartered
2 quarts water
1 teaspoon salt
½ teaspoon pepper
2 cups all-purpose flour
½ teaspoon baking soda
½ teaspoon salt
3 tablespoons margarine, softened
2 tablespoons chopped fresh parsley
¾ cup nonfat buttermilk

Combine first 5 ingredients in a Dutch oven; bring to a boil. Cover, reduce heat, and simmer 1 hour or until chicken is tender. Remove chicken, reserving broth in Dutch oven; discard vegetables. Let chicken and broth cool. Bone and cut chicken into bite-size pieces. Place chicken and broth in separate containers; cover and chill 8 hours. Skim fat from top of broth; bring broth to a boil, and add pepper.

Combine flour, soda, and ½ teaspoon salt; cut in margarine with a pastry blender until mixture is crumbly. Add parsley and buttermilk, stirring with a fork until dry ingredients are moistened. Turn dough out onto a heavily floured surface, and knead lightly 4 or 5 times. Pat dough to ¼-inch thickness. Pinch off 1½-inch pieces, and drop into boiling broth. Add chicken. Reduce heat to medium-low, and cook 8 to 10 minutes, stirring occasionally. Yield: 8 servings.

Chicken Pot Pie

1 (3½-pound) broiler-fryer
2 quarts water
½ teaspoon salt
½ teaspoon pepper
1 celery rib, cut into 2-inch
   pieces
1 medium onion, quartered
1 bay leaf
3½ cups peeled and cubed
   potato (1½ pounds)

1 (16-ounce) package frozen
   mixed vegetables
1 cup fat-free milk
½ cup all-purpose flour
¾ teaspoon salt
1 teaspoon pepper
½ teaspoon poultry seasoning
Butter-flavored cooking spray
5 sheets frozen phyllo pastry,
   thawed

per serving:
Calories: 249
Fat: 5.5g
Protein: 21.5g
Carbohydrate: 25.9g
Cholesterol: 50mg
Sodium: 465mg
Exchanges:
  1½ Starch
  1 Vegetable
  2 Lean Meat

Combine first 7 ingredients in a large Dutch oven; bring to a boil. Cover, reduce heat, and simmer 1 hour or until chicken is tender.

Remove chicken, reserving broth in Dutch oven; discard vegetables and bay leaf. Let chicken cool; skin, bone, and cut into bite-size pieces.

Skim fat from top of broth, reserving 3½ cups broth.

Bring reserved broth to a boil in Dutch oven. Add potato and mixed vegetables; return to a boil. Cover, reduce heat, and cook about 8 minutes or until vegetables are tender.

Combine milk and flour in a jar; cover tightly, and shake vigorously. Gradually add milk mixture in a slow, steady stream to broth mixture, stirring constantly. Cook, stirring constantly, 1 minute or until thickened. Stir in ¾ teaspoon salt, 1 teaspoon pepper, poultry seasoning, and chicken.

Spoon mixture into a 13- x 9-inch baking dish coated with cooking spray; set aside.

Place 1 phyllo sheet horizontally on a flat surface, keeping remaining sheets covered with a slightly damp towel until ready for use. Coat sheet with cooking spray. Layer remaining 4 sheets on first sheet, coating each with cooking spray. Place on top of baking dish, loosely crushing edges around the dish.

Bake at 400° for 20 minutes. Yield: 8 servings.

Stir-Fry Chicken with Vegetables

*Small amounts of potent Asian seasonings deliver a large amount
of flavor in this simple stir-fry. Look for Oriental broth near the canned
chicken broth, and find the dark sesame oil and chili puree with
other Oriental items at your grocery store.*

per serving:

Calories: 287
Fat: 9.8g
Protein: 28.9g
Carbohydrate: 18.3g
Cholesterol: 66mg
Sodium: 1070mg
Exchanges:
  1 Starch
  1 Vegetable
  3 Lean Meat

1 tablespoon cornstarch
¼ cup ready-to-serve Oriental broth
1 tablespoon reduced-sodium soy sauce
4 (4-ounce) skinned and boned chicken breast halves, cut into ½-inch strips
⅓ cup ready-to-serve Oriental broth
¼ cup reduced-sodium soy sauce
2 tablespoons dry sherry
1 tablespoon rice vinegar
1 tablespoon dark sesame oil

1 tablespoon chili puree with garlic
1 tablespoon cornstarch
2 teaspoons sugar
4 teaspoons canola oil, divided
2 large carrots, scraped and thinly sliced
1 green bell pepper, sliced
1 red bell pepper, sliced
1 onion, cut into thin strips
1 tablespoon minced fresh ginger
4 green onions, chopped
Garnish: green onions

Combine first 3 ingredients; add chicken, stirring to coat. Cover and chill 30 minutes.

Combine ⅓ cup broth and next 7 ingredients; set aside.

Remove chicken from marinade, discarding marinade.

Heat 2 teaspoons canola oil in a large nonstick skillet over high heat; add chicken, and stir-fry 5 minutes until tender. Remove chicken from skillet, and set aside.

Heat remaining 2 teaspoons canola oil in skillet; add carrot, and stir-fry 2 to 3 minutes. Add green bell pepper and next 4 ingredients; stir-fry 3 additional minutes.

Stir in broth mixture; bring to a boil. Boil 1 minute or until thickened. Stir in chicken. Garnish, if desired. Yield: 4 servings.

Note: Substitute 1 pound fresh turkey breast for chicken breast halves, if desired.

Turkey with Leek-Onion Stuffing

*Chopped leeks and onions mingle and mellow as
they roast inside this turkey.*

Vegetable cooking spray
1 tablespoon reduced-calorie
   margarine
4 cups coarsely chopped leeks
1 cup chopped onion
1 teaspoon dried whole thyme
1¾ cups canned no-salt-added
   chicken broth, undiluted and
   divided
2 (6-ounce) packages plain
   croutons
⅓ cup chopped fresh parsley
1 tablespoon grated orange rind
½ teaspoon freshly ground
   pepper
1 (10-pound) turkey
1 tablespoon reduced-calorie
   margarine, melted

per serving:
Calories: 282
Fat: 8.2g
Protein: 34.3g
Carbohydrate: 14.8g
Cholesterol: 92mg
Sodium: 273mg
Exchanges:
   1 Starch
   4½ Very Lean Meat
   1 Fat

Coat a nonstick skillet with cooking spray; add 1 tablespoon margarine. Place over medium heat until margarine melts. Add leeks, onion, thyme, and ½ cup broth. Bring to a boil. Cover, reduce heat, and simmer until vegetables are tender. Uncover and cook over high heat until liquid evaporates. Transfer leek mixture to a bowl; add croutons and next 3 ingredients. Add remaining 1¼ cups broth; cover and chill.

Remove giblets and neck from turkey. Rinse turkey under cold water; pat dry. Pack about 7 cups leek mixture into cavity of turkey. Tuck legs under flap of skin around tail, or close cavity with skewers, and truss. Tie ends of legs to tail with cord. Lift wingtips up and over back; tuck under turkey.

Coat turkey with cooking spray; place, breast side up, on a rack in a roasting pan coated with cooking spray. Cover with heavy-duty aluminum foil; bake at 325° for 2 hours. Uncover and baste with melted margarine. Bake 2 hours or until meat thermometer inserted into meaty part of thigh registers 180° and stuffing registers 165°. Let stand 15 minutes before carving.

Spoon remaining leek mixture into a 1-quart casserole coated with cooking spray. Bake at 325° for 25 minutes. Serve with skinned turkey slices. Yield: 20 servings.

Grilled Turkey Breast with Cranberry Salsa

Grilled Turkey Breast with Cranberry Salsa

per serving:

Calories: 322
Fat: 5.6g
Protein: 32.2g
Carbohydrate: 36.5g
Cholesterol: 79mg
Sodium: 240mg
Exchanges:
  1 Starch
  1½ Fruit
  4 Very Lean Meat

1 (6-pound) turkey breast
1 cup cranberry juice cocktail
¼ cup orange juice
¼ cup olive oil
1 teaspoon salt
1 teaspoon pepper
¼ cup chopped fresh cilantro
3 cups frozen cranberries
½ cup honey
2 tablespoons fresh lime juice

½ cup coarsely chopped purple onion
2 jalapeño peppers, seeded and coarsely chopped
½ cup coarsely chopped cried apricot halves
½ cup fresh cilantro leaves
2 large oranges, peeled, seeded, and coarsely chopped

Remove and discard skin and breast bone from turkey breast, separating breast halves; place turkey in a large heavy-duty zip-top plastic bag.

Combine cranberry juice cocktail and next 5 ingredients in a jar; cover tightly, and shake vigorously. Reserve ½ cup marinade; chill. Pour remaining marinade over turkey. Seal bag, and chill 8 hours, turning occasionally.

Process cranberries and remaining 7 ingredients in a food processor until chopped, stopping once to scrape down sides (do not overprocess). Transfer cranberry mixture to a serving bowl; chill.

Remove turkey from marinade, discarding marinade.

Grill turkey, covered with grill lid, over medium-high heat (350° to 400°), about 15 minutes on each side or until a meat thermometer inserted in thickest portion registers 170°, basting occasionally with reserved marinade. Let stand 10 minutes before slicing. Serve with cranberry mixture. Yield: 8 servings.

Game Hens with Chutney-Mustard Glaze

1 (1¼-pound) Cornish hen, skinned and split
Vegetable cooking spray

2 tablespoons chopped mango chutney
2 teaspoons Dijon mustard

per serving:
Calories: 288
Fat: 9.6g
Protein: 37.0g
Carbohydrate: 11.0g
Cholesterol: 113mg
Sodium: 209mg
Exchanges:
 1 Starch
 5 Lean Meat

Place hen halves, cut side down, on a rack coated with cooking spray; place rack in a broiler pan. Combine chutney and mustard, and brush about one-third of chutney mixture over hen.

Bake, uncovered, at 325° for 50 to 60 minutes, brushing twice with chutney mixture. Yield: 2 servings.

Honey-Lemon Cornish Hens

3 (1-pound) Cornish hens, skinned
¼ teaspoon freshly ground pepper
Vegetable cooking spray
½ cup honey

⅓ cup lemon juice
¼ cup low-sodium soy sauce
1 tablespoon margarine
Wild rice (optional)
Garnish: fresh herbs

per serving:
Calories: 267
Fat: 8.1g
Protein: 23.8g
Carbohydrate: 24.5g
Cholesterol: 73mg
Sodium: 353mg
Exchanges:
 1½ Starch
 3 Lean Meat

Remove giblets from hens; reserve for another use. Rinse hens under cold running water, and pat dry. Split each hen in half lengthwise, using an electric knife. Sprinkle evenly with pepper. Place hens, cut side down, on rack of a broiler pan coated with cooking spray.

Combine honey and next 3 ingredients in a small saucepan. Bring to a boil; reduce heat, and simmer 5 minutes.

Brush hens with half of honey mixture. Bake at 350° for 20 minutes. Brush with additional honey mixture, and bake an additional 30 to 35 minutes or until hens are done, basting frequently with remaining honey mixture. Transfer hens to a serving platter. If desired, serve with wild rice, and garnish with fresh herbs. Yield: 6 servings.

Blue Cheese Chicken Salad (page 168)

Salads & Dressings

Maximize your options for healthful eating by selecting one of the many nutritious and delicious salads from this chapter. Discover the colors, textures, and flavors that these various salads have to offer, while providing key sources of vitamins, minerals, and fiber. In addition to salads to serve on the side, you'll find hearty main-dish options. And don't miss our pick of homemade dressings and vinegars that deliver big taste with few calories and little or no fat!

Fresh Fruit with Mint Tea Vinaigrette

Serve this versatile compote on lettuce leaves as a salad, in a large bowl at a brunch or breakfast buffet as a side dish, or in individual dishes as a dessert.

1½ cups water
¼ cup sugar
1 regular-size tea bag
½ cup loosely packed fresh mint
    sprigs
1 tablespoon balsamic vinegar

2 cups cubed fresh pineapple
1 cup cubed honeydew
1 cup cubed cantaloupe
1 cup orange sections
1 cup fresh blueberries

Combine water and sugar in a heavy saucepan; bring to a boil. Add tea bag and mint; remove from heat, and let steep 5 minutes. Remove tea bag; stir in balsamic vinegar, and let stand 5 minutes.

Pour mixture through a wire-mesh strainer into a large bowl, discarding mint. Add fruit, stirring gently to coat. Cover mixture, and chill at least 1 hour. Yield: 5 cups.

Frozen Strawberry Salad

You'll enjoy the ease of this make-ahead dessert salad, and your family will gain the nutritional benefits from the fruit—plus, it tastes yummy.

1 (8-ounce) package fat-free
    cream cheese, softened
½ cup sugar
1 (8-ounce) container reduced-fat
    frozen whipped topping,
    thawed

2 cups frozen no-sugar-added
    whole strawberries, thawed
    and halved
1 (15¼-ounce) can unsweetened
    crushed pineapple, undrained
1½ cups sliced banana (2 medium)

Beat cream cheese at medium speed with an electric mixer until creamy; gradually add sugar, beating until smooth.

Fold in whipped topping and remaining ingredients; spoon into a 13- x 9-inch dish. Cover with aluminum foil.

Freeze until firm. Yield: 12 servings.

Fresh Fruit with Mint Tea Vinaigrette

Marinated Two-Bean Salad

1 cup dried tomatoes in oil
2 (16-ounce) cans kidney beans, rinsed and drained
2 (10-ounce) packages frozen French-style green beans, thawed
6 green onions, chopped

¼ cup balsamic vinegar or red wine vinegar
2 garlic cloves, minced
½ teaspoon salt
¾ teaspoon pepper
Curly leaf lettuce (optional)

per serving:
Calories: 210
Fat: 9.2g
Protein: 8.4g
Carbohydrate: 26.3g
Cholesterol: 0mg
Sodium: 327mg
Exchanges:
  2 Starch
  2 Fat

Drain dried tomatoes, reserving ¼ cup oil. Chop tomatoes.
Combine tomatoes, reserved oil, beans, and next 5 ingredients, tossing well. Cover and chill at least 2 hours. Serve salad over curly leaf lettuce, if desired. Yield: 8 servings.

Marinated Black-Eyed Pea Salad

per ¾ cup:

Calories: 154
Fat: 1.2g
Protein: 8.6g
Carbohydrate: 27.8g
Cholesterol: 0mg
Sodium: 323mg
Exchanges:
  2 Starch

1½ cups water
1 medium onion, halved
½ teaspoon salt
½ teaspoon dried crushed red
    pepper
⅛ teaspoon hickory-flavored
    liquid smoke
1 (16-ounce) package frozen
    black-eyed peas
½ cup commercial or homemade
    raspberry wine vinegar
    (see page 171)

¼ cup water
3 tablespoons chopped fresh
    parsley
1 garlic clove, minced
1 teaspoon olive oil
¼ teaspoon salt
¼ teaspoon freshly ground pepper
½ cup chopped red bell pepper
⅓ cup small purple onion rings

Combine first 5 ingredients in a medium saucepan; bring to a boil. Add peas; return to a boil. Cover, reduce heat, and simmer 40 to 45 minutes or until peas are tender. Remove and discard onion; drain. Rinse with cold water, and drain. Place in a medium bowl; set aside.

Combine vinegar and next 7 ingredients. Pour over peas; toss. Cover; chill 8 hours, stirring occasionally. Stir in purple onion. Serve with a slotted spoon. Yield: 5 servings.

Grilled Vegetable Salad

per 1 cup:

Calories: 103
Fat: 4.9g
Protein: 2.3g
Carbohydrate: 14.6g
Cholesterol: 0mg
Sodium: 116mg
Exchanges:
  3 Vegetable
  1 Fat

⅓ cup white balsamic vinegar
2 tablespoons olive oil
2 shallots, finely chopped
1 teaspoon dried Italian seasoning
¼ teaspoon salt
¼ teaspoon pepper
1½ teaspoons molasses

½ pound carrots, scraped
1 red bell pepper, seeded
1 yellow bell pepper, seeded
2 zucchini
2 yellow squash
1 large onion

Combine first 7 ingredients in a large bowl. Set aside.

Cut carrots and remaining 5 ingredients into large pieces.

Add vegetables to vinegar mixture, tossing to coat. Let stand 30 minutes, stirring occasionally. Drain vegetables, reserving vinegar mixture. Arrange vegetables in a grill basket. Grill, covered with grill lid, over medium-high heat (350° to 400°) 15 to 20 minutes, turning occasionally. Return vegetables to vinegar mixture; toss. Cover; chill 8 hours. Yield: 6 servings.

Roasted Vegetable Salad with Dried Peach Vinaigrette

Use any remaining vinaigrette on fruit or vegetable salads.

2 fennel bulbs, sliced
2 sweet onions, sliced
1 tablespoon olive oil
¾ teaspoon salt, divided
¾ teaspoon pepper, divided
¼ cup chopped dried peach

1 cup peach nectar
1 shallot, minced
¼ teaspoon Dijon mustard
1 tablespoon lemon juice
1 tablespoon olive oil
6 cups torn mixed salad greens

per serving:
Calories: 260
Fat: 5.0g
Protein: 2.7g
Carbohydrate: 22.1g
Cholesterol: 0mg
Sodium: 352mg
Exchanges:
 I Vegetable
 I Fruit
 I Fat

Toss together first 3 ingredients in a shallow roasting pan; stir in ½ teaspoon salt and ½ teaspoon pepper.

Bake at 450°, stirring occasionally, 30 to 40 minutes or until tender. Remove from oven; set aside.

Bring chopped peach and nectar to a boil in a saucepan. Cover, reduce heat, and simmer 5 minutes; cool.

Process peach mixture in a food processor or blender until smooth, stopping to scrape down sides. Pour into a bowl; whisk in remaining ¼ teaspoon salt, remaining ¼ teaspoon pepper, shallot, and next 3 ingredients.

Drizzle roasted vegetables with ¼ cup peach mixture, and toss gently.

Drizzle greens with ⅓ cup peach mixture, and toss gently; arrange greens evenly on 6 individual plates, and top evenly with roasted vegetables. Yield: 6 servings.

Peppery Greens with Raspberry Dressing

A sweet raspberry dressing balances the sharp flavors
of watercress and arugula.

¼ cup cranberry-raspberry juice
   drink
¼ cup seedless raspberry jam
3 tablespoons raspberry vinegar
2 tablespoons olive oil
½ teaspoon salt

⅛ teaspoon freshly ground
   pepper
3 cups watercress leaves
1½ cups arugula
¼ cup freshly shredded Parmesan
   cheese

per serving:
Calories: 140
Fat: 8.4g
Protein: 2.9g
Carbohydrate: 13.5g
Cholesterol: 4mg
Sodium: 400mg
Exchanges:
 ½ Starch
 I Vegetable
 2 Fat

Combine first 6 ingredients in a jar; cover tightly, and shake vigorously.

Combine watercress and arugula; add raspberry dressing, tossing gently to coat. Sprinkle with cheese; serve immediately. Yield: 4 servings.

Seven-Layer Italian Salad

3 cups shredded iceberg lettuce
1 medium-size red bell pepper,
    cut into strips
1 medium cucumber, sliced
2 cups yellow or red teardrop
    tomatoes, halved
1 medium-size yellow bell pepper,
    cut into ½-inch pieces
1 cup thinly sliced celery
¾ cup sliced green onions
¼ cup red wine vinegar

¼ cup water
1 tablespoon vegetable oil
2 teaspoons Dijon mustard
1 teaspoon dried Italian seasoning
1 teaspoon minced fresh garlic
½ teaspoon pepper
¼ teaspoon hot sauce
½ cup (2 ounces) shredded
    nonfat mozzarella cheese
Garnish: red bell pepper rings

Layer first 7 ingredients in a 3-quart bowl. Combine vinegar and next 7 ingredients in a small bowl, stirring with a wire whisk. Pour vinegar mixture over vegetable layers. Sprinkle with cheese. Cover and chill. Garnish, if desired. Yield: 8 servings.

Salad Composé

40 small fresh green beans or
    snow pea pods
20 Bibb lettuce leaves
1 head Belgian endive, sliced cross-
    wise and separated into rings

1 (14.4-ounce) can hearts of
    palm, drained and sliced
1 large tomato, thinly sliced
4 large mushrooms, sliced
Wine Vinegar Dressing

Wash beans; trim ends, if desired. Cook beans in boiling water to cover 30 seconds; drain and plunge into ice water until chilled. Drain; set aside. **Line** 4 salad plates evenly with lettuce leaves; arrange green beans, endive, and next 3 ingredients evenly over lettuce. Serve with Wine Vinegar Dressing. Yield: 4 servings.

Wine Vinegar Dressing

½ cup red wine vinegar
1 tablespoon vegetable oil
½ cup chopped green onions
1 tablespoon fresh minced parsley

½ teaspoon sugar
¼ teaspoon salt
¼ teaspoon pepper

Process all ingredients in a blender 30 seconds. Yield: about ½ cup.

Seven-Layer Italian Salad

Wilted Spinach Salad

per serving:

Calories: 78
Fat: 1.3g
Protein: 7.3g
Carbohydrate: 11.8g
Cholesterol: 7mg
Sodium: 251mg
Exchanges:
  2 Vegetable
  ½ Very Lean Meat

Vegetable cooking spray
2 ounces reduced-fat, low-sodium, honey-flavored ham slices, chopped
12 ounces fresh spinach
2 hard-cooked egg whites, coarsely chopped
4 ounces fresh mushrooms, sliced
1 (8-ounce) bottle fat-free sweet-and-sour salad dressing

Coat a nonstick skillet with cooking spray. Add ham, and cook over medium heat, stirring constantly, until lightly browned. Drain on paper towels; set aside.

Remove stems from spinach; wash leaves thoroughly, and pat dry. Tear into bite-size pieces; arrange one-fourth of spinach on each of 4 individual salad plates. Top each with one-fourth of egg whites and mushrooms; set aside. Bring salad dressing to a boil in a small saucepan over high heat; pour ¼ cup over each salad. Sprinkle evenly with ham. Yield: 4 servings.

Nutty Pineapple Slaw

Crushed pineapple and a sprinkling of peanuts lend delightful texture and sweetness to this slaw. It's pictured as an accompaniment to Honey-Barbecued Chicken Breasts on page 143.

per serving:

Calories: 66
Fat: 1.2g
Protein: 3.2g
Carbohydrate: 10.6g
Cholesterol: 0mg
Sodium: 63mg
Exchanges:
  2 Vegetable

2½ cups shredded green cabbage
1½ cups shredded red cabbage
¾ cup chopped red bell pepper
1 (8-ounce) can crushed pineapple in juice, drained
1 cup nonfat sour cream
2 tablespoons sugar
1 tablespoon dry mustard
3 tablespoons cider vinegar
⅛ teaspoon salt
2 tablespoons unsalted dry-roasted peanuts, chopped

Combine cabbages and red pepper in a large bowl; toss well.
Combine crushed pineapple and next 5 ingredients in a small bowl, stirring well. Add pineapple mixture to cabbage mixture, and toss until blended. Cover and chill. Sprinkle slaw with peanuts just before serving. Yield: 8 servings.

Couscous Salad with
Dried Tomato Vinaigrette

Toasted spices and dried tomatoes give this salad added flavor.
You can add chopped cooked chicken or shrimp to make it a main dish.

1 red bell pepper
½ medium-size purple onion
1 medium cucumber
¼ cup olive oil
3 tablespoons red wine vinegar
¼ teaspoon salt
⅛ teaspoon ground red pepper
1 tablespoon mustard seeds

1 tablespoon cumin seeds
⅓ cup minced dried tomato
¼ cup minced fresh cilantro
1½ cups water
½ teaspoon salt
½ teaspoon black pepper
1 garlic clove, pressed
1 cup uncooked couscous

per serving:

Calories: 231
Fat: 10.2g
Protein: 5.5g
Carbohydrate: 30.1g
Cholesterol: 0mg
Sodium: 364 mg
Exchanges:
  2 Starch
  2 Fat

Place bell pepper on an aluminum foil-lined baking sheet.

Broil 5½ inches from heat (with electric oven door partially opened) about 5 minutes on each side or until pepper looks blistered.

Place pepper in a heavy-duty zip-top plastic bag; seal and let stand 10 minutes to loosen skin. Peel pepper; remove and discard seeds. Dice pepper and onion; peel, seed, and dice cucumber. Set vegetables aside.

Whisk oil and next 3 ingredients in a small bowl.

Cook mustard and cumin seeds in a small skillet over medium heat, stirring constantly, 5 minutes or until toasted; immediately stir into oil mixture. Add tomato and cilantro, stirring well.

Bring water and next 3 ingredients to a boil in a saucepan; stir in couscous. Remove from heat; cover and let stand 5 minutes or until liquid is absorbed. Transfer to a serving bowl; stir in diced vegetables. Drizzle with dressing; toss gently. Yield: 6 servings.

**Couscous Salad with
Dried Tomato Vinaigrette**

Wild Rice Salad

per serving:

Calories: 88
Fat: 2.3g
Protein: 2.7g
Carbohydrate: 15.1g
Cholesterol: 0mg
Sodium: 256mg
Exchanges:
  1 Starch
  ½ Fat

1 (6-ounce) package long-grain and wild rice mix
1 (11-ounce) can white corn, drained
¼ cup chopped fresh parsley
3 green onions, chopped
2 carrots, coarsely chopped
1 cucumber, seeded and chopped
¼ cup lemon juice

2 garlic cloves, minced
1 tablespoon olive oil
½ teaspoon dried dillweed
¼ teaspoon pepper
¼ teaspoon dry mustard
3 tablespoons dry-roasted sunflower kernels
Leaf lettuce

Prepare rice according to package directions, omitting fat. Combine rice mixture, corn, and next 4 ingredients; set aside.

Combine lemon juice and next 5 ingredients; pour over rice mixture, tossing gently. Cover and refrigerate 8 hours. Before serving, sprinkle with sunflower kernels. Serve on lettuce leaves. Yield: 14 servings.

Steak Salad with Peach Salsa

Flank steak, salad greens, and peach salsa make a surprisingly good combination. The secret is the sweet-hot play on flavors in the salsa.

per serving:

Calories: 271
Fat: 15.4g
Protein: 24.1g
Carbohydrate: 9.1g
Cholesterol: 57mg
Sodium: 88mg
Exchanges:
  2 Vegetables
  3 Medium-Fat Meat

1 (1-pound) flank steak
1 tablespoon dark sesame oil, divided
2 tablespoons minced fresh ginger

1 garlic clove, minced
4 cups mixed salad greens
1 tablespoon lime juice
Peach Salsa

Place steak between two sheets of heavy-duty plastic wrap, and flatten to ⅛-inch thickness, using a meat mallet or rolling pin; cut into ½-inch strips.

Combine 2 teaspoons oil, ginger, and garlic; stir in beef strips. Roll strips into pinwheels.

Heat a skillet over high heat; add steak pinwheels, and cook 1 minute on each side or until browned. Turn steak carefully to maintain pinwheel shape.

Toss salad greens with remaining 1 teaspoon oil and lime juice; serve immediately with steak pinwheels and Peach Salsa. Yield: 4 servings.

Steak Salad with Peach Salsa

Peach Salsa

2 peaches
½ red bell pepper
1 jalapeño pepper
2 tablespoons chopped fresh basil

1 tablespoon minced fresh
   ginger
1 tablespoon lime juice
1 teaspoon dark sesame oil

Peel and dice peaches; mince bell pepper. Seed and mince jalapeño pepper.

Toss together peach, minced peppers, basil, and remaining ingredients. Cover and chill mixture at least 1 hour. Yield: 2½ cups.

Blue Cheese Chicken Salad

A small dose of blue cheese delivers big taste in this flavorful chicken salad. It's pictured on page 156.

It's pictured on page 156.

per serving:

Calories: 252
Fat: 12.8g
Protein: 24.7g
Carbohydrate: 9.6g
Cholesterol: 59mg
Sodium: 525mg
Exchanges:
  2 Vegetable
  3 Medium-Fat Meat

4 (4-ounce) skinned and boned chicken breast halves
Vegetable cooking spray
2 teaspoons dried dillweed
¼ teaspoon salt
¼ teaspoon ground white pepper
6 cups romaine lettuce, torn
1 medium cucumber, thinly sliced
1 small green bell pepper, cut into thin rings
2 slices purple onion, separated into rings

2 tablespoons olive oil
1 tablespoon Dijon mustard
1 tablespoon balsamic vinegar
1 tablespoon grated onion
2 medium tomatoes, cut into eighths
2 tablespoons crumbled blue cheese
Garnish: carrot curls

Coat both sides of chicken with cooking spray; sprinkle evenly with dillweed, salt, and white pepper.

Place a seasoned cast-iron skillet over high heat until hot; add chicken, and brown on both sides. Place skillet in a 350° oven, and bake 10 minutes. Cut chicken into thin diagonal slices.

Combine lettuce and next 3 ingredients; set aside.

Combine olive oil and next 3 ingredients; pour over lettuce mixture, and toss. Divide onto plates. Arrange chicken and tomato wedges evenly on lettuce. Sprinkle evenly with blue cheese. Garnish, if desired. Yield: 4 servings.

Grilled Chicken Salad with Mango Chutney

per serving:

Calories: 211
Fat: 4.9g
Protein: 21.4g
Carbohydrate: 22.2g
Cholesterol: 48mg
Sodium: 125mg
Exchanges:
  3 Vegetable
  ½ Fruit
  2 Lean Meat

1 tablespoon olive oil
1 tablespoon reduced-sodium soy sauce
1 tablespoon balsamic vinegar
1 tablespoon rice wine vinegar
1 tablespoon dry sherry
1 tablespoon grated fresh ginger
1 teaspoon ground cinnamon

¼ teaspoon ground red pepper
4 (4-ounce) skinned and boned chicken breast halves
⅓ cup rice wine vinegar
2 tablespoons sugar
8 cups mixed salad greens
Mango Chutney

Combine first 8 ingredients in a shallow dish or heavy-duty zip-top plastic bag; add chicken. Cover or seal; chill 1 hour, turning chicken occasionally.

Remove chicken from marinade, discarding marinade.

Grill chicken, without grill lid, over medium-high heat (350° to 400°) 5 to 6 minutes on each side or until tender.

Combine ⅓ cup vinegar and sugar, stirring until sugar dissolves. Place greens on individual plates; drizzle with vinegar mixture. Place chicken over greens; top with ½ cup chutney. Yield: 4 servings.

Mango Chutney

1 large mango, peeled, seeded, and finely chopped
1 large cucumber, peeled, seeded, and finely chopped
1 large jalapeño pepper, seeded and minced
¼ cup chopped purple onion
1 teaspoon grated fresh ginger
1 tablespoon chopped fresh basil
1 tablespoon rice wine vinegar
1 tablespoon balsamic vinegar
1½ teaspoons olive oil

Combine all ingredients, stirring well. Yield: 3 cups.

Shrimp-and-Couscous Salad

4¼ cups water
1 lemon, sliced
1½ pounds unpeeled large fresh shrimp
½ cup couscous, uncooked
½ red bell pepper, chopped
1 (14-ounce) can artichoke hearts, drained and coarsely chopped
¼ cup reduced-fat mayonnaise
⅓ cup fresh lemon juice
3 tablespoons chopped fresh dill
¼ teaspoon salt
½ teaspoon pepper

per serving:
Calories: 234
Fat: 6.2g
Protein: 19.0g
Carbohydrate: 25.7g
Cholesterol: 113mg
Sodium: 367mg
Exchanges:
 1 Starch
 2 Vegetable
 2 Lean Meat

Combine water and lemon slices in a Dutch oven; bring to a boil. Add shrimp, and cook 3 to 5 minutes or until shrimp turn pink. Drain, discarding lemon; rinse shrimp with cold water. Peel shrimp, and devein, if desired. Cut shrimp in half lengthwise. Cover and chill.

Cook couscous according to package directions; place in a large bowl to cool. Stir with a fork; add shrimp, bell pepper, and artichoke hearts.

Combine mayonnaise and remaining 4 ingredients; stir well. Pour over shrimp mixture, tossing to coat. Cover and chill. Yield: 4 servings.

Creamy Blue Cheese Dressing

½ cup plain nonfat yogurt
½ cup reduced-fat mayonnaise
¼ cup plus 3 tablespoons fat-free
   milk
¼ cup crumbled blue cheese

2 tablespoons lemon juice
½ teaspoon minced fresh garlic
⅛ teaspoon freshly ground
   pepper
Dash of hot sauce

Combine all ingredients in a small bowl, stirring well. Cover and chill. Serve with salad greens. Yield: 1½ cups.

Papaya Seed Dressing

When preparing fresh papaya, don't throw away the seeds. Their peppery flavor adds mysterious pungency to this salad dressing.

1 tablespoon cornstarch
1 (8-ounce) bottle papaya nectar
½ cup sugar
½ teaspoon salt
½ teaspoon dry mustard

½ cup white wine vinegar
2 tablespoons chopped onion
3 tablespoons fresh papaya seeds
   (about 1 papaya)

Combine cornstarch and papaya nectar in a small saucepan, stirring well; cook over medium heat, stirring constantly, until mixture thickens and boils. Boil 1 minute, stirring constantly. Remove from heat; cool
Process sugar and remaining 5 ingredients in a blender until papaya seeds resemble coarsely ground pepper. Stir into nectar mixture; cover and chill at least 2 hours. Serve over mixed fruit. Yield: 2 cups.

Rosy Italian Dressing

½ cup nonfat buttermilk
⅓ cup reduced-fat mayonnaise
¼ cup no-salt-added tomato juice
1 tablespoon grated onion
¼ teaspoon dried whole oregano

¼ teaspoon dried whole basil
¼ teaspoon pepper
¼ teaspoon paprika
1 garlic clove, crushed

Combine all ingredients in a small bowl, stirring well with a wire whisk. Cover and chill. Serve with salad greens. Yield: 1 cup.

Raspberry Wine Vinegar

Use this flavored vinegar in the Marinated Black-Eyed Pea Salad
on page 160 or as a topping to your favorite greens.

3 cups fresh or frozen raspberries
2 (17-ounce) bottles white wine
  vinegar

1 cup sugar

Combine all ingredients in a large saucepan; bring to a boil. Cover, reduce heat and simmer 10 minutes. Pour through a wire-mesh strainer, discarding pulp. Pour into decorative jars or bottles, and cover. Store in refrigerator. Yield: 5 cups.

per tablespoon:

Calories: 13
Fat: 0.0g
Protein: 0.0g
Carbohydrate: 3.0g
Cholesterol: 0.0mg
Sodium: 1mg
Exchanges:
  Free (up to 3 tablespoons)

Shallot-Tarragon-Garlic Vinegar

1 cup fresh tarragon sprigs
10 garlic cloves, divided
4 shallots, divided
2 (17-ounce) bottles white wine
  vinegar

Additional fresh tarragon
  sprigs (optional)

Combine tarragon, 6 garlic cloves, 3 shallots, and vinegar in a large jar; cover securely. Let stand in bright light 1 to 2 weeks.
Pour into a large saucepan, and bring to a boil. Pour through a large wire-mesh strainer into a decorative jar or bottle, discarding solids.
Cut remaining shallot into 4 pieces; alternate pieces with remaining 4 garlic cloves on a wooden skewer. Place skewer in vinegar, and add additional tarragon sprigs, if desired. Cover and store in a cool, dark place. Yield: 3½ cups.

per tablespoon:

Calories: 2
Fat: 0.0g
Protein: 0.0g
Carbohydrate: 0.0g
Cholesterol: 0.0mg
Sodium: 2mg
Exchanges:
  Free (no limit)

Stewed Okra, Corn, and Tomatoes (page 180)

Side Dishes

Accentuate your entrée with any one of these family-pleasing side dishes. Pick from fruit sides, a variety of vegetables, or comforting grain dishes to top off your menu. You'll appreciate the preparation ease of these recipes, which yield outstanding flavor and texture and are loaded with nutrients. Take advantage of fruits and vegetables when they are in season to ensure the highest quality and flavor.

Parson's Curried Fruit

per serving:

Calories: 92
Fat: 0.2g
Protein: 0.7g
Carbohydrate: 22.9g
Cholesterol: 0mg
Sodium: 5mg
Exchanges:
  1½ Fruit

1 (16-ounce) can apricot halves in light syrup
1 (8-ounce) can pineapple chunks in juice
1 (16-ounce) can peach halves in juice, drained
1 (16-ounce) can pear halves in juice, drained
3 tablespoons brown sugar
2 teaspoons curry powder

Drain apricot halves and pineapple chunks, reserving 1 cup total liquid. Set liquid aside.

Combine drained apricots, pineapple, peaches, and pears in an 11- x 7-inch baking dish. Combine reserved liquid, brown sugar, and curry powder in a small bowl; stir well. Pour over fruit mixture. Bake, uncovered, at 350° for 25 minutes or until thoroughly heated and bubbly. Serve with a slotted spoon. Yield: 8 servings.

Pears Baked in Molasses-Port Sauce

Molasses and port wine enrich the taste of baked pears and impart a deep rich color.

per serving:

Calories: 259
Fat: 2.6g
Protein: 0.7g
Carbohydrate: 62.3g
Cholesterol: 5mg
Sodium: 42mg
Exchanges:
  2 Starch
  2 Fruit
  ½ Fat

1 cup molasses
1 cup port wine
1 tablespoon butter, melted
6 pears, peeled and sliced

Stir together first 3 ingredients.

Arrange pear slices in a 13- x 9-inch pan; pour molasses mixture over pear slices.

Bake at 350° for 35 to 40 minutes or until pear slices are tender, basting with molasses mixture every 10 minutes. Remove pear slices from pan, reserving liquid; set aside.

Bring reserved liquid to a boil in a saucepan. Reduce heat; simmer, stirring occasionally, 30 minutes or until of syrup consistency. Drizzle over pear slices. Yield: 4 servings.

Sautéed Pineapple

2 (20-ounce) cans pineapple
   chunks in juice
1 tablespoon reduced-calorie
   margarine
2 tablespoons brown sugar
1 tablespoon rum or ½ teaspoon
   rum extract
½ teaspoon ground cinnamon

per serving:
Calories: 103
Fat: 1.2g
Protein: 0.0g
Carbohydrate: 23.1g
Cholesterol: 0mg
Sodium: 21mg
Exchanges:
   1½ Fruit

Drain pineapple chunks, reserving ¼ cup juice. Set pineapple and juice aside.
Melt margarine in a large nonstick skillet over medium heat; add pineapple chunks, reserved juice, brown sugar, rum, and cinnamon. Bring to a boil; reduce heat, and simmer 5 minutes, stirring frequently. Serve warm. Yield: 6 servings.

Asparagus Strudel

1 pound fresh asparagus spears
Butter-flavored vegetable cooking
   spray
2 tablespoons minced shallot
3 tablespoons all-purpose flour
1 cup fat-free evaporated milk
1 teaspoon lemon juice
½ teaspoon dried whole dillweed
¼ teaspoon salt
¼ teaspoon ground white pepper
¼ teaspoon ground nutmeg
⅛ teaspoon hot sauce
8 sheets commercial frozen phyllo
   pastry, thawed

per serving:
Calories: 105
Fat: 1.8g
Protein: 4.9g
Carbohydrate: 17.4g
Cholesterol: 1mg
Sodium: 206mg
Exchanges:
   1 Starch
   1 Vegetable

Snap off tough ends of asparagus. Remove scales from stalks with a vegetable peeler, if desired. Cut stalks in half; arrange in a steamer over boiling water. Cover and steam 5 minutes. Place asparagus in ice water; set aside.
Coat a small nonstick skillet with cooking spray; place over medium-high heat until hot. Add shallot; sauté until tender. Set aside.
Combine flour and milk in a saucepan; stir until smooth. Cook over medium heat, stirring constantly, until mixture is thickened. Remove from heat; stir in shallot, lemon juice, and next 5 ingredients.
Place 1 sheet of phyllo on a damp towel (keep remaining phyllo covered). Coat with cooking spray. Layer second sheet of phyllo on first sheet; coat with cooking spray. Cut stack in half lengthwise, making 2 rectangles. Drain asparagus. Place one-eighth of asparagus at short end of each rectangle; spoon one-eighth of sauce mixture over asparagus on each rectangle. Fold ends of rectangles over asparagus; roll up, jellyroll fashion. Repeat with remaining phyllo, asparagus, and sauce mixture. Coat phyllo packets with cooking spray; place on a baking sheet coated with cooking spray. Bake at 350° for 30 minutes. Yield: 8 servings.

Garlic Broccoli

per serving:

Calories: 88
Fat: 2.7g
Protein: 4.4g
Carbohydrate: 14.5g
Cholesterol: 0mg
Sodium: 357mg
Exchanges:
  3 Vegetable
  ½ Fat

1½ pounds fresh broccoli
1½ teaspoons dark sesame oil
1½ teaspoons vegetable oil
½ teaspoon dried crushed red pepper

2 garlic cloves, minced
¼ cup reduced-sodium soy sauce
1 tablespoon sugar
1 tablespoon lemon juice
1 tablespoon water

Remove and discard broccoli leaves and tough ends of stalks; cut broccoli into spears.

Arrange broccoli in a steamer basket over boiling water. Cover and steam 5 minutes or until crisp-tender. Remove from heat; keep warm.

Heat sesame and vegetable oils in a small saucepan until hot but not smoking; remove from heat.

Add crushed red pepper, and let stand 10 minutes.

Add garlic and remaining 4 ingredients, stirring to dissolve sugar.

Toss broccoli spears gently with oil mixture just before serving. Serve hot or cold. Yield: 6 servings.

Broccoli and Walnut Sauté

per serving:

Calories: 94
Fat: 5.1g
Protein: 4.6g
Carbohydrate: 10.5g
Cholesterol: 0mg
Sodium: 33mg
Exchanges:
  2 Vegetable
  1 Fat

1½ pounds fresh broccoli
½ cup water
2 tablespoons balsamic vinegar
2 teaspoons cornstarch
1 teaspoon chicken bouillon granules

1 garlic clove, minced
1 cup thin onion strips (cut vertically)
½ cup thin strips red bell pepper
2 teaspoons vegetable oil
¼ cup chopped walnuts, toasted

Remove and discard broccoli leaves and tough ends of stalks; cut broccoli into flowerets. Peel broccoli stems, and thinly slice. Set broccoli aside.

Combine water and next 3 ingredients; set cornstarch mixture aside.

Cook garlic, onion, red pepper, and broccoli in oil in a large skillet over medium heat, stirring constantly, 3 minutes or until broccoli is crisp-tender.

Add cornstarch mixture to vegetable mixture, and bring to a boil, stirring constantly. Cook 1 minute, stirring constantly.

Spoon into a serving dish; sprinkle with walnuts. Yield: 6 servings.

Cabbage with Caraway

1 teaspoon reduced-calorie
    margarine
Vegetable cooking spray
8 cups coarsely shredded cabbage
    (1½ pounds)
1 tablespoon chopped fresh
    parsley

1 teaspoon sugar
1 teaspoon chicken-flavored
    bouillon granules
½ teaspoon freshly ground pepper
1 teaspoon caraway seeds

per serving:
Calories: 39
Fat: 1.0g
Protein: 1.6g
Carbohydrate: 7.3g
Cholesterol: 0mg
Sodium: 194mg
Exchanges:
  1½ Vegetable

Melt margarine in a large nonstick skillet coated with cooking spray. Add cabbage and next 4 ingredients; cover and cook over medium heat 5 minutes. Sprinkle with caraway seeds; cover and cook 1 minute. Yield: 5 servings.

Orange Glazed Carrots

Ground ginger and a smidgen of sugar accentuate the natural sweetness of carrots in this quick and easy side dish.

1 pound carrots, scraped and cut
    into ¼-inch-thick slices
¾ cup canned no-salt-added
    chicken broth, undiluted

2 tablespoons frozen orange juice
    concentrate, undiluted
2 teaspoons sugar
¼ teaspoon ground ginger

per serving:
Calories: 69
Fat: 0.2g
Protein: 1.3g
Carbohydrate: 16.0g
Cholesterol: 0mg
Sodium: 36mg
Exchanges:
  ½ Starch
  2 Vegetable

Combine carrot and chicken broth in a medium saucepan; bring to a boil. Cover, reduce heat, and simmer 10 minutes. Uncover and cook over high heat 5 minutes.

Add orange juice concentrate and remaining 2 ingredients to carrot mixture, stirring well. Cook over medium heat an additional 2 to 3 minutes or until carrot is tender. Yield: 4 servings

Cauliflower Sauté

per serving:

Calories: 69
Fat: 3.7g
Protein: 2.3g
Carbohydrate: 7.8g
Cholesterol: 0mg
Sodium: 157mg
Exchanges:
  2 Vegetable
  ½ Fat

2 cups fresh cauliflower flowerets
½ cup sliced onion
1 garlic clove, minced
1 tablespoon olive oil
1 cup fresh or frozen snow pea pods
1 red bell pepper, cut into strips
½ cup sliced fresh mushrooms
1 teaspoon dried oregano
¼ teaspoon salt

Arrange cauliflower in a steamer basket; place over boiling water. Cover and steam 8 minutes; drain and set aside.

Cook onion and garlic in olive oil in a large nonstick skillet over medium heat, stirring constantly, until tender. Add cauliflower, snow peas, and remaining ingredients; cook, stirring constantly, until heated. Yield: 4 servings.

Fresh Corn Pudding

Enjoy summer's bounty with this old family favorite that incorporates fresh corn and bell pepper.

per serving:

Calories: 102
Fat: 0.8g
Protein: 7.1g
Carbohydrate: 18.0g
Cholesterol: 2mg
Sodium: 185mg
Exchanges:
  1 Starch

2 cups corn cut from cob (about 4 medium ears)
1 tablespoon minced green bell pepper
1½ tablespoons all-purpose flour
2 teaspoons sugar
¼ teaspoon salt
¼ teaspoon mace
Dash of ground red pepper
½ cup egg substitute
1 cup fat-free evaporated milk
Vegetable cooking spray

Combine first 7 ingredients, stirring well. Combine egg substitute and evaporated milk; add to corn mixture.

Spoon mixture into a 1-quart baking dish coated with cooking spray. Place dish in a large shallow pan; add water to pan to a depth of 1 inch.

Bake at 350° for 1 hour or until a knife inserted in center comes out clean. Yield: 6 servings.

Microwave Ratatouille

Pair this colorful side dish with any of the grilled fish recipes beginning on page 66, and make quick work of dinner.

3 cups chopped unpeeled eggplant
2 cups chopped yellow squash
2 cups chopped zucchini
1 red bell pepper, seeded and chopped
1 yellow bell pepper, seeded and chopped
Vegetable cooking spray

1 medium onion, chopped
4 garlic cloves, minced
1½ cups spaghetti sauce
¼ cup coarsely chopped fresh Italian parsley
1 teaspoon dried oregano
1 teaspoon dried thyme
1 tablespoon finely chopped fresh basil

per serving:
Calories: 97
Fat: 3.9g
Protein: 2.9g
Carbohydrate: 15.4g
Cholesterol: 0mg
Sodium: 272mg
Exchanges:
  3 Vegetable
  ½ Fat

Place eggplant in a 9-inch pieplate; cover with a paper towel, and microwave at HIGH 4 minutes. Transfer to a large bowl. Repeat procedure with squash, zucchini, and peppers. Set vegetable mixture aside.

Coat a very large skillet or Dutch oven with cooking spray; place over medium heat until hot. Add onion and garlic; cook, stirring constantly, until tender.

Stir in vegetable mixture, spaghetti sauce, and next 3 ingredients. Cook 4 minutes, stirring occasionally. Stir in basil. Yield: 6 servings.

Fresh Corn Pudding

Green Bean Slaw

Fresh green beans replace cabbage in this twist on the familiar slaw. It pairs well with Oven-Fried Catfish on page 64.

per serving:

Calories: 49
Fat: 0.2g
Protein: 3.7g
Carbohydrate: 9.1g
Cholesterol: 3mg
Sodium: 241mg
Exchanges:
  2 Vegetable

½ pound fresh green beans
¼ small onion, cut into thin strips
    (about ¼ cup)
½ cup thin red bell pepper strips
1 medium cucumber, peeled,
    seeded, and cut into thin
    strips
2½ tablespoons tarragon or other
    herb vinegar
2 tablespoons fat-free cream
    cheese
1 tablespoon fat-free milk
1 teaspoon sugar
¼ teaspoon salt
¼ teaspoon pepper

Wash beans; remove ends. Cook in boiling water 8 minutes or until crisp-tender; drain. Plunge into ice water to stop the cooking process; drain.
Combine beans, onion, red pepper, and cucumber; toss gently, and set aside.
Combine vinegar and remaining 5 ingredients, stirring until smooth. Pour dressing over bean mixture; toss gently. Cover and chill thoroughly before serving. Yield: 4 servings.

Stewed Okra, Corn, and Tomatoes

This nostalgic Southern side dish is ready to serve in 15 minutes. It's pictured on page 172.

per serving:

Calories: 88
Fat: 0.8g
Protein: 4.7g
Carbohydrate: 17.7g
Cholesterol: 4mg
Sodium: 238mg
Exchanges:
  ½ Starch
  2 Vegetable

1½ cups frozen sliced okra
1 cup frozen whole kernel corn
¼ cup chopped reduced-fat,
    low-salt cooked ham
1 teaspoon dried basil basil
¼ teaspoon salt
¼ teaspoon pepper
1 (14½-ounce) can no-salt-added
    stewed tomatoes, undrained
Vegetable cooking spray

Combine first 7 ingredients in a large saucepan coated with cooking spray.
Bring to a boil; cover, reduce heat, and simmer 15 minutes, stirring occasionally. Yield: 4 servings.

Mexican Black-Eyes

Mexican Black-Eyes

1 (10-ounce) package frozen
   black-eyed peas, thawed
Olive oil-flavored vegetable
   cooking spray
½ cup chopped onion
½ cup chopped green onions
½ cup chopped green bell pepper
1 teaspoon minced garlic
1 cup cooked long-grain rice
   (cooked without salt or fat)
1 (14½-ounce) can no-salt-added
   stewed tomatoes, undrained
   and chopped

1 (4.5-ounce) can chopped green
   chiles, undrained
2 teaspoons low-sodium
   Worcestershire sauce
¼ teaspoon pepper
¼ teaspoon dried whole oregano
¼ teaspoon dried whole thyme
⅛ teaspoon salt
⅛ teaspoon hot sauce
2 tablespoons chopped fresh
   parsley
No-oil baked tortilla chips
   (optional)

per serving:
Calories: 83
Fat: 0.3g
Protein: 3.7g
Carbohydrate: 16.9g
Cholesterol: 0mg
Sodium: 56mg
Exchanges:
  1 Starch

Cook black-eyed peas according to package directions, omitting salt and fat. Drain and set aside.

Coat a large nonstick skillet with cooking spray; place over medium-high heat until hot. Add chopped onion, green onions, bell pepper, and garlic; sauté until tender. Add peas, rice, and next 8 ingredients to onion mixture; stir well. Spoon mixture into a 1½-quart casserole coated with cooking spray. Bake, uncovered, at 350° for 30 minutes. Sprinkle with parsley. To serve, spoon mixture into individual serving dishes. If desired, place tortilla chips around edge of each dish, and sprinkle with crushed chips. Yield: 10 servings.

Potatoes au Gratin

3½ cups peeled, finely chopped
  potato
½ cup low-fat cottage cheese
½ cup nonfat buttermilk
1 tablespoon chopped fresh or
  frozen chives
2 teaspoons cornstarch

½ teaspoon salt
⅛ teaspoon pepper
Vegetable cooking spray
¼ cup (1 ounce) shredded part-
  skim mozzarella cheese
⅛ teaspoon paprika

Cook potato in boiling water to cover 8 minutes or until tender (do not overcook). Drain and set aside.

Process cottage cheese and buttermilk in a blender or food processor until smooth. Transfer to a large bowl; stir in potato, chives, and next 3 ingredients. Spoon into a 1-quart casserole coated with cooking spray. Bake at 350° for 20 minutes; sprinkle with cheese and paprika, and bake an additional 5 minutes. Yield: 6 servings.

Roasted Garlic Mashed Potatoes

Yes, this recipe calls for four heads of garlic! Garlic mellows
and takes on a sweet buttery flavor as it bakes, giving
these potatoes extra flair.

4 heads garlic
1 tablespoon olive oil
4 pounds baking potatoes, peeled
  and cut into 1-inch pieces
3 tablespoons reduced-calorie
  margarine

1 cup fat-free milk
1 teaspoon salt
½ teaspoon pepper

Place garlic on a square of aluminum foil; drizzle with oil, and wrap in foil.

Bake at 425° for 30 minutes; set aside.

Cook potato in boiling water to cover 15 to 20 minutes or until tender; drain. Transfer to a large mixing bowl of a heavy-duty electric mixer. Add margarine and remaining 3 ingredients; beat at medium speed 2 minutes or until fluffy.

Cut off ends of garlic; squeeze pulp from cloves. Stir into potato mixture. Yield: 11 servings.

Potato Wedges

4 (5-ounce) baking potatoes
1 tablespoon water
1 teaspoon paprika
½ teaspoon garlic powder
1½ teaspoons vegetable oil

½ teaspoon browning-and-
  seasoning sauce
1 teaspoon dried parsley flakes
¼ teaspoon salt

per serving:
Calories: 123
Fat: 1.9g
Protein: 3.3g
Carbohydrate: 24.2g
Cholesterol: 0mg
Sodium: 157mg
Exchanges:
  1½ Starch

Cut each potato into 8 wedges.
Combine water and next 4 ingredients in an 8-inch square baking dish. Add potato wedges, tossing to coat. Cover with wax paper. Microwave at HIGH 8 minutes or until tender, stirring gently after 4 minutes. Sprinkle with parsley flakes and salt. Yield: 4 servings.

Orange-Sweet Potato Soufflé

A soufflé has a brief moment of glory, so serve this spiced delicacy directly from the oven.

2 cups peeled, cubed sweet
  potato
¾ cup fat-free evaporated milk
½ cup egg substitute, thawed
¼ cup firmly packed brown sugar
1 tablespoon frozen orange juice
  concentrate, thawed and
  undiluted

1 tablespoon Triple Sec or other
  orange-flavored liqueur
  (optional)
½ teaspoon ground cinnamon
½ teaspoon ground allspice
¼ teaspoon salt
¼ teaspoon ground nutmeg
3 egg whites

per serving:
Calories: 132
Fat: 0.3g
Protein: 6.9g
Carbohydrate: 25.8g
Cholesterol: 1mg
Sodium: 200mg
Exchanges:
  2 Starch

Cook sweet potato in boiling water to cover 15 minutes or until tender; drain. Transfer sweet potato to a large bowl. Beat at medium speed with an electric mixer until smooth. Add milk and next 8 ingredients; beat at low speed until blended.
Beat egg whites at high speed with an electric mixer until stiff peaks form. Fold one-third of beaten egg whites into sweet potato mixture; fold in remaining egg whites. Spoon mixture into an ungreased 2-quart soufflé dish. Bake, uncovered, at 325° for 55 minutes or until golden. Serve immediately. Yield: 6 servings.

Fruited Acorn Squash

Fruited Acorn Squash

Acorn squash delivers a rustic presentation—as well as homespun taste—to your fall table.

2 medium acorn squash (about
   2 pounds)
Vegetable cooking spray
¾ cup canned crushed pineapple
   in juice, drained

¾ cup chopped orange
3 tablespoons brown sugar
½ teaspoon ground cinnamon
Garnishes: orange rind curls,
   cinnamon sticks

per serving:
Calories: 167
Fat: 0.4g
Protein: 2.4g
Carbohydrate: 43.1g
Cholesterol: 0mg
Sodium: 10mg
Exchanges:
  1 Starch
  2 Fruit

Cut each squash in half crosswise; remove and discard seeds. Place squash halves, cut side down, in a 15- x 10-inch jellyroll pan lightly coated with cooking spray. Bake, uncovered, at 350° for 35 minutes.

Combine pineapple, orange, and brown sugar; spoon evenly into squash halves. Sprinkle with cinnamon. Bake, uncovered, 10 more minutes or until mixture is thoroughly heated. Garnish, if desired. Yield: 4 servings.

Summer Squash Bake

2 pounds yellow squash, cut into
   ¼-inch-thick slices
½ cup chopped onion
½ cup shredded carrot
½ cup (2 ounces) shredded
   reduced-fat Cheddar cheese
½ cup egg substitute with cheese,
   thawed
1 (4-ounce) jar diced pimiento,
   drained
1 teaspoon low-sodium
   Worcestershire sauce

¼ teaspoon salt
¼ teaspoon pepper
Vegetable cooking spray
3 tablespoons fine, dry
   breadcrumbs (commercial)
1 tablespoon chopped fresh
   parsley
2 teaspoons chopped fresh
   oregano
¼ teaspoon paprika

per serving:
Calories: 62
Fat: 2.1g
Protein: 4.6g
Carbohydrate: 7.1g
Cholesterol: 4mg
Sodium: 164mg
Exchanges:
  2 Vegetable
  ½ Fat

Place squash, onion, and carrot in a steamer basket over boiling water; cover and steam 12 to 15 minutes or until vegetables are tender. Combine steamed vegetables, cheese, and next 5 ingredients in a medium bowl; stir well. Spoon mixture into a shallow 2-quart casserole coated with cooking spray.

Combine breadcrumbs and remaining 3 ingredients in a small bowl; stir well. Sprinkle over squash mixture. Bake, uncovered, at 350° for 25 to 30 minutes or until thoroughly heated. Yield: 10 servings.

Grilled Tomatoes with Basil Vinaigrette

These tomatoes are a zesty accompaniment to grilled fish or chicken, or make a colorful addition to a veggie plate.

per serving:

Calories: 91
Fat: 7.3g
Protein: 1.7g
Carbohydrate: 6.8g
Cholesterol: 0mg
Sodium: 129mg
Exchanges:
  1 Vegetable
  1½ Fat

3 yellow tomatoes
3 red tomatoes
3 tablespoons olive oil, divided
¼ teaspoon salt
¼ teaspoon freshly ground pepper

2 tablespoons white balsamic vinegar
2 tablespoons chopped fresh basil
Garnish: fresh basil sprigs

Cut tomatoes in half; thread onto skewers, alternating colors. Brush with 1 tablespoon oil; sprinkle with salt and pepper.

Grill, covered with grill lid, over medium heat (300° to 350°) 10 minutes, turning skewers often.

Combine remaining 2 tablespoons oil, vinegar, and chopped basil; drizzle over kabobs. Garnish, if desired. Yield: 6 servings.

Steamed Garden Vegetables

Fill your plate with fresh summer abundance from the garden. Pair this dish with Polenta with Black Bean Salsa on page 92.

per serving:

Calories: 74
Fat: 1.0g
Protein: 4.1g
Carbohydrate: 14.7g
Cholesterol: 0mg
Sodium: 119mg
Exchanges:
  3 Vegetable

½ pound carrots with tops, trimmed
½ pound broccoli flowerets
¼ pound zucchini, sliced
¼ pound yellow squash, sliced
¼ pound fresh mushrooms
1 medium-size red bell pepper, cut into strips

1 medium-size green bell pepper, cut into strips
1 medium-size yellow bell pepper, cut into strips
1 teaspoon dried salad seasoning
Garnishes: lemon slices, fresh sage sprigs, parsley sprigs

Arrange carrots in a steamer basket, and place over boiling water. Cover and steam 8 minutes or until crisp-tender; remove and keep warm. Arrange broccoli and next 6 ingredients in steamer basket over boiling water. Cover and steam 6 minutes or until crisp-tender.

Arrange vegetables evenly on dinner plates; sprinkle evenly with salad seasoning. Garnish, if desired. Yield: 4 servings.

Grilled Tomatoes with
Basil Vinaigrette

Couscous with Mixed Fruit

1 cup reduced-sodium, fat-free
   chicken broth
½ cup unsweetened apple juice
½ cup chopped dried fruit mix

½ cup peeled and chopped
   cooking apple
¼ teaspoon salt
1 cup couscous, uncooked

Combine first 4 ingredients in a large nonaluminum saucepan; let stand
15 minutes.

Add salt, and bring mixture to a boil over medium heat. Stir in couscous;
cover and remove from heat. Let stand 5 to 7 minutes or until liquid is
absorbed. Fluff mixture with a fork. Yield: 4 servings.

per serving:
Calories: 288
Fat: 0.0g
Protein: 6.5g
Carbohydrate: 64.4g
Cholesterol: 0mg
Sodium: 162mg
Exchanges:
  2 Starch
  2 Fruit

Garlic-and-Herb Cheese Grits

Serve this 10-minute side dish with grilled
or broiled beef or chicken.

per ¾-cup:

Calories: 161
Fat: 4.1g
Protein: 5.1g
Carbohydrate: 23.7g
Cholesterol: 12mg
Sodium: 112mg
Exchanges:
  1½ Starch
  1 Fat

4 cups reduced-sodium, fat-free
     chicken broth
1 cup quick-cooking grits
¼ teaspoon freshly ground
     pepper

1 (5-ounce) package light garlic-
     and-herb soft, spreadable
     cheese

Bring chicken broth to a boil in a medium saucepan over high heat; gradually stir in grits. Cook, stirring constantly, 5 to 7 minutes or until thickened.
Remove from heat; stir in pepper and cheese. Serve immediately. Yield:
5 cups.

Parslied Rice Casserole

per serving:

Calories: 130
Fat: 1.8g
Protein: 8.5g
Carbohydrate: 19.3g
Cholesterol: 6mg
Sodium: 213mg
Exchanges:
  1 Starch
  1 Very Lean Meat

1 (8-ounce) carton plain nonfat
     yogurt
1 tablespoon all-purpose flour
1½ cups 1% low-fat cottage
     cheese
1 egg white
½ teaspoon hot sauce
⅛ teaspoon salt
⅛ teaspoon pepper
4 cups cooked long-grain rice
     (cooked without salt or fat)

¾ cup (3 ounces) reduced-fat
     Cheddar cheese
½ cup chopped green onions
¼ cup minced fresh parsley,
     divided
1 tablespoon chopped fresh
     cilantro
Vegetable cooking spray

Combine yogurt and flour in a large bowl; stir until smooth. Add cottage
cheese and next 4 ingredients, stirring well. Stir in rice, Cheddar cheese,
green onions, 3 tablespoons parsley, and cilantro.
Spoon mixture into a 2-quart baking dish coated with cooking spray. Bake,
uncovered, at 350° for 30 minutes or until thoroughly heated. Sprinkle
with remaining 1 tablespoon parsley. Yield: 12 servings.

Pecan Wild Rice

2 cups canned no-salt-added
   chicken broth, undiluted
1 cup chopped onion
½ cup wild rice, uncooked
½ cup brown rice, uncooked
3 tablespoons chopped pecans,
   toasted

1 teaspoon pepper
1 tablespoon minced fresh basil or
   1 teaspoon dried basil
¼ teaspoon salt

per serving:
Calories: 152
Fat: 3.8g
Protein: 4.5g
Carbohydrate: 25.3g
Cholesterol: 0mg
Sodium: 145mg
Exchanges:
 2 Starch
 1 Fat

Combine first 4 ingredients in a medium saucepan; bring to a boil. Cover, reduce heat, and simmer 30 minutes. Stir in toasted pecans and remaining ingredients. Cover and simmer an additional 15 minutes or until rice is tender and liquid is absorbed. Yield: 6 servings.

Vegetable Risotto

¾ cup frozen English peas
¾ cup chopped carrot
3 cups canned no-salt-added
   chicken broth, undiluted and
   divided
½ cup dry white wine
⅓ cup finely chopped onion
⅓ cup chopped green onions

1 cup Arborio rice, uncooked
3 tablespoons freshly grated
   Romano cheese
1 (2-ounce) jar diced pimiento,
   drained
2 tablespoons chopped fresh
   parsley

per serving:
Calories: 130
Fat: 1.0g
Protein: 3.7g
Carbohydrate: 25.1g
Cholesterol: 3mg
Sodium: 56mg
Exchanges:
 1½ Starch

Arrange peas and carrot in a steamer basket over boiling water. Cover and steam 8 minutes or until vegetables are tender. Set aside.

Combine 2½ cups broth and wine in a medium saucepan; place over medium heat. Bring to a simmer; cover, reduce heat, and maintain a very low simmer.

Place remaining ½ cup broth in a medium saucepan; bring to a boil over medium-high heat. Add chopped onion and green onions; cook 4 minutes or until tender. Stir in rice. Add ½ cup simmering broth mixture to rice mixture; stir constantly until most of the liquid is absorbed. Continue adding broth mixture, ½ cup at a time, stirring each time until liquid is absorbed (the entire process should take about 30 minutes). Stir in peas, carrot, cheese, pimiento, and parsley; serve immediately. Yield: 8 servings.

Potato-Corn Chowder (page 195) and
Smoked Turkey-Roasted Pepper
Sandwich (page 204)

Soups,
Sandwiches &
Sauces

Heartwarming and satisfying, soup is comfort food at its best. In the next few pages, you'll discover savory soups and stews that are chock-full of fruit, vegetables, and meat. Serve these soups as a main dish or pair them with one of many hearty sandwiches included in this chapter. We guarantee you'll find a winning combination. And check out our sauces that range from marinades to salsas to yummy dessert toppings.

Tropical Gazpacho

Top each bowl of gazpacho with a small scoop of fruit-flavored sorbet for extra refreshment.

2 papayas, peeled, seeded, and chopped
2 mangoes, peeled, seeded, and chopped
2 kiwifruits, peeled and chopped
2 teaspoons grated lime rind

3 tablespoons lime juice
¼ to ½ teaspoon ground cardamom
1 teaspoon vanilla extract
3 (8-ounce) cans papaya nectar
Garnish: carambola slices

Combine all ingredients except carambola slices in a large bowl; cover mixture, and chill. Garnish, if desired. Yield: 5 cups.

Apple Butternut Soup

Vegetable cooking spray
1 tablespoon reduced-calorie margarine
1 cup chopped onion
1 garlic clove, minced
1 tablespoon all-purpose flour
1 (10½-ounce) can low-sodium chicken broth
3 cups peeled, seeded, and cubed butternut squash

1⅓ cups peeled, cored, and coarsely chopped cooking apple
¼ teaspoon dried whole thyme
⅛ teaspoon salt
½ cup low-fat milk
Garnishes: toasted squash seeds, fresh thyme sprigs, nonfat sour cream

Coat a Dutch oven with cooking spray; add margarine. Place over medium heat until margarine melts. Add onion and garlic; sauté 5 minutes or until tender. Add flour, stirring until smooth. Stir in chicken broth and next 4 ingredients; bring to a boil. Cover, reduce heat, and simmer 45 minutes or until squash is tender. Let cool.

Process squash mixture in a food processor 1 minute or until smooth, stopping once to scrape down sides.

Return mixture to pan; add milk. Cook over medium heat until thoroughly heated, stirring occasionally. Ladle soup into individual bowls. Garnish, if desired. Yield: 4 cups.

Tropical Gazpacho

French Onion Soup

per 1 cup:

Calories: 219
Fat: 5.3g
Protein: 9.4g
Carbohydrate: 33.5g
Cholesterol: 28mg
Sodium: 798mg
Exchanges:
 2 Starch
 1 Vegetable
 1 Fat

2 tablespoons butter
Vegetable cooking spray
6 large onions, thinly sliced
   (3 pounds)
2 (10½-ounce) cans beef
   consommé, undiluted
1 (13¾-ounce) can no-salt-added,
   fat-free beef-flavored broth

1⅓ cups water
¼ cup dry white wine
¼ teaspoon freshly ground pepper
7 (1-inch-thick) slices French
   bread
¼ cup grated Parmesan cheese

Melt butter in a Dutch oven coated with cooking spray. Add onion, and cook over medium heat, 5 minutes, stirring often. Add 1 can of beef consommé; cook over low heat 30 minutes. Gradually add remaining beef consommé and next 4 ingredients; bring to a boil, reduce heat, and simmer 10 minutes.

Place bread slices on a baking sheet; sprinkle with Parmesan cheese. Broil 6 inches from heat (with electric oven door partially opened) until cheese is golden brown. Ladle soup into serving bowls, and top each with a toasted bread slice. Yield: 7 cups.

Roasted Red Pepper Soup

per 1 cup:

Calories: 97
Fat: 2.4g
Protein: 3.7g
Carbohydrate: 13.4g
Cholesterol: 11mg
Sodium: 289mg
Exchanges:
 1 Starch
 ½ Fat

4 red bell peppers
1 large onion, chopped
2 garlic cloves, minced
2 (16-ounce) cans reduced-sodium
   chicken broth, divided
¾ cup dry sherry
2 tablespoons all-purpose flour
1 tablespoon butter-flavored
   granules

1 (16-ounce) can whole tomatoes,
   drained
1 cup fat-free milk
1 (8-ounce) carton light sour
   cream
2 tablespoons lemon juice
½ teaspoon salt
½ teaspoon pepper

Place peppers on an aluminum foil-lined baking sheet.
Broil peppers 5½ inches from heat (with electric oven door partially opened) about 5 minutes on each side or until blistered.
Place peppers in a large heavy-duty zip-top plastic bag; seal and let stand 10 minutes to loosen skins. Peel peppers; remove and discard seeds.
Combine onion, garlic, and ¼ cup broth in a saucepan; cook, stirring constantly, until tender. Stir in sherry; simmer 15 minutes, stirring occasionally.

Whisk in flour and butter granules; stir in remaining broth and tomatoes. Simmer 15 minutes, stirring occasionally. Stir in peppers and milk, and cook 2 minutes, stirring constantly.

Process soup in batches in a blender until smooth, stopping once to scrape down sides. Stir in sour cream and remaining ingredients. Return to saucepan, and cook over low heat just until thoroughly heated. (Do not boil.) Yield: 8 cups.

Potato-Corn Chowder

For a satisfying supper, serve this easy chowder
with Smoked Turkey-Roasted Pepper Sandwiches (page 204).
This winning pair is pictured on page 190.

¾ cup chopped green pepper
⅓ cup chopped onion
Vegetable cooking spray
2¾ cups fat-free chicken broth
1½ cups finely chopped potato
1 teaspoon salt

¼ teaspoon pepper
¼ cup cornstarch
2¼ cups fat-free milk
2¼ cups frozen whole kernel corn
1 (2-ounce) jar chopped pimiento, undrained

per 1½ cups:
Calories: 230
Fat: 0.7g
Protein: 9.5g
Carbohydrate: 47.9g
Cholesterol: 3mg
Sodium: 380mg
Exchanges:
  3 Starch

Cook green pepper and onion in a saucepan coated with cooking spray over medium heat, stirring constantly, 5 minutes or until tender. Stir in broth, potato, salt, and pepper.

Bring to a boil; reduce heat, and simmer 5 to 7 minutes or until potato is tender.

Combine cornstarch and milk, stirring until smooth. Gradually add to potato mixture, stirring constantly. Stir in corn and chopped pimiento.

Bring to a boil over medium heat, stirring constantly; cook, stirring constantly, 1 minute or until thickened. Serve immediately. Yield: 6 cups.

Black Bean Soup

per 1 ½ cups:

Calories: 422
Fat: 2.4g
Protein: 21.9g
Carbohydrate: 76.8g
Cholesterol: 0mg
Sodium: 520mg
Exchanges:
  5 Starch
  1 Lean Meat

1 pound dried black beans
4 hot peppers in vinegar, finely chopped
½ cup chopped onion
¼ teaspoon minced garlic
½ cup fresh lemon juice
3 (14¼-ounce) cans reduced-sodium fat-free chicken broth
1½ cups chopped onion
1 tablespoon minced garlic
Vegetable cooking spray
1 (10-ounce) can diced tomatoes and green chiles, undrained
½ teaspoon pepper
½ teaspoon hot sauce
⅔ cup cooked rice (cooked without salt or fat)

Sort and wash beans; place beans in a large Dutch oven. Cover with water to depth of 2 inches above beans; let soak overnight. Drain and set aside.

Combine hot peppers and next 3 ingredients; cover and chill.

Cook chicken broth and beans in Dutch oven over medium-high heat 2½ hours, adding hot water as needed to keep beans covered with liquid.

Cook 1½ cups onion and 1 tablespoon garlic in a skillet coated with cooking spray over medium-high heat, stirring constantly, until tender. Reduce heat, and add tomatoes, pepper, and hot sauce; cook 5 minutes.

Process tomato mixture and 2 cups beans in a food processor until blended; add to remaining beans.

Spoon 2 tablespoons rice into each individual bowl; ladle 1½ cups soup over rice. Top each serving evenly with hot pepper mixture. Yield: 7½ cups.

Firestarter Chili

per ⅔ cup:

Calories: 302
Fat: 9.5g
Protein: 39.0g
Carbohydrate: 13.0g
Cholesterol: 95mg
Sodium: 662mg
Exchanges:
  3 Vegetable
  4 Lean Meat

2 pounds top round steak, trimmed
Vegetable cooking spray
1 cup chopped onion
1 cup chopped green bell pepper
1 jalapeño pepper, seeded and chopped
2 garlic cloves, minced
1 (13¾-ounce) can fat-free, no-salt-added beef broth
1 (10-ounce) can tomatoes with green chiles
1 (8-ounce) can tomato sauce
¼ cup light beer
2 tablespoons chili powder
1 tablespoon ground cumin
1 tablespoon unsweetened cocoa
1 tablespoon creamy peanut butter
1 tablespoon reduced-sodium soy sauce
1 tablespoon hot sauce
1 teaspoon dried oregano
1 teaspoon reduced-sodium Worcestershire sauce
½ teaspoon Hungarian paprika
¼ teaspoon ground ginger
¼ teaspoon ground white pepper

Partially freeze steak; cut into ½-inch-thick cubes, and set aside.
Coat a Dutch oven with cooking spray; place over medium heat until hot. Add steak, onion, and next 3 ingredients; cook until meat browns, stirring often. Stir in beef broth and remaining ingredients; bring to a boil. Cover, reduce heat, and simmer 1½ hours, stirring occasionally. Yield: 4 cups.

Burgundy Beef Stew

Chunks of round steak team with tender potatoes, carrots, and onions to provide a substantial one-dish meal.

2 pounds top boneless round steak
½ teaspoon salt
½ teaspoon pepper
¼ teaspoon garlic powder
1 small onion, chopped
Vegetable cooking spray
1 (8-ounce) can sliced mushrooms, drained
3 cups water
1 bay leaf
1 tablespoon beef bouillon granules

1 teaspoon dried parsley flakes
½ cup dry red wine
2 cups cubed potato
3 carrots, scraped and cut into ½-inch pieces
4 small onions, halved (about ⅓ pound)
3 celery ribs, cut into 1-inch pieces
⅓ cup all-purpose flour
½ cup water

per 1 cup:
Calories: 222
Fat: 4.8g
Protein: 24.8g
Carbohydrate: 19.5g
Cholesterol: 59mg
Sodium: 442mg
Exchanges:
  1 Starch
  1 Vegetable
  3 Very Lean Meat

Trim fat from steak; cut into 1-inch cubes. Sprinkle with salt, pepper, and garlic powder.
Cook meat and chopped onion in a Dutch oven coated with cooking spray over medium-high heat, stirring often, until meat is browned. Add mushrooms; cook 3 to 4 minutes.
Add 3 cups water and next 4 ingredients. Cover, reduce heat, and simmer 1½ hours.
Stir in potato and next 3 ingredients. Return to a boil; cover, reduce heat, and simmer 30 to 40 minutes or until vegetables are tender. Discard bay leaf.
Combine flour and ½ cup water, stirring until smooth. Stir into hot mixture. Cook stirring often, 15 minutes or until thickened. Yield: 10 cups.

Chicken-and-Shrimp Gumbo

Chicken-and-Shrimp Gumbo

Packed with shrimp, chicken, and smoked turkey
sausage, this coastal classic bursts with rich flavor. Browned
flour thickens this gumbo instead of the traditional roux.

4 (6-ounce) bone-in chicken
    breast halves, skinned
2 quarts water
½ cup all-purpose flour
Vegetable cooking spray
1 tablespoon vegetable oil
2 cups chopped onion
1¾ cups chopped celery
1½ cups chopped green bell
    pepper
½ cup chopped green onions
4 garlic cloves, minced
1½ teaspoons dried whole thyme

1 teaspoon dried whole oregano
½ teaspoon pepper
3 bay leaves
1 (13¾-ounce) can no-salt-added
    chicken broth
1 (6-ounce) can no-salt-added
    tomato paste
½ pound smoked turkey sausage,
    sliced
1 pound unpeeled medium-size
    fresh shrimp
6 cups cooked long-grain rice
    (cooked without salt or fat)

per 1½ cups:
Calories: 289
Fat: 6.8g
Protein: 20.4g
Carbohydrate: 35.1g
Cholesterol: 84mg
Sodium: 228mg
Exchanges:
    2½ Starch
    2 Lean Meat

Combine chicken and water in a Dutch oven; bring to a boil. Reduce heat, and simmer 45 minutes. Cover and chill 8 hours. Remove chicken; skim and discard fat from broth, reserving broth. Bone and chop chicken.

Place flour in a 15- x 10-inch jellyroll pan. Bake at 350° for 1 hour or until very brown, stirring every 15 minutes. Set aside.

Coat a Dutch oven with cooking spray; add oil. Place over medium heat until hot. Add onion and next 4 ingredients; sauté until tender. Add thyme and next 3 ingredients. Add browned flour; stir until smooth. Add reserved broth, chicken, canned broth, tomato paste, and sausage. Bring to a boil; reduce heat, and simmer, uncovered, 1 hour. Peel shrimp, and devein, if desired; add to broth mixture. Cover and simmer 10 minutes or until shrimp turn pink. Discard bay leaves. Serve over rice. Yield: 18 servings.

Maryland Crab Chowder

per 1 1/2 cups:

Calories: 295
Fat: 3.5g
Protein: 20.3g
Carbohydrate: 47.1g
Cholesterol: 59mg
Sodium: 647mg
Exchanges:
  2 Starch
  3 Vegetable
  1 Lean Meat

1 onion, chopped
4 garlic cloves, minced
2 celery ribs, chopped
2 carrots, diced
1 tablespoon olive oil
1 cup water
1 cup dry white wine

1 (8-ounce) bottle clam juice
5 new potatoes, diced
3 (14.5-ounce) cans diced
    tomatoes
1 (6-ounce) can tomato paste
1 tablespoon Old Bay seasoning
1 pound fresh crabmeat

Sauté first 4 ingredients in hot oil in a Dutch oven until tender.
Add water and next 3 ingredients to Dutch oven; bring to a boil. Cover, reduce heat, and simmer 30 minutes, stirring mixture occasionally.
Add tomatoes, tomato paste, and seasoning; return mixture to a boil. Reduce heat, and simmer 30 minutes, stirring occasionally.
Drain and flake crabmeat, removing any bits of shell. Stir into chowder. Yield: 9 cups.

Vegetable-Cheese Melts

Sautéed vegetables top a tangy spread on rye and are broiled to perfection in this cheesy delight.

per serving:

Calories: 299
Fat: 11.5g
Protein: 13.2g
Carbohydrate: 36.3g
Cholesterol: 25mg
Sodium: 738mg
Exchanges:
  2 Starch
  1 Vegetable
  1 High-Fat Meat

1 small zucchini, sliced
1 large red bell pepper, cut into
    thin strips
1 small onion, thinly sliced and
    separated into rings
Vegetable cooking spray
1/4 teaspoon ground cumin

1 tablespoon Dijon mustard
1/4 teaspoon dried oregano
4 (1 1/4-ounce) rye bread slices,
    toasted and divided
1/2 cup (2 ounces) shredded colby-
    Monterey Jack cheese

Sauté vegetables in a nonstick skillet coated with cooking spray until tender. Stir in cumin.
Combine mustard and oregano; spread evenly on 2 toast slices, and place on a baking sheet. Top with vegetable mixture, and sprinkle with cheese.
Broil 3 inches from heat (with electric oven door partially open) until cheese melts. Top with remaining toast slices. Serve hot. Yield: 2 servings.

Herbed Cheese Sandwiches

1 (15-ounce) carton part-skim
   ricotta cheese
1 (7-ounce) package crumbled feta
   cheese
½ cup chopped fresh parsley
2 tablespoons chopped green
   onions
1 teaspoon chopped fresh dill
16 slices rye bread
Artichoke-Tomato Salsa
8 lettuce leaves

Combine first 5 ingredients; spread on 8 bread slices. Top with salsa, lettuce, and remaining bread slices. Serve immediately. Yield: 8 sandwiches.

per sandwich:
Calories: 294
Fat: 11.4g
Protein: 15.6g
Carbohydrate: 35.0g
Cholesterol: 39.0mg
Sodium: 653mg
Exchanges:
  2 Starch
  1 Vegetable
  1 High-Fat Meat

Artichoke-Tomato Salsa

2 medium tomatoes, chopped
1 (14-ounce) can artichoke hearts,
   drained and chopped
2 teaspoons olive oil
2 garlic cloves, minced
3 tablespoons chopped fresh basil

Combine all ingredients; cover and chill. Yield: 3 cups.

Mediterranean Picnic Loaf

1 (16-ounce) round loaf
   peasant-style bread
3 large tomatoes
1 large purple onion, thinly sliced
1 green bell pepper, thinly sliced
4 ounces crumbled feta cheese
1 (6⅓-ounce) can solid white
   tuna in spring water, drained
   and flaked
½ cup kalamata olives, sliced
1 cup firmly packed fresh basil,
   chopped
2 tablespoons capers, rinsed and
   drained
2 tablespoons balsamic vinegar
1 tablespoon Dijon mustard
1 tablespoon olive oil
2 garlic cloves, minced

Cut bread in half horizontally; hollow out center of bottom half, leaving a 1-inch-thick shell. Slice tomatoes; cut slices into fourths.
Layer tomato, onion, bell pepper, and cheese in bread shell. Place tuna and next 3 ingredients in bread shell.
Combine vinegar and remaining 3 ingredients; drizzle over mixture in bread shell, and cover with bread top. Wrap filled loaf in aluminum foil, and chill 2 hours. Cut into wedges to serve. Yield: 6 servings.

per serving:
Calories: 311
Fat: 9.2g
Protein: 16.8g
Carbohydrate: 40.1g
Cholesterol: 30mg
Sodium: 976mg
Exchanges:
  2½ Starch
  1 Vegetable
  1 High-Fat Meat

Italian Chicken Sandwiches

per sandwich:

Calories: 279
Fat: 4.6g
Protein: 30.6g
Carbohydrate: 26.3g
Cholesterol: 71mg
Sodium: 379mg
Exchanges:
  2 Starch
  3½ Very Lean Meat

4 (4-ounce) skinned and boned
  chicken breast halves
½ cup reduced-fat Italian dressing
8 (½-inch-thick) French bread
  slices

1 cup shredded romaine lettuce
1½ teaspoons shredded Parmesan
  cheese

Combine chicken and dressing in a heavy-duty zip-top plastic bag; seal and shake to coat.

Chill 2 hours, turning occasionally. Remove chicken, discarding marinade.

Cook chicken and bread slices in a grill skillet over medium-high heat 4 minutes on each side or until chicken is done and bread slices are toasted.

Combine lettuce and cheese; arrange over 4 bread slices. Top with chicken and remaining bread slices. Serve immediately. Yield: 4 servings.

Note: For Italian Fish Sandwiches, substitute 2 (7.6-ounce) packages frozen grilled fish fillets, thawed, for chicken.

Italian Chicken Sandwiches

Ranch Chicken Pitas

½ cup Italian-seasoned
   breadcrumbs
1 pound skinned and boned
   chicken breast halves, cut into
   thin strips
½ cup fat-free milk
1 tablespoon vegetable oil
3 (7-inch) pita bread rounds, cut
   in half

6 romaine lettuce leaves
6 (¼-inch-thick) tomato slices,
   halved
6 slices green bell pepper, cut in
   half
¾ cup fat-free Ranch-style
   dressing

per serving:
Calories: 294
Fat: 5.0g
Protein: 23.3g
Carbohydrate: 37.1g
Cholesterol: 47mg
Sodium: 790mg
Exchanges:
  2½ Starch
  2 Lean Meat

Place breadcrumbs in a large heavy-duty zip-top plastic bag. Dip chicken in milk; add to bag. Seal and shake to coat.

Sauté chicken in hot oil in a large nonstick skillet 7 minutes or until done.

Fill each pita half evenly with lettuce, tomato, bell pepper, and chicken. Drizzle with dressing. Yield: 6 servings.

All-American Turkey Sub

**Layers of turkey, cheese, lettuce, tomatoes, and colorful peppers
stack up to make a meal of towering turkey subs.**

2 tablespoons fat-free cream
   cheese, softened
2 tablespoons nonfat mayonnaise
¼ teaspoon minced chives
⅛ teaspoon onion powder
4 (2-ounce) whole wheat
   submarine rolls, split
4 curly leaf lettuce leaves
2 tablespoons fat-free Italian
   dressing

8 ounces thinly sliced cooked
   turkey breast
8 (¼-inch-thick) slices tomato
4 (¾-ounce) slices reduced-fat
   (2%) process American cheese
4 thin slices green bell pepper
4 thin slices red bell pepper
4 thin slices yellow bell pepper

per sandwich:
Calories: 324
Fat: 8.7g
Protein: 29.2g
Carbohydrate: 33.4g
Cholesterol: 53mg
Sodium: 610mg
Exchanges:
  2 Starch
  3 Lean Meat

Combine first 4 ingredients in a small bowl; stir well. Spread cream cheese mixture evenly on bottom halves of rolls. Combine lettuce and Italian dressing, tossing to coat. Top cream cheese mixture evenly with lettuce leaves, turkey, tomato, cheese slices, and pepper slices; top with remaining halves of rolls. Yield: 4 sandwiches.

Smoked Turkey-Roasted Pepper Sandwiches

Smoked turkey breast, soaked in a salt solution before smoking, lends distinct flavor to these sandwiches (pictured on page 190). If you're watching your sodium, substitute roasted turkey breast for the smoked variety.

per sandwich:

Calories: 280
Fat: 2.9g
Protein: 29.1g
Carbohydrate: 36.3g
Cholesterol: 44mg
Sodium: 1057mg
Exchanges:
  2½ Starch
  3 Very Lean Meat

2 tablespoons fat-free cream cheese, softened
1 tablespoon reduced-fat mayonnaise
1 tablespoon spicy brown mustard
⅛ teaspoon pepper
¼ cup chopped commercial roasted red peppers, drained
2 tablespoons sliced green onions
8 slices pumpernickel bread
¾ pound sliced smoked turkey breast
¼ cup alfalfa sprouts

Combine first 4 ingredients; stir in red pepper and green onions.
Spread mixture evenly on one side of bread slices. Layer turkey and alfalfa sprouts on 4 slices of bread; top with remaining bread slices. Cut in half.
Serve immediately, or wrap each sandwich in heavy-duty plastic wrap, and refrigerate. Yield: 4 sandwiches.

Barbecue Turkey-and-Slaw Sandwiches

per sandwich:

Calories: 287
Fat: 9.9g
Protein: 21.7g
Carbohydrate: 29.4g
Cholesterol: 44mg
Sodium: 517mg
Exchanges:
  2 Starch
  2 Medium-Fat Meat

1 pound ground turkey
½ cup chopped onion
1 (8-ounce) can tomato sauce
1 tablespoon brown sugar
1 tablespoon Worcestershire sauce
1 teaspoon dry mustard
1 teaspoon liquid smoke
½ teaspoon pepper
1½ cups finely shredded red cabbage
½ cup finely chopped Granny Smith apple
1 large carrot, shredded
½ cup plain low-fat yogurt
¾ teaspoon curry powder
½ teaspoon dry mustard
6 reduced-calorie whole wheat hamburger buns

Cook turkey and onion in a nonstick skillet over medium heat until browned, stirring until turkey crumbles; drain.
Add tomato sauce and next 5 ingredients; bring to a boil. Cover and reduce heat; simmer, stirring often, 15 minutes. Keep warm.
Combine cabbage and next 5 ingredients in a bowl. Spoon turkey mixture evenly onto bottom half of each bun; top each evenly with cabbage mixture and remaining bun half. Serve immediately. Yield: 6 servings.

Barbecue Turkey-and-Slaw Sandwich

Barbecue Beefwiches

per sandwich:

Calories: 325
Fat: 8.0g
Protein: 21.1g
Carbohydrate: 39.9g
Cholesterol: 60mg
Sodium: 298mg
Exchanges:
  2½ Starch
  2 Lean Meat

1 (3-pound) lean beef rump roast
Vegetable cooking spray
1½ cups reduced-calorie ketchup
¼ cup plus 2 tablespoons red
    wine vinegar
⅓ cup firmly packed dark brown
    sugar
1 tablespoon dried onion flakes
1 teaspoon liquid smoke
½ teaspoon salt
½ teaspoon pepper

⅛ teaspoon garlic powder
2½ cups finely shredded cabbage
½ cup finely shredded carrot
2 tablespoons white vinegar
2 tablespoons minced sweet
    pickle
1½ tablespoons sugar
1½ teaspoons vegetable oil
⅛ teaspoon celery seeds
12 hamburger buns, split and
    toasted

Trim fat from roast. Coat a Dutch oven with cooking spray; place over medium heat until hot. Add roast; cook until browned on all sides, turning frequently. Remove roast from pan; wipe drippings from pan.

Combine ketchup and next 7 ingredients. Return roast to pan; pour ketchup mixture over roast. Bring to a boil. Cover, reduce heat, and simmer 4 hours or until tender. Remove roast from pan, reserving sauce in pan. Let roast cool slightly. Shred meat with 2 forks, and return to pan. Cover and cook over medium heat until thoroughly heated, stirring occasionally.

Combine cabbage and carrot; set aside.

Combine vinegar and next 4 ingredients in a saucepan; bring to a boil, stirring occasionally. Boil 1 minute. Pour over cabbage mixture, and toss gently. Spoon meat mixture evenly onto bottom half of each bun; top each evenly with cabbage mixture and remaining bun half. Yield: 12 sandwiches.

Cheese-Stuffed Burgers

per burger:

Calories: 259
Fat: 8.6g
Protein: 27.6g
Carbohydrate: 18.9g
Cholesterol: 62mg
Sodium: 357mg
Exchanges:
  1 Starch
  3½ Very Lean Meat
  1 Fat

1½ pounds ground round
2 tablespoons minced fresh basil
2 tablespoons grated Parmesan
    cheese
½ teaspoon garlic powder
⅛ teaspoon pepper

4 ounces reduced-fat mozzarella
    cheese, cut into 6 pieces
Vegetable cooking spray
6 reduced-calorie hamburger
    buns

Combine first 5 ingredients; divide into 12 thin patties. Top 6 patties with cheese. Top with remaining patties; press edges to seal. Place on a rack coated with cooking spray in a broiler pan.

Broil 5 ½ inches from heat (with electric oven door partially open) 5 minutes on each side or until done. Drain on paper towels. Serve patties on buns. Yield: 6 burgers.

Guilt-Free Cheese Sauce

Drizzle this lightened favorite over the vegetable of your choice for added flair the whole family will enjoy.

1 tablespoon reduced-calorie margarine
1 tablespoon all-purpose flour
1 cup fat-free milk
½ cup (2 ounces) shredded fat-free Cheddar cheese

¼ teaspoon ground white pepper
⅛ teaspoon salt
⅛ teaspoon ground red pepper

per 2 tablespoons:
Calories: 20
Fat: 0.8g
Protein: 1.2g
Carbohydrate: 2.4g
Cholesterol: 0mg
Sodium: 68mg
Exchanges:
  Free (up to 4 tablespoons)

Place margarine in a 1-quart glass bowl; microwave at HIGH 30 seconds. Stir in flour with a wire whisk; gradually add milk, whisking until smooth. Microwave at HIGH 6 minutes, stirring at 2-minute intervals, until mixture is smooth and thickened.
Add cheese and remaining ingredients, stirring until cheese melts. Serve over steamed vegetables. Yield: 1 cup.

Mediterranean Sauce

½ cup chopped onion
½ cup chopped green pepper
1 garlic clove, minced
Vegetable cooking spray
1 large tomato, chopped

½ cup dry white wine
4 ripe olives, chopped
⅛ teaspoon hot sauce
¼ cup (2 ounces) crumbled feta cheese

per 2 tablespoons:
Calories: 36
Fat: 2.0g
Protein: 1.4g
Carbohydrate: 2.8g
Cholesterol: 6mg
Sodium: 124mg
Exchanges:
  Free (up to 2 tablespoons)

Cook onion, green pepper, and garlic in a nonstick skillet coated with cooking spray over medium heat, stirring constantly, until tender. Add tomato and next 3 ingredients; cook 5 minutes or until thickened. Sprinkle with feta cheese, and serve over chicken or fish. Yield: 1 cup.

Dried Tomato Pesto

Serve this sauce chilled as a dip for raw vegetables or
steamed shrimp, or toss it over hot pasta.

per 2 tablespoons:

Calories: 53
Fat: 3.9g
Protein: 2.3g
Carbohydrate: 3.2g
Cholesterol: 2mg
Sodium: 195mg
Exchanges:
  ½ Vegetable
  1 Fat

½ cup dried tomatoes
1 cup vegetable broth, divided
½ cup fresh basil leaves
1 garlic clove
¼ cup grated reduced-fat
     Parmesan cheese

2 tablespoons pine nuts
1 tablespoon olive oil
¼ teaspoon salt
¼ teaspoon ground white pepper
1 teaspoon cornstarch

Combine tomatoes and ½ cup vegetable broth in a small saucepan, and
bring mixture to a boil. Remove from heat; let stand 10 minutes.

Process tomato mixture, basil, and next 6 ingredients in a food processor
until smooth, stopping twice to scrape down sides. Set tomato mixture
aside.

Combine remaining ½ cup broth and cornstarch in a saucepan; bring to a
boil over medium heat, stirring constantly. Cook mixture 1 minute, stirring constantly. Stir in tomato mixture. Refrigerate up to 3 days, or freeze
up to 3 months. Yield: 1 cup.

Soy-and-Ginger Marinade

Use this versatile marinade on chicken before grilling.
It's also good for meat and seafood.

per 2 tablespoons:

Calories: 15
Fat: 0.0g
Protein: 0.9g
Carbohydrate: 2.9g
Cholesterol: 0mg
Sodium: 484mg
Exchanges:
  Free (up to 4 tablespoons)

½ cup reduced-sodium soy sauce
½ cup coarsely chopped onion
2 garlic cloves
2 tablespoons coarsely chopped
     fresh ginger

½ teaspoon ground cinnamon
½ teaspoon ground allspice
¼ teaspoon ground cloves

Combine all ingredients; add meat, poultry, or seafood. Cover and chill
30 minutes.

Remove meat from marinade, discarding marinade. Grill as desired. Yield:
1 cup.

Roasted Tomato Salsa

Try this salsa with everything from chips to fish to chicken.

4 dried Anaheim chile peppers
2 pounds Roma tomatoes, halved
Vegetable cooking spray
6 garlic cloves, minced
1 large onion, chopped
1 tablespoon olive oil
1 teaspoon salt
1 teaspoon ground cumin
2 to 3 tablespoons chopped fresh cilantro
Garnish: fresh cilantro sprigs

per 2 tablespoons:
Calories: 20
Fat: 0.7g
Protein: 0.6g
Carbohydrate: 3.3g
Cholesterol: 0mg
Sodium: 102mg
Exchanges:
  1 Vegetable

Seed peppers. Place peppers and boiling water to cover in a saucepan; let stand 30 minutes. Drain. Peel and coarsely chop peppers.

Place tomato halves in a roasting pan coated with cooking spray; bake at 450° for 20 minutes or until blackened.

Sauté garlic and onion in hot oil 3 minutes or until tender.

Process chopped pepper, tomato halves, onion mixture, salt, and cumin in a food processor until mixture is chunky; stir in chopped cilantro. Garnish, if desired. Yield: 3 cups.

Hot Kiwifruit Salsa

1 cup peeled, finely chopped kiwifruit
⅓ cup finely chopped green onions
⅓ cup finely chopped fresh tomatillo
⅓ cup seeded, finely chopped Anaheim chile pepper
2 tablespoons chopped fresh cilantro
½ teaspoon unseeded, finely chopped red or green jalapeño pepper
¼ cup rice vinegar
1 tablespoon unsweetened pineapple juice
1½ teaspoons sugar

per 2 tablespoons:
Calories: 8
Fat: 0.0g
Protein: 0.2g
Carbohydrate: 2.0g
Cholesterol: 0mg
Sodium: 2mg
Exchanges:
  Free (up to 4 tablespoons)

Combine all ingredients in a medium bowl; cover and chill. Serve over fish or chicken. Yield: 2 cups.

Sweet Onion Relish

Add extra zip to your meals with the accompaniment of this relish.

5 pounds sweet onions, chopped
1 cup sugar
2¼ cups white vinegar (5% acidity)
2 tablespoons salt
2 tablespoons celery seeds

Combine all ingredients in a Dutch oven; bring to a boil over medium heat. Reduce heat, and simmer 20 minutes, stirring occasionally.

Spoon relish into hot jars, filling to ½ inch from top of each. Remove air bubbles; wipe jar rims. Cover at once with metal lids, and screw on bands.

Process in boiling-water bath 10 minutes. Let stand 1 week before serving. Store in refrigerator after opening. Yield: 5 pints.

Peach Chutney

5 pounds firm peaches, peeled and chopped
1 lemon
1⅔ cups golden raisins
1 (8-ounce) package chopped dates
2 cups white vinegar (5% acidity)
3 cups sugar
½ cup chopped pecans
1 (2.7-ounce) jar crystallized ginger (½ cup)
1 teaspoon ground ginger
½ teaspoon ground allspice
½ teaspoon ground cinnamon
½ teaspoon ground cloves

Place peaches in a large nonaluminum saucepan.

Cut lemon into fourths, and thinly slice. Add lemon slices, raisins, dates, and vinegar to peaches; bring to a boil over medium heat. Reduce heat, and simmer 5 minutes or until peaches are soft, stirring occasionally.

Add sugar; return to a boil. Reduce heat, and simmer 15 minutes or until mixture is thickened, stirring occasionally. Add pecans and remaining ingredients; cook 5 minutes, stirring occasionally.

Pack chutney into hot jars, filling to ½ inch from top of each. Remove air bubbles; wipe jar rims. Cover at once with metal lids, and screw on bands.

Process in boiling-water bath 10 minutes. Serve with chicken or pork. Store in refrigerator after opening. Yield: 8 half-pints.

Caramel Sauce

This sauce is thinner than commercial caramel sauce
when warm, but it thickens as it chills.

1 cup sugar
¼ cup water
1 tablespoon margarine

¾ cup fat-free evaporated milk
½ teaspoon vanilla extract
Dash of salt

Combine sugar and water in a medium-size heavy saucepan. Cook over medium-low heat 5 minutes or until sugar dissolves. (Do not stir.) Cover, increase heat to medium, and cook 2 minutes. (This will dissolve any sugar crystals clinging to sides of pan.) Uncover and cook 10 additional minutes or until liquid is amber or golden. (Do not stir.)
Remove from heat, and let stand 1 minute.
Add margarine, stirring until margarine melts. Slowly add milk, stirring constantly. (Caramel will harden and stick to spoon.)
Cook over medium heat, stirring constantly, 3 minutes or until caramel softens and mixture is smooth. Remove from heat; stir in vanilla and salt. Cover and chill. Serve sauce over nonfat frozen yogurt or fat-free pound cake. Yield: 1¼ cups.

per 2 tablespoons:
Calories: 104
Fat: 1.2g
Protein: 1.4g
Carbohydrate: 22.2g
Cholesterol: 0mg
Sodium: 50mg
Exchanges:
  1½ Starch

Raspberry Sauce

1 (10-ounce) package frozen
  raspberries in light
  syrup, thawed

Garnish: fresh mint sprigs

Process raspberries in a food processor until smooth. Pour through a large wire-mesh strainer into a bowl, discarding seeds. Chill. Serve with fresh fruit. Garnish, if desired. Yield: 1 cup.

per 2 tablespoons:
Calories: 36
Fat: 0.0g
Protein: 0.2g
Carbohydrate: 9.2g
Cholesterol: 0mg
Sodium: 0mg
Exchanges:
  Free (up to 2 tablespoons)

Chocolate-Mint Ice Cream Pie (page 228)

Desserts

Indulge in this extravagant collection of decadent desserts. We've included samplings of all your favorites—cakes, pies, pastries, frozen desserts, *and* cookies. These recipes are sure to satisfy your sweet tooth without sacrificing your diet. Whether served as a snack or a grand finale, this medley of sweet delights is full of treats you can feel good about.

Very Berry Sorbet

2 cups fresh raspberries
2 cups fresh strawberries, sliced
½ cup sugar
1½ cups sparkling white grape
  juice

Garnishes: fresh raspberries, fresh
  mint sprigs

Place 2 cups raspberries in a wire-mesh strainer; press with back of spoon against the sides of the strainer to squeeze out juice. Discard pulp and seeds remaining in strainer.

Process raspberry juice, strawberries, and sugar in a blender until smooth, stopping once to scrape down sides. Combine fruit puree and white grape juice; stir well.

Pour mixture into freezer container of a 2-quart hand-turned or electric freezer. Freeze according to manufacturer's instructions. Pack freezer with additional ice and rock salt; let stand 1 hour before serving. Garnish, if desired. Yield: 10 servings.

Rum-Raisin Ice Milk

⅓ cup raisins
⅓ cup dark rum
2 large eggs
1 cup sugar

1 teaspoon cornstarch
2 cups fat-free milk
2 cups fat-free evaporated milk
½ teaspoon vanilla extract

Combine raisins and rum in a small saucepan; bring to a boil. Remove from heat; cover and let stand at room temperature 1 hour. Drain raisins, and discard rum. Finely chop raisins, and set aside.

Beat eggs in a medium bowl at high speed with an electric mixer 3 minutes or until thick and pale. Combine sugar and cornstarch; gradually add to beaten eggs, beating constantly.

Transfer mixture to a large saucepan; stir in fat-free milk. Cook over medium heat, stirring constantly, until mixture thickens and just begins to boil. Remove from heat, and let cool. Stir in evaporated milk, vanilla, and raisins. Cover and chill thoroughly.

Pour mixture into freezer container of a 1-gallon hand-turned or electric freezer. Freeze according to manufacturer's instructions. Pack freezer with additional ice and rock salt, and let stand 1 hour before serving. Yield: 11 servings.

Bananas Foster

In this light version, the amounts of butter and sugar are decreased, and the ice cream is replaced with nonfat frozen yogurt—but the flavor and the flames are as authentic as the original.

1 tablespoon butter

¼ cup firmly packed dark brown sugar

⅓ teaspoon ground cinnamon

4 bananas, quartered

¼ cup banana liqueur

¼ cup dark rum

12 ounces vanilla nonfat frozen yogurt

per serving:

Calories: 323

Fat: 5.8g

Protein: 5.5g

Carbohydrate: 64.9g

Cholesterol: 8mg

Sodium: 110mg

Exchanges:

  3½ Starch

  1 Fruit

  1 Fat

Melt butter in a large skillet over medium-high heat; add brown sugar and next 3 ingredients. Cook, stirring constantly, 2 minutes or until bananas are tender.

Pour rum over bananas, and ignite with a long match; cook until flames disappear. Serve immediately over frozen yogurt. Yield: 4 servings.

Bananas Foster

Poached Pear with Raspberry Sherbet

Poached Pears with Raspberry Sherbet

3 large ripe pears
2 teaspoons lemon juice
1 cup white Zinfandel or other
  blush wine
½ cup sugar
½ cup unsweetened apple juice

1 tablespoon lemon juice
1 (1-ounce) square semisweet
  chocolate, melted
1½ cups raspberry sherbet
Garnishes: fresh raspberries, fresh
  mint sprigs

per serving:
Calories: 133
Fat: 2.3g
Protein: 1.1g
Carbohydrate: 29.9g
Cholesterol: 0mg
Sodium: 34mg
Exchanges:
  1 Starch
  1 Fruit
  ½ Fat

Peel and core pears; cut in half lengthwise, and brush with 2 teaspoons lemon juice.

Combine wine and next 3 ingredients in a large saucepan; bring to a boil. Add pears; cover, reduce heat, and simmer 15 minutes or until tender, turning once. Transfer pears and poaching liquid to a bowl; cover and chill.

Drizzle half of melted chocolate evenly onto 6 dessert plates. Transfer pears to plates, using a slotted spoon. Discard poaching liquid. Top each pear with ¼ cup sherbet. Drizzle remaining chocolate evenly over sherbet. Garnish, if desired. Serve immediately. Yield: 6 servings.

Old-Fashioned Banana Pudding

½ cup sugar
3 tablespoons cornstarch
⅓ cup water
1 (12-ounce) can fat-free
  evaporated milk
⅓ cup egg substitute
½ cup nonfat sour cream

1 teaspoon vanilla extract
22 vanilla wafers
3 medium bananas, sliced
3 egg whites
¼ teaspoon cream of tartar
1 tablespoon sugar

per ½ cup:
Calories: 172
Fat: 2.2g
Protein: 6.0g
Carbohydrate: 32.2g
Cholesterol: 1mg
Sodium: 112mg
Exchanges:
  2 Starch
  ½ Fat

Combine ½ cup sugar and cornstarch in a heavy saucepan; stir in water, evaporated milk, and egg substitute. Cook over medium heat, stirring constantly, until mixture boils. Boil, stirring constantly, 1 minute. Remove from heat; fold in sour cream and vanilla.

Place a layer of wafers in bottom of a 1½-quart baking dish. Spoon one-third of pudding over wafers; top with half of bananas. Repeat layers, ending with pudding; place wafers around edge.

Beat egg whites and cream of tartar at medium speed with an electric mixer until foamy. Gradually add 1 tablespoon sugar; beat until stiff peaks form. Spread meringue over pudding, sealing to edge.

Bake at 325° for 25 to 28 minutes. Yield: 10 servings.

Tiramisù

The mascarpone cheese used in Tiramisù is a soft, rich,
buttery Italian cheese made from fresh cream. You'll find this
cheese in the gourmet section at large supermarkets.

1 (3-ounce) package vanilla
  pudding mix
2 cups fat-free milk
1 cup mascarpone cheese
2¾ cups reduced-fat frozen
  whipped topping, thawed and
  divided
1 angel food cake loaf

1½ teaspoons instant coffee
  granules
½ cup hot water
¼ cup brandy
¼ cup Kahlúa or other coffee-
  flavored liqueur
Garnish: cocoa

Combine pudding mix and milk in a saucepan; bring to a boil over medium heat, stirring constantly. Remove from heat; cool.

Add mascarpone cheese; beat at low speed with an electric mixer until smooth. Fold in 1¾ cups whipped topping, and set aside.

Slice cake in half horizontally. Cut each layer into 16 equal rectangles, and set aside.

Dissolve coffee granules in hot water; stir in brandy and Kahlúa. Brush coffee mixture over tops and bottoms of cake pieces.

Line bottom and sides of a 3-quart trifle bowl or soufflé dish with half of cake pieces; cover with half of pudding mixture. Repeat procedure with remaining cake and pudding mixture, ending with pudding mixture. Cover and refrigerate 8 hours.

Spread remaining 1 cup whipped topping over Tiramisù. Garnish, if desired. Refrigerate. Yield: 12 servings.

Tropical Trifle

Pineapple, bananas, and strawberries make up
the refreshing layers in this chilled dessert.

1 (3-ounce) package vanilla
   pudding mix
2 cups fat-free milk
1 (16-ounce) package fat-free
   pound cake
1 (20-ounce) can crushed
   unsweetened pineapple,
   undrained
2 bananas, peeled and sliced

½ cup orange juice
1 (10-ounce) package frozen
   sliced strawberries, thawed
   and undrained
1 (8-ounce) container reduced-fat
   frozen whipped topping,
   thawed
¼ cup flaked coconut, toasted

per serving:
Calories: 258
Fat: 3.2g
Protein: 4.0g
Carbohydrate: 53.3g
Cholesterol: 13mg
Sodium: 280mg
Exchanges:
   1 ½ Starch
   2 Fruit
   ½ Fat

Combine pudding mix and milk in a large saucepan; bring to a boil over
medium heat, stirring constantly. Remove from heat, and cool.

Cut pound cake into 10 slices; cut each slice into 6 cubes.

Combine undrained pineapple and banana slices, stirring to coat. Drain
fruit, discarding liquid.

Place half of cake cubes in bottom of a 2½-quart trifle bowl. Sprinkle with
half of orange juice. Spoon half of strawberries with juice over cake cubes;
spread with half of pudding. Spoon half of pineapple mixture over pudding; spread half of whipped topping over top. Repeat layers, ending with
whipped topping. Sprinkle with toasted coconut.

Cover with plastic wrap, and chill at least 6 hours. Yield: 12 servings.

Chocolate Torte

Chocolate Torte

per serving:

Calories: 349

Fat: 9.5g

Protein: 6.7g

Carbohydrate: 60.0g

Cholesterol: 20mg

Sodium: 260mg

Exchanges:

  4 Starch

  2 Fat

½ cup stick margarine, softened
2 cups sugar, divided
2 egg whites
1 large egg
1 cup nonfat buttermilk
½ cup water
2 cups all-purpose flour
1 teaspoon baking soda
¼ teaspoon salt
¼ cup unsweetened cocoa

Vegetable cooking spray
¾ cup no-sugar-added raspberry spread
⅔ cup unsweetened cocoa
¼ cup cornstarch
1 cup low-fat milk
¼ teaspoon vanilla extract
Garnishes: fresh raspberries, fresh mint sprigs

Beat margarine at medium speed with an electric mixer until creamy; add 1½ cups sugar, beating until fluffy. Add egg whites and egg, one at a time, beating after each addition. Combine buttermilk and water. Combine flour and next 3 ingredients; add to margarine mixture alternately with buttermilk mixture. Mix after each addition.

Pour batter into 2 (8-inch) round cakepans coated with cooking spray. Bake at 350° for 22 minutes or until a wooden pick inserted in center comes out clean. Cool in pans on wire racks 10 minutes; remove from pans. Let cool.

Stir raspberry spread well. Slice each cake in half horizontally. Place 1 layer on plate; spread with ¼ cup raspberry spread. Repeat with next 2 layers; top with fourth layer. Cover and chill.

Combine remaining ½ cup sugar, ⅔ cup cocoa, and cornstarch in top of a double boiler. Stir in milk. Bring water to a boil. Reduce heat to low; cook, stirring constantly, 18 minutes or until of spreading consistency. Stir in vanilla. Cover and chill. Spread on top and sides of cake. Garnish, if desired. Yield: 12 servings.

Lemon Angel Rolls with Raspberry Sauce

Even with the rich lemon curd filling, this dessert has less than seven fat grams per serving. To make these cake rolls, remove the crust of an angel food cake before slicing it. Gently rub the cake with your fingers and the brown crumbs will easily flake off.

1 angel food cake loaf
¼ cup Key Largo liqueur
1 (11¼-ounce) jar lemon curd
Sifted powdered sugar

Raspberry Sauce
Garnishes: lemon twist, fresh mint
    sprigs

per serving:
Calories: 331
Fat: 6.9g
Protein: 4.3g
Carbohydrate: 60.7g
Cholesterol: 65mg
Sodium: 168mg
Exchanges:
  4 Starch
  1 Fat
  ½ Fruit

Remove crust from cake. Cut cake horizontally into 8 slices; flatten each slice slightly with a rolling pin.

Brush cake slices with liqueur. Spread each cake slice with about 1½ tablespoons lemon curd. Starting from the narrow end, roll up cake, jellyroll fashion.

Wrap filled cake rolls in wax paper; chill several hours.

Cut each roll into thirds; sprinkle with powdered sugar.

Spoon 1 tablespoon Raspberry Sauce onto dessert plates; arrange 3 cake roll slices on sauce. Garnish, if desired. Yield: 8 servings.

Raspberry Sauce

1 (10-ounce) container frozen
    raspberries in light syrup,
    thawed

2 teaspoons cornstarch

Process raspberries in a blender until smooth. Pour mixture through a wire-mesh strainer into a small saucepan. Stir in cornstarch; place over medium heat, stirring constantly, until mixture thickens and boils. Boil 1 minute, stirring constantly. Remove from heat, and let cool. Yield: ½ cup.

Banana-Coconut Cake

per serving:

Calories: 230
Fat: 6.5g
Protein: 4.3g
Carbohydrate: 39.3g
Cholesterol: 0mg
Sodium: 241mg
Exchanges:
  2½ Starch
  1 Fat

1¾ cups all-purpose flour
½ teaspoon baking soda
¼ teaspoon salt
⅓ cup sugar
1¼ teaspoons cream of tartar
¾ cup mashed ripe banana
¼ cup fat-free egg substitute

¼ cup fat-free milk
¼ cup stick margarine, melted
1 teaspoon vanilla extract
1 tablespoon flaked coconut
¼ teaspoon ground cinnamon
Vegetable cooking spray

Combine first 5 ingredients in a large bowl; make a well in center of mixture. Combine banana and next 4 ingredients; add to dry mixture, stirring until moistened. Combine coconut and cinnamon; set aside.

Coat an 8-inch square pan with cooking spray. Spoon batter into pan; sprinkle with coconut mixture. Bake at 350° for 20 to 25 minutes or until a wooden pick inserted in center comes out clean. Cool in pan on a wire rack 5 minutes. Remove from pan; let cool on wire rack. Yield: 8 servings.

Caramel-Pineapple Upside-Down Cake

per serving:

Calories: 221
Fat: 5.3g
Protein: 3.3g
Carbohydrate: 41.1g
Cholesterol: 22mg
Sodium: 229mg
Exchanges:
  2½ Starch
  1 Fat

1 (15¼-ounce) can pineapple
   slices, undrained
½ cup sugar
2½ tablespoons water
¼ cup stick margarine, divided
Vegetable cooking spray
9 maraschino cherry halves
½ cup firmly packed brown sugar

1 large egg
1 egg white
1¼ cups all-purpose flour
½ teaspoon baking soda
½ teaspoon baking powder
¼ teaspoon salt
½ cup nonfat buttermilk
½ teaspoon vanilla extract

Drain pineapple, reserving ¼ cup juice. Set aside 5 slices, reserving remaining slices for another use.

Cook sugar and water in a small heavy saucepan over medium-low heat, without stirring, 6 minutes or until sugar dissolves. Cover, increase heat to medium, and cook 1 minute. Uncover and cook 5 more minutes or until golden.

Remove from heat, and let stand 1 minute. Stir in 1 tablespoon margarine. Gradually stir in reserved pineapple juice. (The caramelized sugar will harden and stick to spoon.) Cook over medium heat, stirring constantly, 3 minutes or until caramel melts.

Pour into a 9-inch round cakepan coated with cooking spray.

Place 1 pineapple slice in center of pan; cut remaining slices in half, and arrange in a spoke design around center slice. Place a cherry half in center of each slice; set aside.

Beat remaining 3 tablespoons margarine and brown sugar at medium speed with an electric mixer until creamy. Add egg and egg white, beating well.

Combine flour and next 3 ingredients; add to margarine mixture alternately with buttermilk, beginning and ending with flour mixture. Beat at low speed until blended after each addition. Stir in vanilla. Pour over pineapple.

Bake at 350° for 30 minutes or until a wooden pick inserted in center comes out clean. Cool in pan 5 minutes; invert cake onto a serving plate. Serve warm. Yield: 10 servings.

Frosted Carrot Cake

1 cup firmly packed brown sugar
¾ cup egg substitute
¾ cup nonfat buttermilk
1 (8-ounce) can crushed
    pineapple, drained
2 cups grated carrot
⅓ cup raisins
3 tablespoons vegetable oil
2 teaspoons vanilla extract

1½ cups all-purpose flour
⅔ cup whole wheat flour
2 teaspoons baking soda
2 teaspoons ground cinnamon
¼ teaspoon salt
Vegetable cooking spray
Orange-Cream Cheese Frosting
Garnishes: grated carrot, carrot
    strips, fresh mint sprigs

per serving:
Calories: 213
Fat: 5.6g
Protein: 5.2g
Carbohydrate: 35.9g
Cholesterol: 10mg
Sodium: 282mg
Exchanges:
  2 Starch
  1 Fat

Combine first 8 ingredients in a large bowl. Combine flours and next 3 ingredients; stir into brown sugar mixture. Pour into a 13- x 9-inch pan coated with cooking spray.

Bake at 350° for 30 minutes or until a wooden pick inserted in center comes out clean. Cool in pan on a wire rack. Spread with frosting. Cover and chill. Cut into squares to serve. Garnish, if desired. Yield: 18 servings.

Orange-Cream Cheese Frosting

½ cup low-fat cottage cheese
1 (3-ounce) package reduced-fat
    cream cheese, softened

2 teaspoons vanilla extract
1 teaspoon grated orange rind
1 cup sifted powdered sugar

Process cottage cheese in a food processor until smooth (3 to 5 minutes). Add cream cheese, vanilla, and orange rind; process just until smooth. Add powdered sugar; pulse 3 to 5 times or until smooth. Yield: 1½ cups.

Lemon-Poppy Seed Cake

1 (18.25-ounce) package reduced-
    fat yellow cake mix
½ cup sugar
1 cup egg substitute
⅓ cup vegetable oil
¼ cup water

1 (8-ounce) carton plain nonfat
    yogurt
3 tablespoons lemon juice
1 tablespoon poppy seeds
Vegetable cooking spray
Lemon Glaze

Combine first 7 ingredients in a mixing bowl. Beat at medium speed with an electric mixer 6 minutes. Stir in poppy seeds. Pour batter into a 10-cup Bundt pan coated with cooking spray.

Bake at 350° for 40 minutes or until a wooden pick inserted in center of cake comes out clean. Cool in pan on a wire rack 10 minutes. Remove from pan; drizzle with glaze, and cool on wire rack. Yield: 24 servings.

Lemon Glaze

½ cup sifted powdered sugar

2 tablespoons lemon juice

Combine powdered sugar and juice, stirring until smooth. Yield: ¼ cup.

Banana Cream Pie

25 gingersnap cookies, finely
    crushed
2 tablespoons sugar
½ teaspoon ground cinnamon
2 tablespoons margarine, melted
Vegetable cooking spray
½ cup sugar
3 tablespoons cornstarch

¼ teaspoon salt
1 large egg
1 cup fat-free milk
1 tablespoon margarine
2 teaspoons vanilla extract
2 large bananas, sliced
1½ cups reduced-fat frozen
    whipped topping, thawed

Combine first 3 ingredients; add melted margarine, tossing with a fork until dry ingredients are moistened. Press onto bottom and up sides of a 9-inch pieplate lightly coated with cooking spray.

Bake at 325° for 15 to 20 minutes; cool on a wire rack.

Combine ½ cup sugar and next 5 ingredients in a large heavy saucepan. Cook over medium heat, stirring often, 10 minutes or until thickened and bubbly. Remove from heat; stir in vanilla. Cool; fold in banana slices. Spoon into crust, and spread whipped topping over filling; chill. Yield: 8 servings.

Mocha-Fudge Pie

Mocha-Fudge Pie

You can substitute 2 tablespoons fat-free milk for the Kahlúa in the brownie crust and 1 tablespoon water for the Kahlúa in the topping.

per serving:

Calories: 280
Fat: 5.4g
Protein: 4.4g
Carbohydrate: 50.8g
Cholesterol: 1mg
Sodium: 387mg
Exchanges:
  3½ Starch
  1 Fat

⅓ cup hot water
4 teaspoons instant coffee
   granules, divided
½ (19.85-ounce) package
   reduced-fat fudge brownie
   mix (about 2 cups)
2 teaspoons vanilla extract, divided
2 egg whites

Vegetable cooking spray
¾ cup fat-free milk
3 tablespoons Kahlúa, divided
1 (3.9-ounce) package chocolate
   instant pudding mix
3 cups reduced-fat frozen whipped
   topping, thawed and divided
Garnish: chocolate curls

Combine hot water and 2 teaspoons coffee granules in a medium bowl.
Stir in brownie mix, 1 teaspoon vanilla, and egg whites. Pour into a 9-inch
pieplate coated with cooking spray.

Bake at 325° for 22 minutes. Cool completely on a wire rack.

Combine milk, 2 tablespoons Kahlúa, 1 teaspoon coffee granules, remaining 1 teaspoon vanilla, and pudding mix in a large mixing bowl; beat at medium speed with an electric mixer 1 minute. Fold in 1½ cups whipped topping. Spread pudding mixture over crust.

Combine remaining 1 tablespoon Kahlúa and remaining 1 teaspoon coffee granules. Fold into remaining 1½ cups whipped topping. Spread evenly over pudding mixture. Garnish, if desired. Serve immediately, or store loosely covered in refrigerator. Yield: 8 servings.

Frozen Chocolate Brownie Pie

**Layers of vanilla and chocolate frozen yogurt top the rich
chocolate crust of this pie for a striped sweet.**

¼ cup stick margarine
⅔ cup firmly packed brown sugar
½ cup egg substitute
¼ cup buttermilk
¼ cup all-purpose flour
⅓ cup cocoa
¼ teaspoon salt
1 teaspoon vanilla extract

Vegetable cooking spray
½ gallon vanilla nonfat frozen
   yogurt, softened
1 quart chocolate nonfat frozen
   yogurt, softened
¾ cup chocolate syrup
Garnishes: fresh strawberries,
   chocolate curls

per serving:
Calories: 258
Fat: 4.8g
Protein: 6.9g
Carbohydrate: 46.2g
Cholesterol: 0mg
Sodium: 205mg
Exchanges:
 3 Starch
 1 Fat

Melt margarine in a large saucepan over medium-high heat; add brown sugar, stirring with a wire whisk to blend. Remove from heat, and let cool slightly.

Add egg substitute and buttermilk to pan, stirring well.

Combine flour, cocoa, and salt; add to buttermilk mixture, stirring until blended. Stir in vanilla. Pour into a 9-inch springform pan lightly coated with cooking spray.

Bake at 350° for 15 minutes. Cool completely in pan on a wire rack.

Spread half of vanilla yogurt over brownie; cover and freeze until firm. Spread chocolate yogurt over vanilla yogurt; cover and freeze until firm. Top with remaining vanilla yogurt. Cover and freeze at least 8 hours.

Remove sides of pan; slice pie into wedges. Serve each wedge with 1 tablespoon syrup. Garnish, if desired. Yield: 12 servings.

Chocolate-Mint Ice Cream Pie

Kids of all ages will enjoy this frozen treat. It sports a ribbon of chocolate sandwiched between mint-flavored ice cream atop a crispy chocolate crust. This pie is pictured on page 212.

per serving:

Calories: 226
Fat: 10.4g
Protein: 3.9g
Carbohydrate: 28.6g
Cholesterol: 25mg
Sodium: 112mg
Exchanges:
  2 Starch
  2 Fat

½ cup fat-free evaporated milk
2 tablespoons cocoa
2 tablespoons light corn syrup
1 teaspoon cornstarch
¼ cup crème de menthe, divided
1½ teaspoons vanilla extract, divided
3 (1-ounce) squares semisweet chocolate
2 tablespoons reduced-calorie stick margarine
1¼ cups crisp rice cereal
2 pints low-fat vanilla ice cream, softened
Garnish: chocolate curls

Cook first 4 ingredients in a small saucepan over medium heat, stirring constantly, until mixture comes to a boil. Add 1 tablespoon crème de menthe, and cook 1 more minute. Remove from heat, and add ½ teaspoon vanilla; cool and set aside.

Line a 9-inch pieplate with aluminum foil, and fold excess foil under edge of pieplate.

Melt chocolate and margarine in a heavy saucepan over low heat. Add 1 tablespoon crème de menthe; cook, stirring constantly, 1 minute. Remove from heat; stir in remaining 1 teaspoon vanilla and cereal. Spread over bottom and up sides of prepared pieplate. Freeze until firm (about 20 minutes). Remove shell from pieplate, and remove foil. Place shell in pieplate, and return to freezer.

Combine ice cream and remaining 2 tablespoons crème de menthe; spread half of mixture in shell. Freeze 30 minutes.

Top with cocoa mixture, and freeze 10 minutes. Spread with remaining ice-cream mixture; cover and freeze at least 8 hours. Let pie stand 5 minutes before serving. Garnish, if desired. Yield: 10 servings.

Raspberry-Cherry Cobbler

Serve up a taste of home with this comfy cobbler that's
filled with ruby raspberries and sweet cherries.

1 (16-ounce) package frozen
    unsweetened raspberries,
    thawed
1 (16-ounce) package frozen
    no-sugar-added pitted dark
    sweet cherries, thawed
1 cup sugar
¼ cup all-purpose flour
1 tablespoon lemon juice
⅛ teaspoon ground cinnamon

Vegetable cooking spray
2 cups all-purpose flour
1 tablespoon baking powder
1 teaspoon baking soda
1 teaspoon salt
2 tablespoons sugar
¼ cup reduced-calorie stick
    margarine
¾ cup plain nonfat yogurt
¼ cup fat-free evaporated milk

per serving:
Calories: 225
Fat: 2.7g
Protein: 4.4g
Carbohydrate: 47.1g
Cholesterol: 0mg
Sodium: 403mg
Exchanges:
  2 Starch
  1 Fruit
  ½ Fat

Combine first 6 ingredients; spoon into an 11-x-7-inch baking dish coated with cooking spray.

Combine 2 cups flour and next 4 ingredients in a large bowl; cut in margarine with a pastry blender until mixture is crumbly. Add yogurt and milk, stirring with a fork until dry ingredients are moistened. Turn dough out onto a lightly floured surface, and knead about 10 times.

Roll dough to ½-inch thickness; cut into 12 rounds using a 2-inch cutter. Cut 6 diamonds from remaining dough.

Arrange round and diamond shapes on top of fruit mixture. Bake at 425° for 20 to 25 minutes or until bubbly and golden brown. Remove from oven; lightly coat each biscuit with cooking spray. Yield: 12 servings.

Lemon Squares

Lemon squares are the quintessential Southern treat.
These goodies offer an intense lemony filling that will
bring your guests back for more.

1 cup all-purpose flour
⅓ cup sifted powdered sugar
⅓ cup stick margarine, cut into
   small pieces
Vegetable cooking spray
1 cup sugar
2 tablespoons all-purpose flour
½ teaspoon baking powder
¼ teaspoon salt
3 egg whites
1 large egg
1½ teaspoons grated lemon rind
½ cup lemon juice
¼ teaspoons butter flavoring
2 tablespoons powdered sugar

Combine 1 cup flour and ⅓ cup powdered sugar; cut in margarine with a pastry blender until mixture is crumbly. Press firmly into bottom of an 11 x 7-inch baking dish coated with cooking spray.
Bake at 350° for 20 minutes or until lightly browned.
Combine 1 cup sugar and next 8 ingredients, stirring with a wire whisk until blended; pour over crust.
Bake at 350° for 20 minutes or until set. Cool on a wire rack. Cut into squares, and sprinkle lightly with 2 tablespoons powdered sugar. Yield 2 dozen.

Mocha Brownies

1½ cups sugar
½ cup egg substitute
3 tablespoons Kahlúa or cooled
   strong brewed coffee
¼ cup stick margarine, melted
1¼ cups sifted cake flour
½ cup cocoa
1 teaspoon baking powder
½ cup finely chopped walnuts
Vegetable cooking spray
Garnishes: whole strawberries,
   fresh mint sprigs

Combine first 4 ingredients in a large mixing bowl, stirring well. Combine flour, cocoa, and baking powder; stir into sugar mixture. Fold in walnuts. Spoon batter into a 9-inch square pan coated with cooking spray. Bake at 325° for 30 to 35 minutes or until a wooden pick inserted in center comes out clean. Cool in pan on a wire rack; cut into squares. Garnish, if desired. Yield: 16 brownies.

Lemon Squares

Oatmeal-Raisin Cookies

per cookie:

Calories: 65
Fat: 1.5g
Protein: 1.2g
Carbohydrate: 11.7g
Cholesterol: 0mg
Sodium: 27mg
Exchanges:
  1 Starch

¼ cup stick margarine, softened
½ cup sugar
½ cup firmly packed brown sugar
½ cup egg substitute
2 teaspoons vanilla extract
¾ cup all-purpose flour

¼ teaspoon baking soda
⅛ teaspoon salt
1½ cups quick-cooking oats, uncooked
½ cup raisins
Vegetable cooking spray

Beat margarine at medium speed with an electric mixer. Gradually add sugars, beating well. Add egg substitute and vanilla; mix well.

Combine flour and next 3 ingredients. Gradually add to margarine mixture, mixing well. Stir in raisins.

Drop dough by 2 teaspoonfuls onto cookie sheets coated with cooking spray. Bake at 350° for 10 to 12 minutes or until lightly browned. Remove to wire racks to cool. Yield: 3 dozen.

Chocolate Chip Cookies

per cookie:

Calories: 73
Fat: 2.3g
Protein: 2.2g
Carbohydrate: 11.2g
Cholesterol: 1mg
Sodium: 72mg
Exchanges:
  ½ Starch
  ½ Fat

3½ tablespoons brown sugar
3 tablespoons light-colored corn syrup
1½ tablespoons stick margarine
½ teaspoon vanilla extract
2 egg whites
2 tablespoons water
⅔ cup all-purpose flour
½ cup instant nonfat dry milk powder

½ teaspoon baking soda
¼ teaspoon salt
1 cup quick-cooking oats, uncooked
½ cup semisweet chocolate mini-morsels
Vegetable cooking spray

Combine first 4 ingredients in a medium bowl; beat at medium speed with an electric mixer until light and fluffy. Add egg whites and water, and beat well.

Combine flour, dry milk powder, soda, and salt in a medium bowl, stirring well. Gradually add flour mixture to creamed mixture, mixing well. Stir in oats and chocolate mini-morsels.

Drop dough by level tablespoonfuls, 2 inches apart, onto cookie sheets coated with cooking spray. Bake at 375° for 9 to 11 minutes or until lightly browned. Cool slightly on cookie sheets. Remove from cookie sheets, and cool completely on wire racks. Yield: 2 dozen.

Frosted Sugar Cookies

¾ cup plus 2 tablespoons firmly
　packed brown sugar
½ cup stick margarine, softened
1 large egg
2 tablespoons fat-free milk
2 teaspoons vanilla extract
3 cups all-purpose flour

1½ teaspoons baking powder
½ teaspoon salt
2 teaspoons all-purpose flour,
　divided
Vegetable cooking spray
½ cup sifted powdered sugar
1¼ teaspoons water

per cookie:
Calories: 46
Fat: 1.4g
Protein: 0.7g
Carbohydrate: 7.6g
Cholesterol: 3mg
Sodium: 40mg
Exchanges:
　½ Starch

Beat brown sugar and margarine at medium speed with an electric mixer until light and fluffy. Add egg, milk, and vanilla; beat well.

Combine 3 cups flour, baking powder, and salt, stirring well. Gradually add flour mixture to creamed mixture, mixing well. Cover and chill at least 2 hours.

Divide dough in half. Work with one half at a time, storing remainder in refrigerator. Sprinkle 1 teaspoon flour evenly on work surface. Turn dough out onto floured surface, and roll dough to ⅛-inch thickness. Cut with a 2-inch cookie cutter, and place cookies 2 inches apart on cookie sheets coated with cooking spray.

Bake at 350° for 6 to 8 minutes or until edges of cookies are lightly browned. Remove from cookie sheets, and let cool on wire racks. Repeat procedure with remaining flour and remaining half of dough.

Combine powdered sugar and water. Pipe frosting around the edges of half the cookies; spread frosting on the tops of remaining cookies. Yield: 6 dozen.

Peanut Butter Balls

1½ cups vanilla wafer crumbs
1 cup sifted powdered sugar
2 tablespoons cocoa
½ cup plus 1 tablespoon light-
　colored corn syrup

¼ cup plus 2 tablespoons creamy
　peanut butter
2 tablespoons sifted powdered
　sugar

per candy:
Calories: 53
Fat: 1.8g
Protein: 0.8g
Carbohydrate: 8.5g
Cholesterol: 0mg
Sodium: 28mg
Exchanges:
　½ Starch

Combine vanilla wafer crumbs, powdered sugar, and cocoa in a large bowl, and stir well. Combine corn syrup and peanut butter, stirring well. Add to crumb mixture, mixing well.

Shape mixture into 1-inch balls. Sprinkle evenly with 2 tablespoons powdered sugar. Store in an airtight container. Yield: 44 candies.

Metric Equivalents

The recipes that appear in this cookbook use the standard United States method for measuring liquid and dry or solid ingredients (teaspoons, tablespoons, and cups). The information in the following charts is provided to help cooks outside the U.S. successfully use these recipes. All equivalents are approximate.

EQUIVALENTS FOR DIFFERENT TYPES OF INGREDIENTS

A standard cup measure of a dry or solid ingredient will vary in weight depending on the type of ingredient. A standard cup of liquid is the same volume for any type of liquid. Use the following chart when converting standard cup measures to grams (weight) or milliliters (volume).

Standard Cup	Fine Powder (ex. flour)	Grain (ex. rice)	Granular (ex. sugar)	Liquid Solids (ex. butter)	Liquid (ex. milk)
1	140 g	150 g	190 g	200 g	240 ml
¾	105 g	113 g	143 g	150 g	180 ml
⅔	93 g	100 g	125 g	133 g	160 ml
½	70 g	75 g	95 g	100 g	120 ml
⅓	47 g	50 g	63 g	67 g	80 ml
¼	35 g	38 g	48 g	50 g	60 ml
⅛	18 g	19 g	24 g	25 g	30 ml

LIQUID INGREDIENTS BY VOLUME

¼ tsp				=	1 ml		
½ tsp				=	2 ml		
1 tsp				=	5 ml		
3 tsp	=	1 tbls		=	½ fl oz	=	15 ml
		2 tbls	= ⅛ cup	=	1 fl oz	=	30 ml
		4 tbls	= ¼ cup	=	2 fl oz	=	60 ml
		5⅓ tbls	= ⅓ cup	=	3 fl oz	=	80 ml
		8 tbls	= ½ cup	=	4 fl oz	=	120 ml
		10⅔ tbls	= ⅔ cup	=	5 fl oz	=	160 ml
		12 tbls	= ¾ cup	=	6 fl oz	=	180 ml
		16 tbls	= 1 cup	=	8 fl oz	=	240 ml
		1 pt	= 2 cups	=	16 fl oz	=	480 ml
		1 qt	= 4 cups	=	32 fl oz	=	960 ml
					33 fl oz	=	1000 ml = 1 l

DRY INGREDIENTS BY WEIGHT

(To convert ounces to grams, multiply the number of ounces by 30.)

1 oz	=	1/16 lb	=	30 g
4 oz	=	¼ lb	=	120 g
8 oz	=	½ lb	=	240 g
12 oz	=	¾ lb	=	360 g
16 oz	=	1 lb	=	480 g

LENGTH

(To convert inches to centimeters, multiply the number of inches by 2.5.)

1 in				=	2.5 cm		
6 in	=	½ ft		=	15 cm		
12 in	=	1 ft		=	30 cm		
36 in	=	3 ft	= 1 yd	=	90 cm		
40 in				=	100 cm	=	1 m

COOKING/OVEN TEMPERATURES

	Fahrenheit	Celsius	Gas Mark
Freeze Water	32° F	0° C	
Room Temperature	68° F	20° C	
Boil Water	212° F	100° C	
Bake	325° F	160° C	3
	350° F	180° C	4
	375° F	190° C	5
	400° F	200° C	6
	425° F	220° C	7
	450° F	230° C	8
Broil			Grill

Index

235